INTERNED

The Curragh Internment Camps in the War of Independence

James Durney

MERCIER PRESS

Website: www.jamesdurney.com
Twitter: @jamesmdurney

MERCIER PRESS
Cork
www.mercierpress.ie

© James Durney, 2019

ISBN: 978 1 78117 588 0

A CIP record for this title is available from the British Library

This book is sold subject to the condition that it shall not, by way of trade or otherwise, be lent, resold, hired out or otherwise circulated without the publisher's prior consent in any form of binding or cover other than that in which it is published and without a similar condition including this condition being imposed on the subsequent purchaser.

No part of this publication may be reproduced or transmitted in any form or by any means, electronic or mechanical, including photocopying, recording or any information or retrieval system, without the prior permission of the publisher in writing.

Printed and bound in the EU.

CONTENTS

Acknowledgements … 5
Introduction … 7
1 Internment … 9
2 The Rath Camp … 19
3 The Men Behind the Wire … 41
4 'No Place Like Home' … 62
5 Sport and Pastimes … 91
6 Truce Outside, Dissent Inside … 106
7 A Tunnel to Freedom … 126
8 The Foggy Dew … 143
9 Prison Breaks … 168
10 *Fé Ghlas ag Gallaibh* – Locked Up by Foreigners … 191
11 And the Gates Flew Open … 212
Appendix I: List of Internees, Hare Park Camp … 223
Appendix II: List of Internees, the Rath Camp … 227
Appendix III: Escapers from the Rath Camp … 274
Appendix IV: Songs of Freedom … 280
Endnotes … 285
Bibliography … 306
Index … 313

*This book is dedicated to my grandson
Flynn James Reddy*

ACKNOWLEDGEMENTS

A big thanks to Mario Corrigan and Karel Kiely of the Local Studies and Genealogy Department, Newbridge Library, for all their help and for permission to use images from the Library Collection; thanks to Kevin Timmons for access to the autograph book of Jack Timmons; Michael Kenny for facilitating access to the autograph books and other ephemera held in the National Museum of Ireland (NMI); Sandra Heise, NMI, Collins Barracks, for access to the NMI collection; Diarmuid Bracken, Local Studies Section, Tullamore Library, Co. Offaly, for background information on Offaly internees and for facilitating contacts with local historians; Caitlin Browne, Local Studies Section, Roscommon Library, for background information on Roscommon internees; Maureen Costello, Local Studies Section, Mayo Library, for background information on Mayo internees; Aisling Mitchell, Local Studies Section, Galway Public Libraries, for background information on Galway internees; Aisling Doyle, Gaelic Athletic Association Museum, Croke Park, Dublin; Phillip McConway for his research and information on Offaly internees; Áine Delahunt for access to and use of her father's autograph book from the Rath Camp; Fr Peter Clancy for access to and permission to use photographs from his collection; Jim Doyle, president of the 1916–21 Club, for permission to use his photograph of Fr Smith; Irish Life and Lore for the use of a photograph of Tom Byrne; Ronan Lee and John Stack for the information on Nellie Kearns; Brian McCabe, Kill Local History Group, for sourcing photos and a song from local internees; and Liz Gillis for her quote for the front cover.

Thanks also to my publisher, Mary Feehan, who has been supportive of this project from the start, and I thank the editorial staff at Mercier Press for their keen edits and comments.

INTRODUCTION

From 1916, faced with armed insurrection and revolutionary claims to democratic legitimacy, the British government responded with increasingly harsh emergency powers against Irish republicans. An important weapon in the government's fight against republican violence was internment, or imprisonment, without trial. The purpose of this was to contain people believed by the British authorities to be a threat, without bringing charges against them, or having the intent to file any.[1]

It was in the immediate aftermath of Bloody Sunday, on 21 November 1920, that the British authorities decided to open internment camps in Ireland, facilitating a record use of imprisonment without trial. These camps, rather than established prisons, quickly became the largest holding centres of political prisoners. By late June 1921, 3,311 men were interned in the camps, constituting just over half of all those then incarcerated because of the War of Independence. As conditions in the country became more militarised, the circumstances of most imprisoned men came to appear similar to those of prisoners of war, a status the British authorities did not want to grant them. From the start of the conflict the British government had refused to concede that there was a war in Ireland, as claimed by Irish republicans, and by strengthening the police rather than the military it could justify the conflict as mere 'civil disorder'. However, the opening of internment camps and the use of the military as guards helped to dispel this myth.

Despite the negative optics, internment was an easier option for the British than the long-drawn-out process of court-martialling republicans. In addition, republican prisoners had regularly demanded their transfer from convict prisons to special camps as part of their campaign for recognition as prisoners of war. Consequently, the British authorities believed that the camps would be more secure and that prisoners would be less trying, and more easily managed, if held in specially designed internment camps. However, Irish republicans in the Curragh internment camps proved enthusiastically that this was not to be.

1
INTERNMENT

The outbreak of war between Britain and Germany in August 1914 led to the enactment of the Defence of the Realm Act 1914, for the purposes of securing public safety in Britain and Ireland. The act, usually referred to as DORA, governed all citizens in Britain and Ireland during the years 1914–18. The legislation gave the government executive powers to suppress published criticism, control civilian behaviour, imprison without trial, and to commandeer economic resources for the war effort. DORA was amended and extended six times as the First World War progressed, and when war broke out in Ireland, with subsequent amendments, became the most relevant enactment for the suppression of political violence there.[1]

On the outbreak of the European war, the leaderships of the Irish Volunteers and the Ulster Volunteer Force pledged their support for the British war effort, mainly to strengthen their respective hands at the post-war bargaining table. The Irish Volunteers, however, split on this issue, and a minority group, heavily influenced by the secretive Irish Republican Brotherhood (IRB), began planning an insurrection to exploit Britain's wartime difficulties.

At Easter 1916 this IRB-influenced group, together with the Irish Citizen Army, occupied positions in the centre of Dublin and declared an Irish Republic. The immediate British response was to issue two proclamations. One announced the imposition of martial law; the other, under Section 1 of the Defence of the Realm (Amendment) Act 1915, suspended the right to jury trial for breaches of the regulations, and thus created in Ireland an extensive court-martial jurisdiction.[2]

Militarily, the Rising was a failure. In the aftermath, a total of 3,340 men and seventy-nine women were taken prisoner or rounded up in countrywide raids. A lack of evidence against those arrested, however, meant that most of them were interned rather than prosecuted. But British intelligence had left much to be desired, as many of the prisoners were innocent, and 1,424 were released within a fortnight without charge.[3] Fifteen of the prisoners were court-martialled and executed by firing squad during 3–12 May 1916. The rest were held under the Defence of the Realm Act 14B (internment without trial) and transferred to prisons in Britain.[4]

Twenty-five men arrested in Co. Kildare were initially held at Hare Park Camp, first built in 1915 to billet large numbers of troops training on the Curragh. The camp took its name from its location on the edge of the former Kildare Hunt Club Hare Park site. The Kildare prisoners were held at Hare Park until 8 May, when they were conveyed from the Curragh to Richmond Military Barracks in Dublin; from there they were subsequently deported to prisons in England.[5] Their internment was short-lived, as most of the prisoners were released unconditionally in December 1916.

The Curragh Camp continued to be a place of detention for republicans as Sinn Féin and the Irish Volunteers reorganised in early 1917 and began to confront Britain's Irish policy. When Thomas Ashe, the Easter Week hero of the Battle of Ashbourne, was arrested in Dublin in August 1917, having made what was termed a seditious speech in Ballinalee, Co. Longford, he was conveyed to the Curragh Camp and detained in the cells adjoining the guardroom at Keane Barracks. James Grehan, from Co. Laois, was arrested for illegal drilling and housed in a neighbouring cell. Michael Collins, then of the Irish National Aid Association, travelled from Dublin to the Curragh to visit both men – Collins was at that time a largely unknown entity to the British authorities. How it must have rankled with Dublin Castle some years later, when Collins had become such a thorn in their side, to know that he had visited the centre of the British military in Ireland.[6]

In the general election of December 1918, Sinn Féin successfully supplanted the Irish Parliamentary Party (IPP), winning seventy-three seats from a total of 105 and receiving 46.9 per cent of the vote island-wide. They quickly moved to set up an alternative parliament on 21 January 1919, known as Dáil Éireann – 'National Assembly' – and declare an Irish Republic.[7] On the same day the Volunteers, now increasingly known as the Irish Republican Army (IRA), began their military campaign against the crown forces with an attack on the Royal Irish Constabulary (RIC) in Soloheadbeg, Co. Tipperary, which left two policemen dead. Though it was not sanctioned by general headquarters (GHQ), this was the first deliberate killing of state security forces by the IRA.[8]

The escalation of the war from 1919 led to the strengthening of the Defence of the Realm Act, but the use of DORA legislation in response to the Irish conflict was nearing the end of its life, as the power to issue regulations was only exercisable 'during the continuance of the present war', meaning the First World War. It was a war emergency law that was meant to lapse at the end of hostilities in Europe. The old Crimes Act was used to create Special Military Areas, which allowed the authorities to control movement and ban public events, but without DORA it was impossible to continue interning republicans.[9]

In January 1920 a new internment policy was implemented, involving co-operation between the military and police. The British government put into effect a policy of moving prisoners to English jails to diminish any threat or influence they would have on the campaign in Ireland. On 5 April prisoners in Dublin's Mountjoy Gaol began a mass hunger strike, demanding that DORA internees should be treated as political prisoners. Viscount French, the Lord Lieutenant of Ireland, said there would be no concessions to the prisoners, but the situation reached a crisis point with the resignation of the prison's chief medical officer. The strikers turned down an offer of 'ameliorative' treatment; more men joined the strike bringing the number to ninety. A one-day labour strike added to the tension and distressing scenes were witnessed outside the prison as relatives and supporters awaited news. Dublin Castle then conceded the hunger strikers' demand for political status, only to be presented promptly with a demand for their release; when liberation on parole was offered, the internees demanded unconditional release. On advice from the British government, the authorities in Mountjoy relented and transferred the hunger strikers en masse to hospitals for convalescence as a precursor to immediate release. The military programme of arrests since January, the impact of which had been growing steadily, was thrown into turmoil.[10]

New legislation was needed, and the Restoration of Order in Ireland Act (ROIA) was introduced on 9 August 1920 to deal with the rising republican violence and the collapse of the British civilian administration. (The army would pronounce ROIA procedures 'too slow and cumbrous to be really effective against a whole population in rebellion'.) The act permitted the government to continue, under a new label, most of the restrictions imposed under DORA.[11] In most cases this alteration was carried out by the substitution of the phrase 'restoration or maintenance of order in Ireland' for 'the public safety or defence of the realm'.[12] Consequently, DORA 14B, allowing internment without trial, became Restoration of Order in Ireland Regulation (ROIR) 14B.[13]

Over seventy regulations were made under the ROIA Act – civil law was practically revoked. Military and naval authorities were empowered to jail any Irish man or woman without charge or trial under Section 3 (6). Section 3 (1–5) provided for the replacement of trial by jury with courts martial in those areas where IRA activity was prevalent, and an extension of the jurisdiction of courts martial to include capital offences. In addition, military courts of inquiry were substituted for coroners' inquests. This was mainly because (up to August 1920) thirty-three coroners' inquests had indicted military or police personnel for murder. In addition, the regulations provided for the withholding of grants, otherwise payable from public funds, from local authorities that refused to discharge statutory obligations.[14]

However, the introduction of ROIA was followed by a general increase in IRA activities, which culminated in the shooting dead of twelve British intelligence agents on 21 November 1920 in Dublin. The immediate British response was to resort to internment on an unprecedented scale and an overall intensification of the counter-insurgency drive, with full use made of the new regulations. On 22 November orders were given to 'arrest all leaders of the IRA and other "wanted men" and to intern them, should conviction for offences be unobtainable in Ireland'. From that point, if there was not enough evidence to secure a conviction, the military authority was assigned to forward the names of known republicans for internment.[15]

'The great round-up,' the *Irish Independent* reported, 'of prominent Sinn Feiners and public men in the provinces within the last few days appears to have been on a larger scale than that after the 1916 insurrection. The hundreds of arrests which have taken place do not appear to have been the result of anything found on the premises of the men, as in many cases the men were asked for and no search was made.'[16]

In the two weeks following Bloody Sunday, 500 internment orders were made and hundreds of men rounded up.

According to *The Freeman's Journal*, a 'high authority' source said: 'We are going over Ireland with a fine-comb.' The new internees were to be held in internment camps 'until such time as they can be safely tried'.[17]

The *Donegal News* of 4 December said: 'At the present moment there are close on seventeen hundred Irishmen locked up in British jails, and the present intention is to round up something like five thousand. Preparations have been made for the reception of that number, and it is the belief of [Sir Hamar] Greenwood and his advisers that when five thousand Irishmen are in prison, the Sinn Fein movement will be effectively smashed.'

Temporary internment camps were hastily opened at Dollymount, on the north coast of Dublin Bay, and Collinstown, in north Co. Dublin, where the British Army had established a training camp and an airfield during the First World War. Meanwhile, a permanent camp was being prepared at Ballykinlar, on Dundrum Bay in Co. Down.[18] The former British military training camp there had been identified as the most appropriate location for this and thus became the first mass internment camp in Ireland when it opened in early December 1920 to receive its first batch of prisoners from Arbour Hill Prison in Dublin.[19]

There were two internment camps at Ballykinlar, usually distinguished as Camp I and Camp II. Though these two camps adjoined each other for a short distance at one end, being separated only by the double fence of barbed wire that surrounded each camp, they were isolated from each other, and communication between the prisoners in one camp and those in the other was forbidden. Three sides of the camp were surrounded by the sea, which simplified the problem of guarding the prisoners. Each camp held (when full) 1,000 prisoners. These were divided, for purposes of administration, into four companies (250 men in each), and each company was housed in ten huts (twenty-five men to each hut). In addition to the huts in which the men slept, the camp buildings included large central huts for use as a chapel, dining hall, recreation area (for concerts, etc.), canteen, cookhouse and workshops.[20]

On 27 November a *Belfast Newsletter* correspondent wrote: 'The internment indicates the acceptance in a certain sense of the Republican Army's declaration of a state of war and their demand for treatment as prisoners of war.' The *Belfast Telegraph* concurred: 'Men will be liable to be interned without trial, and membership of the Irish Republican Army will be sufficient reason for this treatment.'[21]

The British system of internment against Irish republicans was described as follows:

> [Army] Divisions submitted to GHQ lists of men they wished to intern, giving their believed rank in the IRA. These lists were examined at GHQ and forwarded to the Chief Secretary with application for internment warrants. Owing to delay in the issue of warrants and the congestion which would have occurred in divisional areas had the arrested men been retained until the warrants were received, divisions were authorised to

ship to Ballykinlar batches of men whose internment had been approved, as and when shipping facilities became available, the internment warrants were then sent direct from GHQ to the Commandant of the internment camp.[22]

The main difficulty experienced was found to be one of identity, and in many cases the civilian authorities did not know enough about the suspect to put the correct name on the requisite form, so the military authorities sometimes had trouble in fitting the warrants to the individuals arrested. Many men were interned wrongfully, while others were interned under an incorrect name. The military authorities insisted on attributing an IRA rank to all of those interned – though they were not as successful as they believed in doing this and gave officer ranks to many who were not. Likewise, members of the British government were keen to claim that all the internees were 'believed to be active members of the Irish Republican Army'.[23]

Internment powers continued to be used on a massive scale as the War of Independence entered the new and most crucial year of 1921. According to Dublin Castle, by the last week of December 1920, 995 internment orders had been issued and 800 men interned at Ballykinlar, which at that time only had a capacity of 1,000.[24] By 17 January 1921 the number of internees had risen to 1,478 and, with no let-up in arrests, additional internment places had to be established.[25] In January 1921 an internment camp was opened at the former military installation at Bere Island in Co. Cork.[26]

The following month another camp was opened at Fort Westmoreland, the military fortress on Spike Island in Cork Harbour, which before 1885 had been the chief depot for Irish convicts. It was expected to accommodate 500 men and, because of its location, was believed to be escape-proof.[27]

In the week ending 21 February 1921 a further 507 men had been arrested, bringing the total number of internees to 1,985.[28] Greater capacity was required to deal with this growing number of detainees. To supplement this, another internment camp was constructed on the Curragh plains some 400 metres north-west of the Gibbet Rath to house about 1,300 men. Known as the Rath Camp, it took its name from the historic Gibbet Rath – a large Viking-era enclosure which was also the scene of a massacre of rebels during the 1798 rebellion.[29] On 12 March 1921 the *Leinster Leader* reported: 'Another internment camp, conducted on the same lines as the Ballykinlar Camp, has been opened at the Rath, Curragh. A large number of prisoners have been transferred from the Hare Park Camp to the Rath, where no visits are allowed.'[30]

2
THE RATH CAMP

In the first three months of 1921 crown forces arrested a considerable number of republicans. Numbers interned rose from 1,478 for the week ending 17 January, to 2,569 for the week ending 21 March.[1] The internment camp at Ballykinlar had reached its capacity and instructions were received from British GHQ to prepare a further internment camp at the Curragh military base in Co. Kildare for the reception of internees from the British 5th Division and the Dublin District Division areas.[2]

Located about 3 miles from the garrison town of Newbridge, the Curragh is a natural, grassy, treeless plain of about 4,658 acres. It is not a flat tract of land, but has a series of hills and hollows, and in parts is studded with gorse bushes. At one time the Curragh was a sheet of water, hence its sandy and uneven soil. From east to west it measures about 5 miles in length and it is 2 miles in breadth. The adjacent racecourse has been in operation since 1741.[3]

The Curragh plain has been the site of military activity from prehistoric times and was the scene of the worst atrocity of the 1798 Rebellion. On 29 May 1798 a force of about 400 rebels, pursuant to an agreement made between them and General Ralph Dundas, the officer commanding the British forces in the midlands, had gathered at the Gibbet Rath to lay down their arms. By this stage the rebellion in Co. Kildare was practically over. Patrick O'Kelly, one of the rebel leaders, wrote that, once their arms had been dumped, the rebels were forced to kneel and beg the king's pardon. The British commander at the scene, Major General Sir James Duff, said in a letter to Lieutenant General Lake that he was 'determined to make a dreadful example of the rebels'. He ordered his men to 'charge and spare no rebel'. Duff attempted to justify the actions of his men:

> Kildare two o'clock p.m. – We found the rebels retiring from the town on our arrival, armed. We followed them with the dragoons. I sent some of the yeomen to tell them, on laying down their arms, they should not be hurt. Unfortunately, some of them fired on the troops; but from that moment they were attacked on all sides – nothing could stop the rage of the troops. I believe from two to three hundred of the rebels were killed. We have three men killed and several wounded.[4]

An estimated 350 rebels were killed at Gibbet Rath, most of them trying to escape the armed yeomen and dragoons.[5] Gibbet Rath became a byword for British duplicity and another massacre in a long litany of crown force atrocities, so it was an appropriate place to house the rebels of another generation.

The significance of the position of the Rath Camp was not lost on its occupants. Micheál Ó Laoghaire wrote in his witness statement: 'Interned in the vicinity of such a sacred place with our martyred dead sleeping beside us should, to my mind, be an inspiration to us as I am sure their proud spirits hovered within and around our Camp, watching over us and praying for our liberation as well as the freedom of Ireland.'[6]

As a result of Britain's involvement in the Crimean War (fought from October 1853 to February 1856, in which an alliance comprising Britain, France, the Ottoman Empire and Sardinia defeated the Russian Empire), the Inspector General of Fortifications, Sir John F. Burgoyne, issued instructions in 1855 that a temporary camp for 10,000 infantry be built on the Curragh to train for action in the Crimea.[7] Subsequently, the camp became permanent and included both a Catholic and an Anglican church, a school and a post office. The Curragh Camp was used to train troops for both the regular and the reserve of the British Army in various duties for overseas service. During the First World War the camp was a great centre of military activity.

When the Easter Rising broke out in 1916, the 3rd Reserve Cavalry Brigade at the Curragh was in Dublin within five hours. According to Augustine Birrell, the chief secretary of Ireland, 'the rebellion failed from the beginning, because the soldiers were there before the end of the [first] day in quite sufficient force from the Curragh and Belfast'.[8] And while British troops, many of them Irish-born, were leaving the Curragh for Dublin, others were preparing the huts at Hare Park Camp for an influx of men arrested in the wake of the Rising. Consequently, the first use of the Curragh Camp for detainees was for the twenty-five men from Co. Kildare who were arrested during and after the Rising and held in the camp before being sent to Dublin for processing, sentencing and deportation to prisons in England.[9]

In March 1920 an auxiliary police depot was established at Hare Park Camp to train British recruits to the RIC. Hundreds of recruits, known as 'Black and Tans', received a six-week police training course at Hare Park before a dedicated training centre was established at Beggars Bush Barracks in Dublin.[10] Following this, Hare Park was once again adapted to accommodate republican prisoners.

By mid-February 1921 there were forty-nine men interned there, among them Fr Smith, the Catholic curate (CC) of Rahan, Co. Offaly, who played a prominent part in religious ministering to the internees. The four huts at Hare Park could accommodate twenty-eight men each. Bedding consisted of a mattress, pillow and three blankets. A week later it was deemed to be 'full', with 149 prisoners. To supplement it, construction began on what was to become the Rath Camp, around 450 yards to the east.[11]

The huts in Hare Park were open from 7 a.m. to 9 p.m., although one report said the prisoners were locked up after the 6.30 parade in the evening. Visits were allowed and visiting times for family and friends were Mondays and Fridays from 11.30 a.m. to 12.30 p.m.[12] Edith Garland, a Cumann na mBan member from Newbridge, Co. Kildare, was a regular visitor and rarely missed visiting day. She moved among the prisoners with a cheery word, a message from outside friends or a smuggled note, and always with a parcel of good provisions to supplement the prison food.[13]

At the time, the British Army in Ireland was in the throes of demobilisation and reorganisation on a peace footing. Ireland was grouped into three divisions – the Northern, the Midland and Connaught, and the Southern. In the autumn a fresh sub-division was made creating four districts – the Dublin, Northern, Midland, and Southern divisions, with the Midland district extending westward to include the Connaught sub-district. The army's 5th Division, under the command of Major General Sir Hugh Sandham Jeudwine, with headquarters at the Curragh Camp, was responsible for the Midland (excluding the Connaught sub-district), Dublin and Northern districts. Brigadier General Percy Cyriac Burrell Skinner, commanding the Curragh Brigade and area, was, by virtue of his seniority, officer commanding (OC) the Curragh garrison.[14] He was responsible for the implementation of the new internment camp at the Curragh. Troops from the 5th Division made up the camp guards.

The Rath Internment Camp was designed to hold 1,000 prisoners and was laid out on the southern fringe of the Curragh Camp directly opposite the grandstand of the racecourse. It consisted of about 10 acres of the Curragh plain enclosed in a rectangle of barbed-wire entanglements. There were two fences encircling the camp, each 10 feet high and 4 feet wide. Between the fences was a 20-foot-wide corridor patrolled by sentries, which the prisoners called 'No Man's Land'. At each corner of the compound stood high blockhouses from which powerful searchlights lit up the centre passage and played on the huts. Sentries armed with rifles and machine guns manned these watchtowers twenty-four hours a day, calling out 'All is well' on the stroke of the hour throughout the night. No. 1 post would begin: 'No. 1 post and all is well.' No. 2 would repeat this for their post, and Nos 3 and 4 would follow suit. This 'All is well' continued through the night, every night.

Inside the rectangular enclosure there were some fifty to sixty wooden huts (20 feet by 60 feet), which served as sleeping quarters, and huts used for a hospital, a canteen (dining hall), a cookhouse, a chapel and a library. There was also a hut used for British military stores, and a sports ground large enough to provide a football pitch and space for exercise. The wooden huts were arranged in four symmetrical rows, referred to as 'A', 'B', 'C' and 'D' lines.

Beyond the main barrier, the camp was surrounded by a further fence consisting of five single strands of barbed wire about 4 feet high, not designed to keep the prisoners in, but rather to prevent animals approaching the main enclosure. Nevertheless, it was a further obstacle to the possibility of escape. The Rath Camp was regarded as escape-proof. To add to the difficulties of intending escapers, a large searchlight was mounted on the watchtower of the main military camp. During the hours of darkness, the beam from the searchlight lit up the entire Curragh plain.[15]

The construction of the camp by the Royal Engineers took a great deal of time and labour as the engineers were concerned with making the camp secure. On the other hand, the huts had previously been used as an emergency camp and were hastily erected and hastily evacuated, so when the internees arrived the accommodation was not in good condition. The roofs were leaking, the floors draughty, the surroundings, especially in wet weather, sodden, and the so-called roads rough and overgrown with weeds. Although the capacity of the camp was for a wartime battalion of about 1,000 men, when it was eventually filled with internees there were around 1,300 men, which led to overcrowding.[16]

By the beginning of March 1921 the camp was ready for business. The *Leinster Leader*, a weekly newspaper published in Naas, carried a report in its 12 March issue that 'another internment camp, conducted on the same lines as the Ballykinlar Camp, has been opened at the Rath, Curragh.' The newspaper went on to report that fifty prisoners from the west, including a priest, passed through Naas on their way to the Curragh, and thirty prisoners from Athlone Military Barracks were transferred to the Rath Camp, along with a further seventeen prisoners from Maryborough Gaol.[17] The editor of the *Leinster Leader* at that time was Michael O'Kelly, who had been arrested and held at Hare Park during Easter Week. Within a few months O'Kelly had joined his comrades at the Rath Camp.

Notices were posted in national newspapers that parcels for prisoners at the camp should be carefully packed in wooden boxes or canvas and strong brown paper. The list of contents and address were to be enclosed in the parcel, and all parcels were to be plainly addressed, both on the cover and on a tie-on label. The observance of these rules, the notice said, would facilitate the delivery of parcels without delay or loss. Parcels contained a variety of tinned goods, home-made cakes, cigarettes, clothing and playing cards. Such parcels arrived in the camp quite regularly and in good condition. They made life a little more bearable and gave prisoners goods to barter with each other. Letters from home were also received regularly; prisoners could send out one letter per week.[18]

One of the first republican prisoners to arrive at the Rath Camp was Joseph Lawless:

> It must have been about the first or second week of March 1921 that we were moved from Arbour Hill to the Curragh. Looking up some old letters of mine … I found one which seemed to have been written from the Rath Camp immediately, or within a day or [so] of my arrival there. This was dated 3rd March 1921 and so established the approximate date of our arrival, which I had thought to be about a month later.
>
> We were paraded that morning in the main hall of Arbour Hill Prison and a list of about a hundred and fifty names called out, which represented more than half of the prisoners left in the prison at the time. The Governor then read to us the terms of our internment order and we were informed that the place of our internment was to be the Rath Camp on the Curragh of Kildare. Through the narrow iron gate covering the doorway of the prison we could catch a glimpse of the awaiting escort and hear the buzz of their vehicles as they pulled into position near the entrance …
>
> Any ideas of escape en route were quickly dissipated as we were lined up on the roadway outside the prison and the line

THE RATH CAMP

of lorries for our conveyance pulled up to where we stood on the footpath. The escort consisted of a full company of troops, a platoon in front, a platoon in rear, and the remaining platoons divided amongst the lorries on which we were to travel. In addition to this there was an armoured car in front of the convoy as well as one in rear, and a couple of tender-loads of Auxiliaries cruised around the convoy until we were clear of the environs of the city. From there on to the Curragh an aeroplane from the military aerodrome at Baldonnell flew in circles above us keeping watch for any possible attempt at rescue. When we entered upon the Curragh Plain, near Ballymany crossroads, the aeroplane landed ahead of us and, the convoy being halted, we watched the pilot coming across to have his duty order signed by the officer commanding the convoy.

… People who have lived their lives in more or less enclosed places, particularly in cities, are, I think, bound to get a certain agraphobic [*sic*] feeling of isolation when they first find themselves in a wide open space unbounded by walls, hedges or fences of any kind. But I had also another feeling, induced by the view of the barracks and the other military establishments set upon the ridge in the middle of the plain. Here seemed to be the unassailable heart of the powerful enemy of our nation. Here were military forces in strength, and from where they could sally forth at will to crush the puny efforts of the native people.

I did not at the time, of course, arrange my thoughts as I have written them here, but this represents the feelings we had and explains why there was little conversation between us as we were driven through the Curragh Camp, past Harepark [*sic*] Camp and halted at last, to dismount outside the newly erected internment camp just west of the Gibbet Rath.[19]

A hut that acted as a guardroom, manned by a military guard, stood near the entrance gate between the barbed wire and the road. The remainder of the troops engaged in the guarding and administration of the camp were quartered in a hutment camp about 200 yards on the south side of the internment camp. The guard was provided by the 2nd Battalion, the Suffolk Regiment, of which headquarters and two companies had been moved from Boyle, Co. Roscommon, at the end of February. According to the official history of the 5th Division, the first internees arrived on 2 March.[20] Lawless, who had been appointed vice-commandant of the republican prisoners, wrote:

> I think we were the first batch of prisoners to arrive at the new camp, the construction of which was not quite finished when we arrived. It is possible that some few may have arrived before us on the same day or the day before, but my recollection is that we went into occupation on the first line of huts and began immediately to elect our own commandant and administrative officers. Peadar McMahon became the prisoners' commandant and I his vice-commandant ... We thought it peculiar when we first arrived that we were urged by the military authorities to proceed immediately with the election of leaders, and when this had been done, to find that they were so solicitous as to provide specially arranged quarters for the prisoners' commandant and his staff. They refused, however, to recognise our military titles as commandant and vice-commandant and insisted upon addressing us and referring to us at all times as 'Internee Supervisor' and 'Assistant Internee Supervisor'.[21]

THE RATH CAMP

The British commandant of the internment camp was Colonel John Connor Hanna, Royal Artillery, who joined the British Army in 1892, was mentioned twice in dispatches and was awarded the Distinguished Service Order (DSO) and the French *Croix de Guerre* (War Cross) during the First World War. He was born in Madras, India, in 1871, the eldest son of Francis B. Hanna, an engineer, and Elizabeth Connor of Kilcoole, Co. Wicklow.[22]

Hanna's aide-de-camp, or adjutant, was Lieutenant Hubert Frederick Vinden, 2nd Suffolk Regiment, who had served as an officer on the Western Front during 1915–17, taking part in the Battle of the Somme (1916) and the Battle of Arras (1917). He arrived in Ireland with his battalion in January 1921 and, after a few weeks in Boyle, they were detailed to the Curragh Camp. He said, 'I thought this was a happy choice, as our senior officers who had been "inside" in Germany should know the ropes of guard duties and the wiles of prisoners trying to escape.' However, the military quickly found that the staffing of the camps was a considerable drain on manpower and morale. Lieutenant Vinden soon felt he was too inexperienced for the job and described the shortcomings of guard duty for regular soldiers:

> Aid to the civil power is one of the most unpleasant tasks which can fall to soldiers, and our colonel, Arthur Peeples, was most alert to the pitfalls for the military. If anything went wrong, it would be blamed on the soldiers and officers … Colonel Peeples wanted to avoid being in command of the regiment and at

the same time be in charge of the internment camp, while the regiment only provided the guards required for it. He appointed me to be staff captain to the commandant and this brought me in a very welcome extra five shillings a day.[23]

The internees appointed their own OC as well as a camp council to run all their affairs in the camp. Captain Micheál Ó Laoghaire, OC Liverpool Company, Irish Volunteers, said:

> When we arrived in the Camp, A Line was only full [*sic*] but, from that day on, prisoners began to arrive daily from Dublin, Tullamore, Galway, Mayo, Sligo, Roscommon, Leitrim, Kildare, Meath and Wicklow, with the result that the Camp that looked to us on our arrival as derelict and desolate in a few weeks became a hive of living men.
>
> Then the work of re-organisation had to begin. We were lucky in this respect for we had in the Camp several prominent I.R.A. men who knew each other and there was not much difficulty in renewing comradeship and fidelity. Volunteer officers from their own particular areas would vouch for their Volunteers and so, in a short time, we had a good idea of who was who.
>
> The next important step was the election of officers. A meeting of hut leaders was held and the following officers were elected:
>
> Camp Commandant – Peadar McMahon
> Vice Camp Commandant – Joe Lawless
> Camp Quartermaster – Micheál Ó Laoghaire (myself)
> Line Officers –   Mick McHugh   A Line,
>   Tom Derrig   B Line,

> late James Victory   C Line,
> Joe Vize   D Line

A medical officer was appointed in charge of the hospital. The first man appointed was the late Dr. O'Higgins of Stradbally (father of the late Kevin O'Higgins) who was afterwards released. Dr. O'Higgins was Coroner for Leix at the time and was very prominent and well respected. The authorities offered him his release if he would undertake to sign a bond for £200 (or £300) which the doctor refused to do. They approached him again a short time afterwards and reduced the bond. He not only refused but told them, with all the indignation at his disposal, that if they did not release him unconditionally his bones would rot in the Camp compound before he would sign any undertaking. A week later he was released unconditionally. Dr. Brian Cusack was appointed M.O. [Medical Officer] and Dr. Fehily [*sic*] Assistant M.O. (both prisoners).

… The actual management of the Camp, including the hospital, was now handed over to us. A medical Corporal and Orderly (British soldiers) were the only two soldiers who slept inside the Camp. The British M.O. called in daily. The work was carried out by our own medical men and students under whose care patients were tended and treated.

I took over the food stores from Lieutenant Mallett, British Camp Quartermaster, including weighing-scales, tables and butcher's knives.[24]

The reason the doctor and others refused to sign a bond for their release was because this only allowed for a conditional release, in which the signee could be rearrested if deemed to be once again involved in republican activities. The prisoners refused to accept anything but an unconditional release.

The internees were treated like prisoners of war but were not recognised as 'belligerents', as this would have afforded them, and the republican movement, a recognition the British authorities were not willing to concede. Nevertheless, the internees were given great leeway in organising their own lives. Line captains reported all grievances to the internees' OC, who in turn placed them before the British OC. The military supplied the food, but the internees had their own cooking staff. Roll call took place each morning and evening, and a general inspection at midday.

Collinstown Camp and prisons such as Arbour Hill were used as clearing stations for prisoners until a consignment was ready for dispatch to Rath or Ballykinlar. Dr Brian A. Cusack was a medical doctor from Oldtown in north County Dublin, who moved to Galway where he became involved in the IRB. He was a sitting Teachta Dála (TD) for North Galway when he was arrested and taken to Collinstown and subsequently Arbour Hill:

> One day in Arbour Hill one of the Military Police put his hand on my shoulder. I objected to this and I told him so in no uncertain manner. I was taken before the Governor and the next day I was transferred to the Curragh. This was a welcome change as in Arbour Hill we were three to a cell and in the Curragh we had plenty of open air and better conditions. I was kept in internment until after the Truce was signed.

> There were a number of doctors in the internment camp in the Curragh as prisoners. A British Medical Officer – an Irishman and a very capable man [–] visited the Camp one day and asked me if I would take charge of all medical institutions within the Camp. I agreed to do so under certain conditions, the principal one of which was that all our sick prisoners be sent for treatment to 3 Dublin Hospitals. He said 'We cannot do that'. However, he really did all he could to facilitate us.[25]

As more men arrived, there was a pressing need for organisation, and the camp leadership soon took over these responsibilities. Tom Byrne, a Boer War and Easter Week veteran, wrote:

> We ran the camp ourselves, making our own paths out of concrete blocks. In other ways, too, we were allowed within limits to improve our housing conditions. But such concessions were purely domestic and there was no leniency in the manner in which we were guarded for our jailers were constantly on the watch to offset attempts at escape. To try and catch us out there would be sudden swoops on the huts with intensive searches and the barbed wire was being constantly strengthened.[26]

The routine of the camp was dictated by two disciplinary systems. On the one hand, the British regulations set the times when the internees were locked up and let out, the number of letters they might write and the amount of food provided. But the internees also had their own disciplinary system, imposed from the beginning. Micheál Ó Laoghaire said:

The first essential was the appointment of reliable Hut Leaders who were known and trusted. In this connection, so far as I know and remember, all the hut leaders were trusted men and carried out carefully the duties assigned to them. There were about thirty men in each hut under the charge of the hut leader whom they appointed themselves. His duties openly were to maintain law and order in the hut, detail men for duty and keep a watching brief over them, always reporting anything he thought important, at the same time becoming acquainted with his men and ascertaining, if possible, the views of every man in the hut. His fellow-Volunteers he coached on those lines also. In this way, he was soon able to give an account of each man in the hut. This, of course, only referred to men who were not known to any Volunteer in the Camp. When his suspicions were aroused, he kept the suspects, naturally unknown to themselves, under observation and their correspondence was seized in our own post office and examined. From information like this, we were able to associate directly or indirectly 28 prisoners. When some of them were openly accused, they fled from the Camp under the protection of the military. This was the work of our Intelligence men and they usually held their meetings in my stores.

The 28 spies and suspects referred to were removed from the Camp and we never saw them again. To my knowledge, there were in that 28 at least two who could definitely be condemned as spies and the remaining suspects were always associating with them. Of the two, one was a member of a Volunteer unit in Dublin and the other was a member of the Casement Brigade in Germany.

The Volunteer prisoners were now organised into their own areas, that is to say, the areas from which they came before being interned, and elected their officers. They too held their meetings in my stores. This meant that I had to keep at all times unauthorised persons from entering the stores, with the result that they gave me the name of the 'Black and Tan'.[27]

However, on the issue of British spies in the camp, Lieutenant Vinden claimed:

Thinking over our time on the Curragh, I have realized how frightfully 'green' we were. We never even thought of putting agents in the cage through whom we could have hoped to get some information.[28]

The leadership did their best to keep the men busy and entertained, and hut leaders allotted duties, or 'fatigues', to the men under their charge. These fatigues were mainly aimed at keeping the huts clean, hygienic and orderly but, as always, not everyone embraced the idea of discipline.

In Hare Park, with few exceptions, the prisoners held were largely from Counties Kildare and Carlow. While internment was the punishment for men suspected of republican involvement, those arrested under arms or involved in physical 'rebel' activity were sentenced by court martial. Sentenced prisoners were immediately transferred to penal institutions in Ireland and Britain. Thomas Martin, who was arrested on 30 March 1921 as he travelled with two companions from

Carlow to Kildare, held overnight in a cell at Kildare RIC Barracks, fingerprinted and photographed the next morning, and moved under escort to Hare Park Camp, would see many of his fellow prisoners sentenced by military courts to hard labour during the six weeks he spent in the camp.[29]

Martin himself was not court-martialled but was asked to sign a bond, upon which his release would be assured. He refused to do so. In mid-April, with six other men, he was handed over to an armed guard of seven soldiers, who marched them to their new abode – the Rath Camp. Much to Martin's distaste, he was appointed hut leader of his billet and made responsible for the enforcement of the rules. Some of his fellow prisoners found the rigid discipline of the camp too much for them and their lack of response caused Martin to report them to the internee commandant. As punishment, the prisoners were awarded additional fatigues. Soon afterwards, Martin resigned from what he called this 'rotten job' and sought a transfer to another billet.[30]

By the end of April there were around 400 internees in the Rath Camp. Because of its location on the broad, flat Curragh plain, the camp was open to the elements, so conditions varied depending on the weather and time of year. The open air was often a relief to men who had spent time in cells in traditional prisons, and the space afforded each prisoner was far more than in a conventional prison. However, the huts were not comfortable. Made of wood, they were cold places in the winter, despite the cramped conditions. Bedding was basic and was damp most of the time. The roofs leaked and were in bad need of repair. On wet nights the internees rearranged the positions of their beds to avoid the incoming rain. When the prisoners were asked to supply skilled workmen from among their number to carry out any repairs that the camp authorities were willing to sanction, the workmen in question, who were trade union members, let it be known that they were not prepared to carry out work that would deprive local workmen of employment.[31]

A month after the camp had opened, the propaganda war began. On the one side, internees complained that money and parcels sent to them had not arrived. On the other, Lieutenant Vinden maintained that the internees were raising numerous trivial grievances. One of these was a complaint about prisoners' parcels being opened and cakes cut, which, Vinden said, was being done for good reason – the camp staff had found knives, files, letters and money in some parcels and cakes.[32]

It was mainly police and military documentary evidence that enabled the British to obtain and hold, in the face of appeals, the vast number of internees, and which led to successful prosecutions of many republicans.[33] Internees' letters were heavily censored by their own leaders, so contained very little of value to British intelligence.[34] In an attempt to gather more intelligence, microphones and dictaphones were used to a certain extent in the camp. Their value, however, depended on the types of buildings in which they were situated, and they were quite useless in the camp's wooden huts, where every noise was magnified. Though the practice was not particularly effective, the prisoners believed microphones were installed everywhere and this hampered their attempts to escape or to communicate with their friends outside.[35] One wire and bug found behind the bed of the prisoners' camp commandant led to the British quarters. The prisoners – to their amusement and the guards' embarrassment – used this wire as a clothes line.[36] Joe Lawless takes up the story:

> Sometime in the middle of that summer, when a prolonged period of intense sunshine had baked and shrivelled the ground, a few of us were lying on the parched grass at the back of our hut one day. Idly gazing at the ground, someone suddenly noticed a slight depression which formed a narrow line running from the direction of the Camp Administrative Offices towards our hut. Speculating vaguely as to what this might mean, it gradually gained a sinister significance as we realised that neither water nor sewage pipes could be the cause of the mark as neither of these services were installed in the huts. Lying closely together so as to conceal our purpose we, therefore, began a small excavation with a penknife, discovering about six or eight inches down what appeared to be a pair of insulated telephone cables and, having severed these, the hole was carefully closed again.
>
> Following the mark, we then traced the cables to the side of our hut where, concealed in a carefully prepared board of the inner partition, we found two microphones. One had been placed at the head of our bed to catch our bedtime conversation I suppose, and the other above a table, where presumably we might be expected to hold secret meetings.
>
> Other microphones were then located in the outer part of

our hut and, I think, in one of the other huts nearby, all of which were removed, and I kept two of them as souvenirs until I had to abandon them on my escape. I do not know whether the enemy intelligence staff learned anything by this means, but they took no action about the destruction of the system.[37]

Interrogations of internees were not particularly effective either. Intelligence officers in the camp conducted them, but they were hampered by a lack of local knowledge. Prisoners took advantage of this and often gave incorrect names and addresses to obstruct their interrogators. Many republicans changed their names to Gaelic versions, while the British authorities always used the English version. One example of this was the prisoners' commandant, Peadar McMahon, who had been arrested in Dublin in early 1921. He was a member of the Dublin Brigade and had served as a training officer in several counties in 1919 and 1920, including Kildare and Mayo, but British military intelligence was unaware of his importance as all his reports had been signed in Irish. It was not until after the Truce was signed in July 1921 that they were alerted to McMahon's standing.[38]

The British government was keen to claim that all the internees were active IRA Volunteers. In view of the interrogation methods used to obtain admissions of membership, these claims were often far from accurate.[39] For example, Cornelius Buckley, a sixty-year-old shopkeeper from Kilcock, Co. Kildare, was arrested and interned in the Rath Camp in early 1921. Although a republican supporter and a brother of Sinn

Féin TD Domhnall Ua Buachalla, at his age he was not an IRA member or even an active republican.[40]

The 5th Division's history later recorded that for internment to succeed it would be better if prisoners were interned outside the country: 'Prisoners interned among their own kin are bound to be objects of sympathy to them, and incentives to resistance. Moreover, their security is infinitely more difficult to ensure, and an unnecessarily large number of troops is used up in providing for it.'[41] However, the situation in Ireland in 1921 was a learning process for both sides and the internees were quick to absorb how to exercise control of the camp for their own ends and for the most important feature of prison life – escape.

3

THE MEN BEHIND THE WIRE

The internees in Hare Park Camp and the Rath Camp were all male and had an age range from sixteen to over seventy, but the majority were in their twenties and thirties. At its peak, the Rath Camp held 1,500 men, but not all of the internees were active Volunteers; many were Sinn Féin members, some were republican supporters, others were trade unionists and some were family members of republicans with no connection to any of the republican organisations. In his witness statement, Micheál Ó Laoghaire claimed that 'there were about fifty per cent of the prisoners who were never associated in any Irish-Ireland movement'.[1]

The core problem was intelligence, which made the internment process very difficult as police lists were out of date and the information supplied to the military was imprecise. By the summer of 1920, because of boycott and ostracisation by the republican movement and the public, the RIC had been effectively neutralised and practically removed from intelligence gathering. In the military's opinion, the police had not attempted to determine the units, formations and disposition of the Volunteers' personnel, leaving it up to military intelligence to identify the status of individuals listed for arrest. At this point, the military realised that it would have to construct its own full-scale intelligence system to do so, which would take months, if not years.[2]

Internees who felt they had been wrongly arrested could make representations against their internment to an Advisory Committee set up in January 1921. The Advisory Committee was created specifically to review the applications of internees who considered their detention to be mistaken or unwarranted. The composition of the committee was judicial: Chairman (Justice) Sir John Ross; His Honour Judge Doyle, King's Counsel (KC), Recorder of Galway; and W. Sullivan, Resident Magistrate (RM). This committee did not review all cases, but heard the appeal of any internee who claimed to be innocent. It appears to have attracted little interest from internees – by the end of June 1921 there were only twenty-four appeals awaiting a hearing, a figure representing approximately 0.6 per cent of those interned.[3] Initially, Volunteers were not permitted to apply for release, though men deemed to be important for the outside campaign were later given permission to apply.

Dublin had the highest number of internees in the Rath Camp, with 273. In August 1920 the British authorities set up a Raid Bureau in the city to co-ordinate the raiding of premises and the collecting of information on republican activists. Between then and the Truce in July 1921, 6,311 raids were carried out in the Dublin district, an average of nearly nineteen a day. By 7 May 1921, 3,594 suspects from Dublin had been interned, the largest number from any British military district.[4]

Every county in Ireland was represented in the Curragh

internment camps apart from Fermanagh and Waterford. Excluding Dublin, most internees in the Rath Camp, however, were from the Midland counties of Offaly (142), Kildare (100), Laois (110) and Westmeath (81), and the western counties of Mayo (143), Galway (94) and Roscommon (88). There were also thirteen internees with addresses in England: eight from Liverpool, three from London and two from Manchester.[5] The English IRA men included Liverpool Company Commander Micheál Ó Laoghaire, who had been arrested after the burning of timber yards and warehouses in Liverpool and Bootle. Ó Laoghaire had also shot and wounded a policeman who had attempted to arrest the Volunteers involved. He was deported to Ireland and imprisoned in the Bridewell, Mountjoy and Arbour Hill prisons before being transferred to the Rath Camp in March 1921.[6]

The War of Independence was a nationalist revolution reinforced by the overwhelming Sinn Féin election result of December 1918, and the men who led, and fought, during this revolution were in the main urban, educated, skilled and in the early stages of their working careers. The educational attainments of the Volunteers seem high, and numerous conspicuous IRA men had had a university education, including several who were interned at the Rath Camp. The uncompromising and anti-British Christian Brothers had educated the majority, but there were some who were educated in non-religious surroundings, men such as Desmond FitzGerald, Rory O'Connor and Frank Burke. Many received their radical education in Gaelic League classes, while others came from families that had 'kept the faith' from Fenian times and saw themselves as carrying on an inherited tradition.[7] Nearly every county and city had its leading republican families and many Volunteers were brothers, cousins or neighbours. Micheál Ó Laoghaire said:

> There were some personalities interned in the Camp, including the late Joe McBride (a brother of Major McBride), Tom Byrne (of South African fame who fought with the Boers under Major McBride), Joe Vize (Director of Purchases), Liam Ó Briain (Professor of Galway University), several T.D.s (too numerous to mention) and prominent medical men. There were a few badly wanted men who had passed the net of British Intelligence without being recognised and several, of course, with assumed names.[8]

The IRA commandant of the Rath Camp, Peadar McMahon, joined the Irish Volunteers on their inception at the Rotunda, Dublin, on 25 November 1913 and was posted to C Company, 2nd Battalion, Dublin Brigade. Born in 1893 in the townland of Coose, near Ballybay, Co. Monaghan, he worked in Dublin as a shipping clerk and became involved in the Gaelic League and then in the Irish Volunteers. At the outbreak of the Easter Rising he became separated from his unit and served at St Stephen's Green under Citizen Army commanders Michael Mallin and Constance Markievicz. On Mallin's recommendation, he was promoted to second lieutenant and took part in the occupation of the Royal College of Surgeons when the rebels were driven from St Stephen's Green.

McMahon was the bearer of the surrender document to Thomas MacDonagh in Jacob's Biscuit Factory, where he rejoined his unit and subsequently surrendered. He was detained at Knutsford Prison in England and later at Frongoch Internment Camp in Wales. On his release he joined the family bakery of the sister of executed leader Ned Daly in Limerick. While living there he reorganised the city and county battalions of the Volunteers, and was adjutant of Limerick Brigade until 1918. In 1919 he joined the GHQ organising staff as a commandant and extended his operations into the counties of Kildare, Kilkenny, Leitrim, Cavan and Mayo. In December 1920 he was arrested in Brunswick Street, Dublin, by the Auxiliaries and taken to Dublin Castle. After interrogation he was transferred to Arbour Hill Prison and subsequently to the Rath Camp, where he was elected commandant.[9]

McMahon's second-in-command, or vice-commandant, was Joseph Lawless. He had been arrested on 8 December 1920 at Swords, Co. Dublin, and taken to the temporary internment camp at Gormanstown. A few days before Christmas, Lawless and other prominent republicans, including Emmet Dalton and Peadar Kearney, were transferred to Arbour Hill Prison. Lawless said, 'We were not charged with any specific offence, nor were we served with internment orders, but merely held in custody at the pleasure of the British military authorities.' In Arbour Hill, Joseph Lawless was joined by his father, Frank, his brother Colm, and two of his uncles, Ned and Jim Lawless, all of them republican activists.[10]

Joseph Lawless was born in 1897 at Saucerstown in Fingal, north Co. Dublin. The Lawless family were prominent republicans and Joseph became interested in the nationalist movement at a young age. He was an active member of Na Fianna, the Gaelic League and the Gaelic Athletic Association (GAA). In 1914, while working in Dublin as an engineer's apprentice, Lawless joined the Irish Volunteers. He was a member of C Company, 1st Battalion, Dublin Brigade, and took part in the landing of arms from the yacht *Asgard* during the Howth gun-running. In 1915 Joseph became a lieutenant in the Swords Company of the 5th Battalion, taking part in numerous exercises and events, including the funeral of Jeremiah O'Donovan Rossa at Glasnevin Cemetery, Dublin. Later that year, he was sworn into the IRB by his father.

During the Easter Rising, Lawless took part in an attack on the Rogerstown viaduct, the ensuing attacks on Swords and Donabate RIC Barracks, the seizure of Garristown Barracks and the Battle of Ashbourne. Following the Rising he was sent to Knutsford Prison in England and eventually transferred to Frongoch until his release just before Christmas 1916. He returned to Ireland and became active in the reorganisation of the Volunteers in the Fingal area, as well as taking part in the anti-conscription campaign and the 1918 general election. In 1919 he took part in the hugely successful arms raid on Collinstown Aerodrome. As brigade engineering officer, he was involved in the production of bombs and other ordnance for the Volunteer companies in north Co. Dublin. He also set up two companies as fronts: a bicycle shop at 198 Parnell

Street, which housed a munitions factory, and a motor rental company, which supplied cars to the Dublin Brigade.[11]

Lawless had a lucky escape when two of the most notorious and murderous British intelligence operatives, Captain William 'Tiny' King and Captain Jocelyn 'Hoppy' Hardy, were pursuing him because of his connection to the Parnell Street bomb factory. King and Hardy were responsible for the torture and murder not only of several Irish republicans, but also of innocent civilians. Lawless was saved from their in-depth interrogation methods when the military detachment at Arbour Hill refused to hand him over to King, who had arrived at the prison to take him to Dublin Castle. According to Lawless, King was under the influence of alcohol at the time and was very upset at not being able to gain access to his charge. There had been an attack on the British military that day, with bombs similar to those found at Parnell Street, and Lawless was to be 'interrogated' to find out who was responsible.

Prisoners were routinely transferred from Arbour Hill to Ballykinlar and other areas of detention, and at the end of January 1921, when Con O'Donovan, the prisoners' OC, was moved, Joseph Lawless was elected in his place. Rory O'Connor, a member of GHQ staff, maintained that he was the senior officer and should, by rank, automatically be OC, but O'Connor, according to Lawless, was not popular with the men and so was passed over. Lawless soothed O'Connor's wounded pride by telling him it would not do to elect him OC, thereby alerting the enemy to his prominent position. In accordance with the practice, the name of the prisoners' OC was forwarded to the British governor of the prison and the two would iron out any difficulties that arose.

However, this was not the end of the affair. When the Rath Camp opened to receive prisoners from Arbour Hill, both Lawless and O'Connor were in the first batch of 150 men to be transferred. O'Connor, who had been involved in the escapes of republican prisoners from several prisons, asked Lawless if he had made plans for a mass escape during the move to the Curragh. Lawless replied that he had not, and explained that they were certain to be heavily guarded, so it was not possible to make any pre-arranged plans:

> I assured him that, of course, if any opportunity showed itself on the way we would do what we could about it when the chance arose. He [O'Connor] then took up the heavy attitude with me and, speaking as a member of the General Staff, warned me that it was my duty as the prisoners' commandant to organise an escape. Poor Rory was evidently still suffering from the snub to his dignity of my election as commandant against his candidature, and I regretted the necessity for a further snub when I replied that the matter rested safely in my hands. It was clear, however, that Rory was likely to cause trouble and I discussed this quietly with Peadar McMahon and a few others while we waited. We concluded that nothing was likely to happen until we arrived at the Curragh, but then we would be in a position of a new community and Rory would most likely try to gain an ascendency and have himself elected as camp commandant. We agreed that we would not allow this to happen, but I said

that I would not stand as a candidate for election and suggested Peadar McMahon as more suitable. Peadar tried to persuade me to accept election to the appointment, and only agreed to accept it himself on condition that I would act as his vice-commandant or second in command.

All this may sound a bit like parish pump politics, but the position was that the general body of prisoners would accept any reasonable rule of leadership provided that there were no divided councils. If opposing factions were allowed to arise then the men would be unable to decide what was the right thing to do and a division in our ranks would thus be exposed to the enemy. It was therefore up to the senior I.R.A. officers among the prisoners to make the decision and present this to the general body – for rectification in the form of an election.[12]

While he was interned at the Rath Camp, Lawless took a set of invaluable historic photographs, now part of the National Museum of Ireland's collection. He took thirty-five photographs inside the camp, doing so covertly and most probably using a Vest Pocket Kodak, covering everyday activities such as taking exercise, washing clothes, attending mass, tuberculosis patients being treated in the camp hospital, and cooking meals. These activities contrast with the background to the photographs showing watchtowers and barbed wire. Lawless took a photograph of one of the guards, Sergeant Roper, who heard the click of the photo being taken but did not know who had the camera. He became very alarmed when an internee, Ed McEvoy, said that the photograph would be used to identify him to the prisoners' friends on the outside.[13]

Rory O'Connor was born in Kildare Street, Dublin, in 1883 and educated at St Mary's College, Dublin, Clongowes Wood College, Co. Kildare, and University College Dublin (UCD), graduating in Arts and Engineering. He also attended the College of Science, Merrion Street, Dublin. O'Connor worked as a railway engineer in Canada before returning to Ireland in 1915 at the behest of the IRB. He worked as a civil engineer with Dublin Corporation, and was involved with the Gaelic League and Irish Volunteers. His precise role in the Rising is unclear, but he was wounded by sniper fire during reconnaissance at the College of Surgeons. On his recuperation from his wounds, O'Connor was prominent in the successful Sinn Féin parliamentary by-election campaign in Roscommon.

Appointed to the Volunteers' GHQ staff as director of engineering in March 1918, he held the post throughout the War of Independence. He was also involved in the planning and execution of prison escapes in both Ireland and Britain, most notably the daring daylight escape of Piaras Béaslaí, Austin Stack and four others from Strangeways Prison in Manchester. For this he bore the unofficial (and jocular) titles of 'OC of escapes' and 'director of jail deliveries'. Not long after arriving in the Rath Camp, he made his own successful escape.[14]

One of the most important men in the camp was the journalist Desmond FitzGerald. He was born in 1888 in West Ham, London, to a Co. Cork father and a Co. Kerry mother, who had met in London. FitzGerald was educated at West Ham Grammar School, and while employed as a clerk in the civil service began to write poetry and did some journalism. He became friendly with the group of poets known as the Imagists, including F. S. Flint, T. E. Hulme, Hilda Doolittle, Edward Storer and Richard Aldington. In 1911 Desmond eloped with the daughter of a Presbyterian unionist, Mabel McConnell, who had worked briefly in London as a secretary to George Bernard Shaw and George Moore, and they settled in Brittany. Two years later, the FitzGeralds moved to Ventry, in West Kerry, to enable Desmond to perfect his Irish-language skills. Some time later, he began to organise the Irish Volunteers in West Kerry and became a member of the IRB, remaining in the Irish Volunteers following the split with John Redmond.

In January 1915 the FitzGeralds moved to Bray, Co. Wicklow, when an order issued under DORA banned Desmond from Kerry. The cause of the expulsion was Mabel's decision to feed her hens at night, which, according to the Department of Agriculture, increased egg production. The wavering light of Mabel's lantern, seen from the RIC station across the bay, convinced the police that Desmond FitzGerald was signalling to German submarines. Soon, though, FitzGerald was organising the Irish Volunteers in Wicklow, and in October 1915 he was arrested and sentenced to six months' imprisonment for making a seditious speech and discouraging recruitment to the British Army. He completed his sentence just three weeks before the Rising, in which both he and Mabel participated, taking part in the occupation of the General Post Office (GPO).

Singled out as a leader among the republican prisoners,

FitzGerald served over a year in four English prisons before being released in mid-1917. In May 1918 he was in Cootehill, Cavan, canvassing for Arthur Griffith in a by-election, when he was arrested in connection with the 'German Plot' – an alleged conspiracy existing between Sinn Féin and the German Empire to start an armed insurrection, but really an excuse by Dublin Castle to arrest the republican leadership. The German Plot prisoners were released in March 1919 and a month later FitzGerald was named director of publicity for Dáil Éireann, the Irish parliament, which had been established the previous January. To ensure that the Dáil government's case was represented effectively abroad, he constantly lobbied international journalists based in London and Dublin. In November 1919 the publicity department began to produce an underground daily newspaper, the *Irish Bulletin*, again with a foreign audience in mind and with the primary aim of influencing press coverage of Ireland.

The *Irish Bulletin* was published from various locations without a break until after the Truce, but FitzGerald's activity with the newspaper was interrupted in February 1921 when he was arrested while visiting his wife and children at their home. Mabel rushed to inform the press, fearing that he might be assassinated. He was held in Dublin Castle and Arbour Hill Prison, before being transferred to the Rath Camp, where he became the camp librarian.[15] Lieutenant Vinden often talked with FitzGerald, who spoke with a markedly English accent.[16] Vinden said, 'I … spent many an hour in the evenings walking round the cage with him.

He poured out the woes of Ireland going back to the days of Cromwell and the Battle of the Boyne ... All I could do in response was to apologise for their actions.' However, Vinden stressed 'we did talk of other things'.[17]

Christopher Stephen Andrews – 'C.S.' or 'Todd', as he was more commonly known – was among a batch of fifty prisoners brought from Arbour Hill Prison in early March 1921 to the Curragh. 'We found we were in the Rath Internment Camp,' Andrews wrote in his memoir *Dublin Made Me*, 'which, as prisoner 1569, hut 32, became my address for the next five months.' Andrews was born in 1901, in the Summerhill area of Dublin. At that time Summerhill was becoming a slum and Todd recorded that he was 'born into the lower middle class of the population'. In 1910 the family moved to Terenure village, a mixed community of Protestants and Catholics. He briefly attended P. H. Pearse's school, St Enda's, but completed his education at Synge Street Christian Brothers School (CBS). His schooling by the Christian Brothers was apolitical but nationalistic, and shaped the young Todd's thinking. He joined Na Fianna Éireann in 1912 but left the organisation when one of his teachers preached against secret societies. The executions of the 1916 leaders 'imprinted on my young mind an abiding hatred of British domination in Ireland'.

In March 1917, when he was fifteen, Todd Andrews joined the Rathfarnham Company of the Irish Volunteers. He chose Rathfarnham because it was outside Terenure and the local police would not know him. Many of the Volunteers of

Rathfarnham, or E Company, were veterans of Easter Week, as St Enda's was situated in the area. Andrews attended UCD in 1919 while remaining an active member of the IRA. In April 1920 he was arrested, but was released after ten days of a hunger strike in Mountjoy Gaol. He was arrested again in March 1921, by members of the Igoe Gang, a group of RIC men drawn from different parts of the country, and was interrogated in Dublin Castle; however, he was spared a beating because his interrogators, to his amusement, regarded him as a harmless enthusiast.

Andrews remembered receiving his internment order with some relief as it was 'a fairly certain guarantee that the British had nothing against you for which you could be tried by court martial'.[18] From November 1920 a court martial could mean execution if a Volunteer was arrested carrying arms. There was also the added danger of being killed when apprehended by the crown forces. Arrival at a camp meant that a prisoner had survived the risky hours following arrest, when beatings, mock executions, torture and the use of captives as hostages were common. In a strange way the internees and their families regarded the prison camps as havens, despite the hardships and dangers of incarceration.[19]

Republican public representatives were easily recognisable and provided convenient targets for internment, though many were not active Volunteers. During its existence, the Rath Camp housed fourteen elected members of the Dáil. Among them was Tom Derrig, a native of Westport, Co. Mayo. Derrig was born in 1898 and educated at the Christian Brothers

School at Westport, at University College Galway (UCG) and at UCD. At an early age he showed strong republican leanings and, when a student at UCG in 1915, he assisted with the organisation of a corps of the Irish Volunteers. He took part in the Rising and was arrested, deported to Britain and interned at Frongoch in Wales. He was released in August 1916 and subsequently graduated from college and became the headmaster of the Ballina Technical School.

Derrig continued to organise the Volunteers on a military basis in both Mayo and Galway until he was arrested and sentenced, on retrial at Belfast Assizes (the jury in Green Street in Dublin having failed to agree), to a term of imprisonment, which he served in Belfast and Derry. He was released in time to take an active part in the general election of December 1918, when Sinn Féin overwhelmingly defeated the IPP.[20] At that time, Derrig was commandant of the West Mayo Brigade of the Irish Volunteers, a position he held until his arrest by a military and police raiding party on the Monday night after Bloody Sunday. While imprisoned in the Rath Camp, Derrig was elected a Sinn Féin TD for Mayo North and West.[21]

One of those directly involved in the Bloody Sunday killings, which had led to internment and the establishment of the Rath Camp, was James McNamara. A native of Longhill, near Foynes, Co. Limerick, McNamara moved to Dublin seeking employment. He subsequently worked as a barman and became a member of E Company, 1st Battalion, Dublin Brigade. On Easter Monday he and other staff members of

Mooney's, Parnell Street, left their work and took part in the Rising. McNamara fought in the Four Courts, Church Street and North King Street during Easter Week. After the surrender, he was deported to Knutsford Prison in England along with his brother, Patrick, who was also a member of the Four Courts garrison. They were subsequently interned in Frongoch until December 1916.

James McNamara rejoined his company on his release, and on 1 March 1918 was selected to serve on a special mission to London under the command of Cathal Brugha, with orders to shoot the British prime minister and members of the cabinet if conscription were introduced in Ireland. However, the assassination squad was called back to Ireland when the plan to implement conscription was withdrawn. After the Bloody Sunday killings of British officers on 21 November 1920, McNamara and three others – James Boyce, Michael Tobin and Thomas Whelan – were charged with the shooting of Captain G. T. Baggallay, a courts martial officer.[22]

A witness picked out McNamara, whom he had seen with a group of men at the corner of Herbert Place and Upper Mount Street, near the scene of Baggallay's killing at 119 Lower Baggot Street. The eyewitness said the men were out of breath as if they had been running; he also picked McNamara out because he had red hair. In his defence, McNamara said he was at nine o'clock mass in Kingstown and had a witness to corroborate this. The charges were dropped because of the flimsy evidence, but McNamara was considered an active republican and was hauled off to the Curragh. He was considerably lucky – Thomas

Whelan, despite his innocence, was convicted, sentenced to death and hanged on 13 March 1921.[23]

Fr Patrick Smith, CC, Rahan, Tullamore, Co. Offaly, became one of the most important men in the camp. Arrested on 3 March 1921 at the parochial house, he was brought by military lorry to Tullamore and later conveyed to Hare Park Camp.[24] Patrick Smith, who was born at Kilskyre, Kells, Co. Meath in 1877, was a curate in Tyrellspass, Co. Westmeath, where he helped to form a local unit of the Irish Volunteers. He was also a fluent Irish speaker and at one stage was president of the Meath Irish-Speaking Priests Association. After the 1914 split in the Irish Volunteers, Fr Smith became one of the leaders of the Tyrellspass Company but was moved to another parish just before the Easter Rising.[25]

Liam Ó Briain arrived from GHQ in Dublin to Tyrellspass with orders for manoeuvres for Easter Week 1916 and inquired in the street for Fr Smith, only to discover that he had been moved to Castlepollard, 27 miles away, as a curate. Ó Briain continued to Tullamore, Co. Offaly, with the result that the Tyrellspass Volunteers failed to mobilise for the Rising. (He later met Fr Smith in the Curragh when they were both interned.)[26]

In Castlepollard, Fr Smith was embroiled in controversy when, on 24 September 1917, at Sunday mass the organist played 'God Save the King' and 'La Marseillaise'. Fr Smith took offence at the playing of the English national anthem and according to onlookers physically removed the organ player. The schoolmistress was also involved and she, along with Fr Smith, was 'tried' before three parish priests. The people outside the church cheered Fr Smith and proclaimed that the organ was bought with their money, but during the first week of October Fr Smith was moved to Rahan, Co. Offaly, where his republican activities led to his arrest and incarceration in 1921.[27]

In the Curragh, Fr Smith was highly thought of by the internees. Todd Andrews described him as 'one of our prize prisoners (if that is the appropriate word)':

> To us in the IRA the Catholic religion meant as much emotionally as did the Movement. We were disappointed that, except for some individual priests and one or two bishops, we had not got the support of the Church. De Valera tried, without success, to get the Hierarchy to issue a statement recognising the Government appointed by Dáil Éireann as the legitimate government of the Irish people. The presence of a priest in the camp was a consolation to us; he helped to sustain our morale. We had, I think, a subconscious fear that we might be denounced by the Church as the Fenians were. Somehow Father Smith as a fellow prisoner, sharing our common lot, gave us an assurance that this would not happen. To be deprived of the sacraments would have created a conflict of loyalties for us. We did not want to have to choose.[28]

Micheál Ó Laoghaire said of Fr Smith that he 'was our beloved sagart':

> He was that fine type of man that, if you met him in the street,

you would stand to look after him. His personality, physique and stance commanded not only respect but awe. He was a man of at least 6' 3" in height, beautifully developed. Stand-offish and domineering would be the first impression one would form of him. Hard, one would think, to approach but, when one had got in contact with him, one very soon realised that those impressions were wrong. He commanded the respect of the Camp and even the most hardened sinners amongst us always paid him his due respects. He was not only sagart aroon ['the dear priest'] but an Irishman as well who always guided his fellow-prisoners in their stand for freedom and who, though a priest first, if it came to a point when he had to assert himself physically, would have no hesitation in doing so. I only met him once after our release and he said to me, 'I am neutral, for the unfortunate split has driven my boys into different camps. Seeing this, I could take no sides. You were all my boys!'[29]

One of the leading sportsmen of the era, Frank Burke, was a prisoner at the Rath Camp for nine months. He was born in Carbury, Co. Kildare in 1895, and in September 1909 was sent as a boarder to St Enda's College, which had been founded the previous year by Pearse in Cullenswood House, Oakley Road, Ranelagh. In 1910 the school was transferred to the more spacious grounds of The Hermitage, Rathfarnham. There was another Frank Burke at St Enda's when he arrived, so Pearse called him Fergus. On 25 November 1913, when the public meeting was held at the Rotunda in Dublin 'to establish a corps of Irish Volunteers', Burke attended as a steward.

On Easter Monday 1916 Burke made his way to the GPO on a tram with the rest of the Rathfarnham Volunteers. His first few days were spent on the roof of the GPO. After the evacuation of that building he manned a barricade in Moore Street, and on Saturday morning was one of the group in Sackville Lane who were preparing to attack the British barricade less than 30 yards away in Parnell Street when the decision to surrender was made. On 1 May he was deported to Stafford Detention Barracks and later transferred to Frongoch Camp in Wales.

Prisoners designated as 'Class A' were internees 'who in the opinion of the Police should not be released'. The RIC Special Branch report for Burke declared: 'release will tend to further the cause of Sinn Feinism'. Most of the rebel prisoners had been freed over the previous months, but some were held until the end of the year. Burke was released on 23 December. When the schools reopened in January 1917 he returned to St Enda's to teach. Despite his internment, he served as headmaster from then until the school closed in 1935.

Frank Burke was one of the most outstanding all-rounders in GAA history, winning two All-Ireland hurling medals and three All-Ireland football medals, all with Dublin. On Bloody Sunday, 21 November 1920, he was marking Mick Hogan when the Tipperary captain was fatally shot by British forces.[30] Fourteen people were killed that day, including one football player and three children under the age of fifteen. An inquiry was set up and it was suggested that the initial shots came from inside the grounds and that the crown forces were fired on first. This was quickly discredited as all the spectators were searched and only one revolver was found.

While fleeing from the grounds, Burke was struck on the head with a revolver by a policeman, who told him to go to the dressing room. He and the other Dublin players were corralled in the dressing room, where they were searched and their watches, cigarettes and money taken. They were then allowed to leave. Burke made his way back to St Enda's to make sure all his students were safe as he had given permission for some of them to go to the game. Apart from one minor injury, all the students had returned safely.

Frank Burke was arrested on 21 March 1921 at Rathfarnham and was initially taken to Arbour Hill Prison before being transferred to the Curragh. In the Rath Camp he helped to organise Gaelic football games to keep up discipline, fitness and morale.[31]

4
'NO PLACE LIKE HOME'

The aim of internment was containment rather than punishment or rehabilitation, so men were detained at the pleasure of the British government with no release date in sight. Life in the Curragh internment camps was dreary and monotonous, with the same surroundings, the same dull routine, day after day, week after week. While visitors were permitted at Hare Park, none were allowed at the Rath Camp apart from two priests from Kildare town, who came in weekly to hear confessions. In her witness statement, Brigid Brophy, 1st lieutenant in the Carlow town Cumann na mBan branch, said she 'visited prisoners at Hare Park internment camp, the Curragh, Co. Kildare, and supplied them with food and clothing'.[1] Morale in both camps was maintained with concerts put on by the prisoners, the playing of sports, planning escapes and letter-writing. Valuable sources of pleasure were the local newspapers, which kept men informed of what was happening in their home districts. All of the Irish daily newspapers, and periodicals such as *Ireland's Own*, were allowed in the camps. Copies were passed around until they practically fell apart.[2]

Sylvester Delahunt from Tuckmill, Straffan, Co. Kildare, was arrested on 1 March 1921 and interned in Rath Camp until December of that year. His autograph book of the time includes a quote from Richard McDermott of Athenry, Co. Galway: 'Rath Camp is nice, but there's no place like home.'[3]

The actual management of the Rath Camp was handed over from the start to the internees. Micheál Ó Laoghaire took over the food stores from Lieutenant Mallett, the British camp quartermaster. According to Ó Laoghaire, rations provided by the military were a genuine source of grievance:

> He [Mallett] then handed to me a copy of the ration scale and said that he would supply me with rations according to that scale. The scale, with some deductions, was similar to the one in use by the British army at the time. It looked good enough on paper but, when put to the test, there were always snags arising, such as, short weights (a daily occurrence), no vegetables, rancid margarine, fish (when supplied) sometimes putrid and the bread ration insufficient. This caused a lot of trouble and, although reported daily, nothing was ever done to put matters right.
>
> On one occasion a consignment of fish arrived which was definitely bad. I got our own Medical Officers to inspect it, as well as the British Medical Officer. All were unanimous that the fish was not fit for human consumption and the British M.O. gave his certificate to that effect. The fish was sent back to the Curragh only to be returned again by orders of the D.M.S. as he considered the fish was perfectly good. When the internees who were waiting for their dinner heard the result, a party of them there and then swept the fish off the lorry, carried the boxes to the barbed wire and emptied the contents on and over the wire, leaving it there to smell, stench and decay under the broiling sun of a summer's day.
>
> The margarine was generally rancid and scarcely ever

> touched. No fresh vegetables were supplied, always split peas in lieu, with the result that these commodities began to accumulate in my stores and in the cookhouse, so much so that I was able to hand over to the White Cross and the Newbridge Cumann na mBan, when the Camp was closed, about 4 tons of split peas and beans, 1,500 lbs of rancid margarine and 700 or 800 lbs of tea for disposal, but not without a big fight with the British Camp authorities …[4]

The lack of provision for the disposal of offal also often resulted in the remains of beasts being left outside the cookhouse door, a situation that was undoubtedly unhygienic and probably malodorous. The internee medical men complained that while the food was supposed to be the same as that served to their guards, only inferior meat was given to the prisoners. The milk supply arrived late in the morning, which caused much inconvenience. Rice had been promised to the internees on the recommendation of their medical doctor, Francis P. Ferran (Foxford, Co. Mayo), but its supply was again insufficient. (Ferran was also OC 4th Battalion, North Mayo Brigade.)[5]

When Todd Andrews arrived in the camp in early March 1921 he found:

> We got a great welcome from our fellow internees who helped us to settle in and got us tea and sandwiches. They showed us how to make up our beds which consisted of a bed board and hard cushions, called 'biscuits', a pillow and blankets. We had no sheets. It took us only a few days to settle into the routine of camp life.

Life in the camp was, in a physical sense, far from unpleasant. Indeed for the first few weeks I found it agreeably exciting meeting new people including some national personalities, exploring the library which was surprisingly good, playing football, learning the procedure for receipt of letters and parcels and examining the canteen …

From time to time rows or disputes between prisoners had also to be settled though these were rare as a great sense of camaraderie prevailed and morale was very high. The main function of our O/C was to deal with the British O/C concerning our constant grievances about the quality of the food. Theoretically, according to the British regulations, we were supposed to rise at 6.30 a.m. to be ready at 7 a.m. and standing by our beds to be counted. We were counted twice a day by a Sergeant accompanied by a couple of soldiers with fixed bayonets. The second count took place a half an hour before sundown when we were locked up for the night.

After we were locked up a few of the prisoners with good voices usually started a sing-song. The songs were heavily patriotic, the most popular being 'Down by the glenside', 'All round my hat I wear a tri-coloured ribbon-o', 'The grand old dame Brittania' [sic]. 'The Soldier's Song' was often sung but it had no special significance and never rated as the National Anthem. Last thing in the evening before going to sleep the whole hut joined in saying the Rosary aloud. Not one decade but five decades. There was always someone who knew what five mysteries were appropriate to any given day. The Rosary was much more than a prayer. It came to be a secular slogan interwoven into the fabric of the Movement.

In fact the morning count never took place until 8 a.m. when we were let out for breakfast. We had complete freedom until we were locked up in the evening. After breakfast we did whatever fatigue we were assigned to, for cleaning up the hut. Once per week it was washed out thoroughly with Jeyes Fluid. The latrine fatigue was the least popular. Not much less popular was the washing up of the plates, mugs and knives and forks. It had to be done in cold water. The food, although it was the same food as the soldiers got, was, except for the tea and bread, abominable. It was assumed, rightly, that everyone liked extremely strong tea with plenty of sugar in it. The bread was good, freshly baked every day. The margarine stank and was quite uneatable. The meat might have been good before it was cooked but the cooking ruined it. The potatoes were rotten and the cabbage, which was the only other vegetable supplied, was invariably worm eaten. We would certainly have been hungry except for the generous parcels received from home.

In the huts we formed 'messes' of three or four prisoners, who shared their parcels in common. There was always a shortage of cigarettes because not every 'mess' got them from home and even if you had money they were not sold in the camp canteen. The canteen, which was run by the British (payment being made in camp chits) had a limited but very useful stock. Buttons, needles, thread, darning wool, matches, shaving soap, razor blades were the main items. We got quite useful at darning socks, sewing on buttons and mending tears in our clothes.

We had very little contact with our guards. Periodically they would patrol the camp at night. Sometimes, if they had read of some successful attack by the IRA, they would bang on our huts with their rifle butts, wakening us and swearing at us. Sometimes they would conduct exhaustive searches of the huts during the day. They belonged to a Scottish Regiment – I am not sure if it was the King's Own Scottish Borderers or the King's Own Scottish Light Infantry – but their attitude to us was very hostile. In the course of the searches they never passed without calling you a bastard or threatening you with their bayonets. They were all young conscripts who seemed to loathe us and they treated us very differently from the Lancashire Fusiliers whom I had encountered in Dublin. They were particularly offensive when they succeeded in finding an escape tunnel of which there was always at least one being dug by one or other of the Companies into which the internees were organised. When a tunnel was found the whole camp was punished by the stoppage of parcels and the closure of the canteen. Once we had a fine of five shillings per man imposed because bed boards were missing; they had been used either for fuel in the stove with which each hut was furnished or as pit props for the tunnels. As not everyone got money from home, those who did refused to accept any in protest. The British replied by closing the canteen and stopping the newspapers. We got the Irish newspapers fairly regularly and I had the *Sunday Observer* sent to me weekly directly from O'Kennedy's, the newsagents in Terenure. It arrived most weeks, as did a sports paper called *All Sports*.[6]

Due to the canteen being closed as a punishment for the escape attempts in mid-May, prisoners urged relatives to send in extra commodities usually purchased in the canteen to cover the shortfall.[7]

Despite the hardships of internment, camp life suited some prisoners, like Todd Andrews:

> I had no difficulty in putting in the day in the camp. I worked out a satisfactory way of life for myself getting gradually on friendly terms with different internees. I often went to the library, spending my time looking through the books and talking to the assistant librarian, a man named [John P.] Cotter who was also the champion chess player in the camp. I regret that I never learned to play chess. The nominal head of the library was Desmond FitzGerald, the most important prisoner in the camp, a well-known national figure.[8]

Joe Lawless, who had been interned in Frongoch, found there was a great difference between the Welsh camp and the Rath Camp. He later recalled, 'In the former we were in a foreign land in which we could count upon no friends around us, and our effort in the Rising was spent for the moment. In the Rath we were still in our own land with friends close to us on every side and the fight was still in progress throughout the land.' He occasionally received a letter from his father, Frank, who was interned in Ballykinlar Camp. Lawless even had some fond memories of his time in the Rath:

> An odd memory of the camp that persists with extraordinary clarity after all the years is that of the trumpeters of the Huzzar Regiment which was our garrison. About six of these carried out daily practice during the summer mornings beside the great

mound of Gibbet Rath, a couple of hundred yards from the east side of our enclosure. The music of the various trumpet calls in blended harmony was something new to our ears. In contrast with the strident tone and limited range of the bugle calls to which we had become accustomed, this sounded really beautiful and, added to the scene of a rising sun flashing upon the highly polished brass trumpets, as the trumpeters' arms rose and fell in unison, gave a sharp thrill to the very appreciative audience within the wire enclosure. The various trumpet calls of British cavalry regiments have become familiar to my ears since then, and I still appreciate their musical arrangement, but the notes of a trumpet always recall to my mind those days in the summer of 1921, when the thoughts that arose at its sound took us far beyond wire and away from the age in which we lived.[9]

Fintan Murphy, one of four republican prisoners arrested in London and deported to Ireland for detention, did not have such warm memories and described camp life as a 'slow death process'. The effects of confinement were so bad that he had seen 'strong, young, country lads unable to answer roll call in the morning, and later on, faint shortly after beginning exercise in the field'. He blamed the process of locking the internees in the huts from 6 p.m. to 7.30 a.m., and said such conditions would 'wreck the health of many of the young men' interned.[10]

Most of the internees adapted to their confinement, but some suffered mental stress and health breakdown. Noise in and about the huts was non-stop from morning to night, and most internees found sharing a hut with two dozen other men very trying. The biggest test of camp life was mental rather than physical. When it was noticed that a prisoner was feeling despondent or in a melancholy state, fellow internees would rally around him to try to boost his spirits. It was harder, mentally, on the older prisoners who had families, farms or businesses to run. They worried about their wives and children, how they were coping without them; or were apprehensive about the farm, how it was being run; or a business, how it was surviving. With no physical visits, news was gained by letter, but at the whim of the camp authorities letters could be censored or banned as a punishment. For some, the seeds of insanity or consumption were sown in the close confinement of the internment camps.

Although no prisoners died of the dreaded diseases that were prevalent in Irish society at the time, the highly infectious tuberculosis bacillus (TB) thrived in the crowded and poorly ventilated huts in the Curragh Camp housing both military servicemen and internees. During the period January to December 1921 eleven British soldiers, all of them young and in the prime of life, died at the Curragh Camp from illness, mainly consumption (TB), while another half-dozen died of self-inflicted injuries or were shot (accidentally or on purpose) by their fellow servicemen.[11]

Internees also contracted TB, and while none died, the long-term effects certainly contributed to their early demise. For example, Joseph Leo Tonge, of St Mary's Avenue, Rathfarnham (3rd Battalion, Dublin Brigade) was arrested on

23 March 1921 and held in Hut 16, B Line. According to his pension application he 'contracted TB while interned' at the Rath Camp 'where his health broke down'. He was released from internment on medical grounds on 20 November 1921, and subsequently reported to his battalion commandant, who, through the White Cross, sent him to Newcastle Sanatorium, Co. Wicklow, from where he was discharged in May 1922 'fit for work'. He was transferred from the IRA to the National Army on 8 June 1922 and was assigned to the Pay Office in Portobello Barracks, Dublin. Tonge was discharged from the National Army in January 1924, deemed medically unfit. He entered Crooksling Sanatorium, Brittas, Co. Dublin and from 29 February was in receipt of 10 shillings a week from the White Cross Disablement Committee. He died at Harold's Cross Hospice, Dublin, on 6 April 1926, aged twenty-eight, of 'phthisis', an old term for pulmonary tuberculosis.[12]

Another internee, Michael Horan from Mullingar, died on 20 June 1924 in the County Hospital from phthisis and syncope (fainting). He was twenty-two and his death was deemed attributable to the ten months, from February to December 1921, that he spent in Hare Park and the Rath Camp, as the hardship and poor conditions he endured led to the illness that caused his early death. Horan, a railway employee and quartermaster of the 1st Battalion, Mullingar Brigade, was arrested in February 1921 and brought to the Curragh. He developed a 'heavy cold', which led to pulmonary tuberculosis, from 'sleeping in wet blankets' and was transferred from the Rath Camp hospital to the TB hut. Thomas Lennon oversaw the TB hut and attributed Horan's illness to conditions at the camp. Horan was released during the general amnesty on 9 December 1921. He was arrested again in June 1922 but was subsequently released because of ill health.[13]

There were up to thirty men housed in each hut, which were built to accommodate a maximum of twenty-five. Dr Cusack said twenty men would fit comfortably and, to prevent outbreaks of diseases which thrived in areas of high congestion, such as consumption, he ordered that no more than twenty-five men should be in each hut. Tents were erected to relieve overcrowding, which were fine until the wet weather came. When rain fell, the water pooled on the ground around the tents and soaked its way into the interior. Rain also leaked into the tents, with the result that the beds became wet, and many prisoners were forced to try to sleep under these conditions.[14]

The camp drainage system was far from satisfactory, and the piping system provided for sanitation was insufficient to carry away the waste satisfactorily. In the hot summer weather conditions were extremely bad, almost unbearable, and there were fears of an outbreak of fever.

A further problem developed when the canteen shop was closed again, this time because, according to the military, some knives and forks were missing. However, the prisoners claimed the closure was because they refused to buy any goods they thought originated in Belfast, in sympathy with the Belfast Boycott in place throughout southern Ireland. In fact, some cutlery was missing and was returned, but the authorities refused to reopen the canteen.

On 24 May, on a pretext that he wanted to address the internees in their huts, the British adjutant led an armed search of prisoners and their belongings. That night, the internees refused to answer the roll call and had to be counted individually (905 of them in total). The following morning, the internees again refused to answer the roll call and were locked back into their huts. The prisoners forced open the hut doors and took what food they could find in the cookhouse before the military guard drove them back in at bayonet point.

This violation of discipline led immediately to the military commandant, Colonel Hanna, informing the prisoners' commandant, Peadar McMahon, that he had issued an order that all correspondence to or from the camp would cease; no incoming parcels would be delivered and all food supplies would cease to be delivered until discipline was restored. As there were by then no usable doors on the huts, sentries were placed outside until 6.30 a.m. In retaliation, the prisoners went on 'strike', refusing to do any work in the camp or obey any orders given by the military. Many men remained in bed all day in protest, refusing to attend the roll call; others basked in the summer sunshine. Tobacco supplies ran out and used tea leaves were gathered and smoked.[15]

The poor conditions in the Rath Camp led to a heated exchange between Sir Hamar Greenwood, Chief Secretary for Ireland, and Liberal MP Major Murdoch Mackenzie Wood in the House of Commons on 9 June 1921. The former front-line officer asked Greenwood whether he was aware that 'serious discontent exists among internees in Rath

Internment Camp with regard to conditions prevailing there; whether the food ration has been reduced, that the receiving and sending of letters and parcels have been stopped, and that military pickets have been preventing internees from cooking food previously received from friends; whether Rath Camp is treated differently from others in these matters, and if so, why that should be so?'

Greenwood replied that 'Rath Internment Camp is subject to the same rules as other internment camps in Ireland, namely, those laid down in the Royal Warrant for the treatment of prisoners of war. Following an outbreak of concerted insubordination, measures were taken, in accordance with those rules, for the restoration of discipline, and these measures included a curtailment of rations and of privileges.'

Wood asked: 'Does the Right Hon. Gentleman consider that it is a civilised method of punishing prisoners to put them on famine rations?'

Conservative Lieutenant Colonel Martin Archer-Shee interjected: 'Is it not a fact that among these internees are a great many people who have committed the most foul murders?'

Several MPs loudly demanded that the internees be tried for murder, to which Greenwood replied: 'They are not tried for the same reason that you cannot try the same Sinn Féin men in London when they have committed murders, namely, the difficulty of getting any evidence.'

Major Wood then asked: 'If these men are hungry and have not enough to eat, and their friends send them parcels, why should the authorities interfere to prevent them from eating and cooking what is sent to them?'

Greenwood replied: 'The internment camps in Ireland are entirely under military control, and I have every confidence in the administration of the military officers.'[16]

Hamar Greenwood was no stranger to controversy. As chief secretary he was closely identified with the aggressive use of the Black and Tans and the Auxiliaries, and after the burning of Cork city centre by the Auxies in December 1920 had suggested that it was the citizens of Cork who had burned their own city and not the crown forces.[17]

On the seventh day of the prisoners' 'strike', a 'truce' was agreed and normal conditions were restored: the playing of football, debating classes, and mail and food deliveries were reinstated.[18]

In August as many as 600 cases of infectious disease attributable to food poisoning occurred in the camp. Around 300 men were confined to bed during one outbreak; some were seriously ill, and Laurence O'Callaghan, of Main Street, Naas, was reported as being in a very dangerous condition.[19] His family received a telegram from the Rath Camp to this effect. O'Callaghan had been arrested on 26 March 1921 and interned without charge or trial. He was eventually released in November as a result of continuing ill health.[20] The interned medical men, Dr Francis Ferran and Dr Brian Cusack, protested about the conditions to the camp authorities, and an investigation took place at the insistence of the British War Office. While this was being conducted there was a temporary improvement, but nothing permanent came out of the inquiry.

There was also the possibility of the arrival of a highly contagious and potentially catastrophic disease in the camp. In a batch of prisoners from Boyle, Co. Roscommon, were two cases of men with typhoid and, in order to prevent the spread of such a deadly disease throughout the camp, the two had to be isolated. A less serious, but more common health issue with prisoners (and also with IRA Volunteers in active service units and flying columns) was scabies.[21]

There was a hospital hut for internees in the Rath Camp, where prisoners were treated for minor ailments and injuries resulting from everyday camp life during their detention. Those contracting more serious illnesses, and those wounded or injured on active service, were taken to the nearby Curragh Military Hospital.

One of the Rath Camp hospital's patients was John J. Martin, who lost an eye in an accident on 3 April 1921. He stated that he ran into a man carrying a length of timber on his shoulder and a spike of wood penetrated his left eye. Peadar McMahon, however, said the accident occurred when two men were wrestling over a length of wood and Martin came on the scene and was struck accidentally. The eye was severely damaged and was removed in the camp hospital the following day, with Martin subsequently being fitted with a glass eye. Martin was a member of the 1st Battalion, Dublin Brigade and a hut leader at the time. He was later a quartermaster in the camp and one of the organisers of the September tunnel escape.[22]

Mick Ryan and Larry O'Neill were injured during their capture at Ballymurphy, Co. Carlow, on 18 April 1921. Ryan had a shattered shoulder and spent three months in the Rath Camp hospital. Along with six others captured – Patrick Gaffney, Patrick Fitzpatrick, William McKenna and Thomas, James and Michael Bchan – he was subsequently court-martialled at Keane Barracks in the Curragh Camp around the time of the Truce. As a result of a spirited legal defence, the eight men were found not guilty of endangering the safety of crown personnel by the 'discharge of firearms, and the aiding of such an act', but at the end of July they received lengthy prison sentences on explosives charges and for possession of guns. As sentenced prisoners, they were sent to convict prisons: Mountjoy in Dublin, and Dartmoor and HMP Liverpool in England. Mick Ryan, of Tullow Street, Carlow, was given fifteen years but was freed when all convicted republican prisoners were released on 12 January 1922; he returned to the Curragh during the Civil War, when he was interned in Hare Park Camp.[23]

Jack Hunt was captured when the No. 2 Leitrim column was ambushed at Selton Hill by British troops on 11 March 1921. Five Volunteers were killed outright, while another was mortally wounded and died later that night. Four men escaped, and Hunt, from Rinnacurran, Carrick-on-Shannon, was the only one of the survivors captured. He was wounded in the leg but refused medical attention. He was moved to Boyle, where a military doctor attended to him, but his leg did not improve with treatment, so he was moved to the Curragh

Military Hospital. He eventually recovered, though his knee always gave him trouble and he was left with a limp. Hunt was tried and subsequently charged with carrying arms and levying war. He was sentenced to ten years' imprisonment.[24]

Michael Molloy, from Drumcullen, Co. Offaly, was accidentally wounded in the left foot by a shotgun blast from a fellow Volunteer before he was interned. His toe had to be amputated and he subsequently received medical treatment for his injury in the camp hospital.[25]

Other injured Volunteers needed hospital treatment for beatings received after they had been taken into custody. Thomas Berry, from Tullamore, was captured on 20 June 1921 after an attack at Geashill, Co. Offaly, on Black and Tans on a train. He was initially held in Tullamore Prison, where he was badly beaten on the head with rifle butts, and was subsequently transferred to the Rath Camp in August. He needed treatment throughout his time there. Berry was released in December 1921 in the general amnesty and subsequently received more medical care.[26]

Six republican prisoners held in Strokestown demesne after the Scramogue ambush in March 1921 were beaten by a dozen soldiers. One of the prisoners, William Mullaney, of Culleenaghamore, Kilglass, Strokestown, gave this account:

> They struck us with revolvers and rifle butts and bed crutches. We were kicked and beaten. They left and returned again in half an hour and attacked us again. We got kicks in the face and back and I got a kick on the hand which left it powerless. I was

also struck on the head with a stick and was knocked almost unconscious. As I went to rise from the floor I got a blow of a poker across the bridge of my nose. Two nights later we were again attacked by soldiers and though we were badly injured they refused our request for a doctor. We were later taken to Longford, then to Athlone and from that to the Curragh Camp from where, after spending seven weeks in bed, I was discharged on the recommendation of a medical board.[27]

For the majority of Volunteers, who did not have to spend their days in the hospital, or did not have camp jobs like fatigues, cooking, etc., there were other ways to pass the long days. Military classes were held in the camp and experts gave lectures in explosives, handling of arms and tactical exercises. They were always well attended and were never discovered, despite a British intelligence officer named Bultitude and an army sergeant whom the internees nicknamed 'White Liver' being specifically employed within the camp to unearth clandestine activity.

However, Bultitude found other reasons to punish the men and that punishment could be severe. Attached to the camp was an isolation and detention hut, where some men were detained in solitary confinement for several months. The British guards referred to the internment camp as 'the cage' and this detention hut was known as 'the sub-cage', because it was cut off from the rest of the camp by high corrugated iron fences. Micheál Ó Laoghaire maintained: 'This was a most uncalled for act and caused a rightful feeling of resentment throughout the Camp, but the Intelligence officer, Bultitude, and his Camp touts had to show some results for their daily visits. Men were confined to this isolation hut because the British Intelligence authorities thought they were organising within the Camp for the I.R.B.'[28]

Desmond FitzGerald, speaking to a reporter from *The Freeman's Journal* on his release in July 1921, described the conditions of the sub-cage. He was one of fourteen men singled out for incarceration there as a disciplinary punishment and said that some of the British officers behaved quite well towards their captives, but others showed their hostility in various ways. Communication with the main camp was prohibited, and exercise was conducted in a small uncovered yard.

FitzGerald also pointed out that the military regime in the camp was more severe than conditions in an ordinary British convict prison, where no authority could inflict a punishment of more than three days on a bread and water diet on any prisoner. As a capable journalist with the *Irish Bulletin*, FitzGerald was used to producing republican propaganda, and circulated this and other prison incidents to the national and international media. The maximum punishment in a convict prison, he said, was apparently not enough to satisfy the military authorities at the Curragh. And he informed readers that when he left the Rath Camp, thirteen of his fellow internees 'had not had a square meal for a week'.[29]

The prospect of freedom was, of course, foremost in the minds of many prisoners, and some began plotting to escape as soon as they arrived. Tomás Ó Maoláin from Mayo said:

Prisoners of war in those days could usually be placed in one of two main categories: (1) Those who just settled in and decided to make the best of a bad lot, and (2) Those whose mental register was 'I'm getting out of this joint just as fast as I can'.[30]

Tipperary businessman Lieutenant Daniel Ryan, F Company, 2nd Battalion, Dublin Brigade, was one of the latter. The Igoe Gang arrested Ryan near St Stephen's Green, Dublin, on 28 January 1921, the day after he took part in a gun and bomb attack on a military lorry in which one soldier was injured. After interrogation and the customary beating for Volunteers caught with arms, he was transferred from Dublin Castle to Arbour Hill, and subsequently to the Curragh. He described how he arrived at the Rath Camp (although he referred to it as Hare Park Camp) in a convoy of military trucks, with two British Army aeroplanes patrolling overhead, on a bitterly cold March morning:

> As we proceeded on our journey, we amused ourselves by singing national songs, and the soldiers of the escort laughed when an officer put a gun up to one of our boys and told him to stop singing rebel songs. To the great delight of the soldiers, our party sang a parody of 'Rule Brittania' [*sic*] which infuriated the officer still more.
>
> We arrived at our destination about 5.30 p.m., weary and hungry. We were duly searched and allotted our places in the huts. A crowd of us who were old members of the Dublin Brigade had no desire to be separated, and we luckily succeeded

in remaining together. We were about the first batch of prisoners to arrive at Hare Park Camp. For the first week, on account of our changed addresses, we received none of the usual parcels from our friends outside, and to say that we were often hungry during that week would be putting it mildly.

A friend in the enemy's camp invariably proves a valuable possession. In our case he turned out to be an exceptionally valuable one. When strolling around the camp one morning after breakfast, I accidentally opened the door of a hut which appeared to be in the course of construction, and to my great surprise and delight, who rushed over to me but the late Jerry Gaffney who was an active member of 'E' Company, 2nd Battalion, Dublin Brigade, and who was then employed as a carpenter at the Curragh Camp. After a warm handshake, Jerry produced a packet of cigarettes and we discussed the question of getting into communication with G.H.Q. as early as possible. I arranged with him to bring in a couple of loaves of bread and some cigarettes daily, and he did not spare himself in this respect. He also conveyed to me letters that the censor had not the pleasure of reading. That went on for a week or more, and then we discussed thoroughly the question that was uppermost in my mind, that of escape.

With Gaffney's assistance there was a sporting chance of getting out.[31]

The next question for Ryan was who was to go with him, so he approached one of the senior officers he knew in the camp, Rory O'Connor of GHQ. Ryan said O'Connor was using an assumed name and, like many other important men, had kept his identity a secret from the enemy. Ryan continued:

> He [O'Connor] had often planned escapes for others. Now he was to have the pleasure of planning his own.
>
> I told him that I saw a possible chance of escape but I would not disclose my plans until one condition was entered into – i.e. that I should be one of the two or three to escape. That was the greatest number I estimated could hope to get out without arousing suspicion. To this he smiled and said: 'That's the spirit; you can do more outside than here. There are too many locked up.' He added that he had been thinking of a possible way of escape since his arrival.
>
> I immediately revealed my plans to him. I told him about my meetings with Jerry Gaffney and to what extent the latter was prepared to go to help us.[32]

The two would-be escapers met Jerry Gaffney the following day in a disused hut at the end of the compound and discussed in detail the proposed escape. The entry and exit of the workmen was controlled by a pass system, and guards supervised their work. It was arranged that Gaffney and another man would stay away from work on the given day and Ryan and O'Connor would escape in the guise of the two workmen. Only a select few were told of the impending escape, among them Christopher Kenny of Rathangan, Co. Kildare, who persuaded another carpenter to stay away from work on the day selected. As per regulations, Dan Ryan informed the vice-commandant of the camp, Joe Lawless, of the contact he had made. Lawless in turn informed his superior officer, the camp commandant, Peadar McMahon.[33]

Meanwhile, over the following days Gaffney smuggled in workmen's dungarees and various articles of a tradesman's outfit, along with fake discs and passes to get through the military security at the gate. They decided that Friday, being payday amongst the workmen, would be the best day to chance their luck, and that 5.30 p.m. was the ideal time to escape as the workmen left at that time for home each evening. Then, at about 3.30 p.m., O'Connor approached Ryan while he was strolling around and told him, to his great disappointment, that the escape was off because the roll would be called in the camp at 6.30 p.m. and they would be missed within an hour of their departure. Later that evening Ryan and O'Connor had a quick meeting in the old hut and arranged to make the attempt the following day, Saturday 12 March. That morning, Ryan and O'Connor answered roll call at 6.30 a.m. and had breakfast at 8.15 a.m. Saturday was a half day for the workmen. Ryan said:

> Saturday came, and after breakfast Rory and I had a long discussion.
> About 12.30 p.m. we both rambled away from the general body of the prisoners and made our way to the hut in which all our requisites were hidden. We dressed in the dungarees, smeared our faces with dust to make ourselves look like workmen, got our discs and passes ready, and after putting the finishing touches to our personal appearance we silently opened the door of the hut

and, with a saw and tools under our arms, followed in the train of about a dozen workmen to the exit gates. We had to pass through two gates, with a full guard on each, and the majority of the workmen were well known to the guards on each gate.

As we approached the gate I could feel my heart beating quickly, my breathing became jerky and my senses began to weaken. At the exit I brazened myself up, produced my pass and disc, which were examined and found to be in order by the sentry at the first gate. We next approached the second gate and, to my horror, I recognised the sentry on duty. This particular soldier was always sympathetic and when passing me in the camp invariably greeted me with the remark, 'Hard lines, old man'. I could feel myself sagging when he looked at the card and disc and then looked at me. Fortunately, I had a cap pulled down on the right-hand side of my face. He again looked at the disc and at me – these few seconds seemed like an eternity – and then he said, 'All right, pass on'. I have often wondered since if he did really recognise me. The gate was opened and we passed out through it.

We slouched away down the road, keeping a distance from the workmen. When we got out of sight of the camp, we made our way across fields in the direction of Kildare railway station. In an old cowhouse we discarded our dungarees and tools and endeavoured to make ourselves look a little presentable. Rory turned to me and said, 'Thank God, they have been caught napping again.'

After half an hour's plodding across the fields, we arrived at Kildare railway station in time to catch a train to Dublin. Rory went to the booking office and purchased two first-class return tickets for Dublin. Not that we intended to return, but in case we were missed before roll call, and inquiries were made at the station, this would help to turn the enemy off the scent.[34]

Ryan and O'Connor got off the train at Lucan village and walked about a mile from the railway station to the old steam tram which ran from Lucan to Parkgate Street, on the edge of Dublin's Phoenix Park. When they were about halfway along the road, they saw a tender-load of Auxiliaries coming towards them. O'Connor said with dread: 'I'm afraid it's all up, but walk on.' They casually walked on, and as the tender drew near it pulled up. One of the Auxiliaries asked if they were on the right road for Newbridge, to which O'Connor replied, 'Yes.' The tender continued on its way. The two escapers arrived in Dublin at about 3 p.m., and after a warm handshake and arranging to meet later, parted company at Parkgate Street:

> I went to my digs, no doubt a risky thing to do, and when my landlady opened the door she nearly collapsed. However, the welcome was splendid.
>
> That night, with Rory I had the pleasure of meeting and being congratulated by Michael Collins, Gearóid O'Sullivan and other members of the G.H.Q. staff, all of whom were delighted to get a first-hand account of the first escape of prisoners from an internment camp in Ireland.[35]

The escape of the two prisoners was discovered at roll call that evening and from then on there was a considerable tightening of security measures, so that no similar attempt was possible for a long time.[36]

The details of the escape remained secret for some time, the newspapers knowing nothing of the facts, commenting that it was a 'mysterious affair'. The facts were simple enough. Daniel Ryan had arrived at the Rath Camp on 6 March and, with Rory O'Connor, had walked out through the main gate six days later.[37] Their escape within two weeks of the camp opening firmly established that it was not escape-proof and was a great morale boost to the prisoners, as well as a huge propaganda coup for the republican movement.

Bigger escapes were then planned. Some adventurous prisoners had, soon after their arrival, considered the prospect of digging a tunnel out of the camp, but the practical details were difficult to resolve. Joe Galvin of Mount Talbot, Co. Roscommon, had the idea of digging a tunnel under the huts and barbed-wire fences, and discussed it with a few trusted prisoners. Almost every trade and profession was represented in the camp, and for tunnelling work mechanics were the most sought after. However, the internees also had an ace up their sleeve. Jim Brady, from Bailieboro, Co. Cavan, had worked in the Arigna coalmines in Co. Roscommon and with his experience he became the chief strategist. Galvin said, 'when we discussed the matter with him, he was of the opinion that it was possible. We decided to try.'[38]

John F. 'Jack' Conroy, of The Neale, Ballinrobe, Co. Mayo, brought Brady to acting quartermaster Hugh Byrne with the idea of an escape tunnel. (Byrne was acting quartermaster while John J. Martin was recovering from his eye injury.) The idea seemed far-fetched but possible to Byrne, so he began drawing up plans.[39] Galvin said:

> Occasionally a working party of soldiers came into the camp to lace more and more barbed wire into the boundary fences. We were lucky that they arrived a few days later. They had about four wire cutters with them. We were very interested and very innocent-looking admirers of their work and when they left for dinner we had a cutter in our possession. We decided to start. At this time only about seven prisoners were aware of what was being planned – Brady, Todd Andrews, Hugh Byrne, Liam Murphy, J. Shaughnessy, J. J. Martin and myself.[40]

Several prisoners began the construction of a tunnel. They drilled down under their hut, which was raised on concrete blocks and had a crawl space of 12–18 inches. After they had reached a depth of about 4 feet, they started to tunnel towards the barbed wire. A considerable quantity of timber was required for shoring up the roof, and this could only be obtained by secretly removing the odd board here and there from huts and other structures in such a way as not to cause suspicion. It was found that bed boards provided the most suitable material and, as many men preferred to use two boards instead of three to sleep on – allowing the straw-filled mattress to form a hollow in the middle – a considerable number of boards were made available from this source.[41]

In the first week of May, however, the tunnel was discovered. A party of the King's Own Scottish Borderers rushed into the compound and began a thorough search of a line of huts, leading the prisoners to conclude that knowledge of the construction had been discovered by one of the 'stool-pigeons' who had been planted in the camp by the authorities. But in fact it was a letter that had been smuggled out which had led to the authorities' knowledge of a tunnel in progress. The letter was picked up in a raid in Mary Street, Dublin, and contained a great amount of detail about the plan that was underway:[42]

A Chara

There is a chance of a number of men escaping from here. There is a tunnel dug under the wires. There is double barbed wire round this camp at 13ft in height. The tunnel goes on beyond that all right, but about 30 yards further out a fence has recently been erected. This is a simple wire fence as for a sheep pen, but barbed wire is now being passed about this. This only gives a short time to get out, as it is impossible to carry the tunnel that far out.

The arrangement is that at night a number of men will pass through the tunnel which will be opened into the field that the Rath is in (to the east of the camp). It is doubtful if this can be done without their being seen coming out of the earth by the sentries. But it is possible. After that the trouble will be to get away. As it will have to be at night, the motors are hardly feasible. Would it be possible to get a goods train going to Dublin? Or can you offer any other suggestions? At least those escaping should be told the direction to go in and the places to avoid. There is also the question as to who should go. Can you send a list of those you want to get out? You might send instructions as soon as possible. There will also be the question of money for the men who do get out; money is taken from us here.

The boys who are working on the tunnel say they have gone nearly as far as they can. They will have reached the limit in a few days.

You understand that the men will appear in the field where the Rath is. There is something there that looks like a dug out. They may have a guard there at night as well as the sentries in the boxes at the corner of the camp.

I think that if assistance cannot be got from the outside, it would be better for you to say that the whole thing should be called off. It will be necessary for the men not only to get out but also to get far away, as they have so many troops here that they could comb out any place nearby thoroughly, if they had an idea that the men were there.

Do Chara,

D.F.[43]

The tunnel was elaborately propped with bed boards sawn into suitable lengths by using sharpened dinner knives, and an air shaft of stove pipes was inserted. The tunnel was almost finished when 'dozens of guards were brought in with a great number of trench diggers. One whole line of huts was isolated, they were digging for about five days before they found the tunnel. Then they got more excited. Guards were on all night. It took about three days to fill in the tunnel.'[44] As a punishment, all privileges were withdrawn; the prisoners responded by refusing food for nine days. Privileges were then restored, but there was a major tightening of security.[45] Further tunnelling, for the time being, was suspended.

5
SPORT AND PASTIMES

During the revolutionary period, there was a strong sporting culture in the prisons and internment camps, with the playing of Gaelic games at the forefront. From 1916 the GAA publicly supported the plight of prisoners at both the national and local level, and contributed to various prison welfare funds. The GAA was founded in 1884 and from the beginning had been infiltrated by militant republicans.[1] A royal commission established by the British government to uncover the causes of the 1916 Rising concluded that the Irish Volunteers had gained 'practically full control' over the organisation.[2]

Gaelic games served many important functions – programmes were initiated by the camp leaders to stimulate the men physically, mentally, politically and culturally. For many internees, Gaelic games provided much-needed relief and staved off the boredom that normally accompanies lengthy periods of detention. Gaelic games were also used as a symbolic statement by those interned and were played as a means of reaffirming an Irish nationalist identity.[3] The boredom of prison life and the lack of other distractions ensured that even former sceptics adopted Gaelic games. Soccer-playing Todd Andrews said of his time in the Rath Camp:

> We played a lot of football – Gaelic of course, since foreign

games were forbidden … We organized a football league competition between the Companies. I was good enough to be picked on the 'D' Company team. The league matches were of high standard as the teams were studded with All-Ireland players from different counties. The games were very tough.[4]

Gaelic football competitions were organised and played in both the Rath and Hare Park camps. The various huts formed Gaelic football teams and played matches with footballs produced in the camp or donated by local football clubs.[5] Camp authorities encouraged the games as a welcome outlet for energies and aggression that might otherwise be directed at them; however, while football, throwing the stone, and running and jumping were common, hurling was not encouraged by the authorities because of the potential for hurley sticks to be used as weapons. Hurling was played in the Rath Camp, probably after the Truce, though most counties in the camp could not field a full hurling, or even a football, team.[6]

On 25 May the internees turned out to watch the final of the Rath Camp Football Championship. GAA stalwart Frank Burke was the captain of A Company, who were favourites to win. D Company, captained by Tom Burke of Drogheda, Co. Louth, were the underdogs, but were the surprising winners with a scoreline of 1 goal 7 points to 2 goals 3 points. A report of the match was sent out to the *Leinster Leader*, which said:

First-class football was very prominent … Tom Burke, captain of the once famous Louth team, and captain of D Company,

SPORT AND PASTIMES

took the free, and nicely judging his kick, scored the winning point, amidst thunderous cheers ... The cheers that followed after D Company's victory could be heard for miles around.

Frank Burke, Carbury, captained the losing team and stood out on his own throughout the game. The Gaels of Kildare will be glad to see that even though the cream of Ireland's G.A.A. men are in internment camps they keep the old ball rolling.[7]

Frank Burke seemed to play on several teams, and captained B Company when they were beaten in the junior football final by C Company. Silver medals – donated by the GAA county board – were presented to the winners, including Tom Wilmot of Athgarvan, Co. Kildare, whose brother William had been killed in action on the Western Front in March 1916, while serving with the British Army.[8] Andrew Boyle of Dublin said:

> I was on the C Line team captained by the lovable character Tom Behan (later executed at the Curragh), when we beat Frank Burke's team ... Dick O'Connor or 'Tiny' Dunne, our six-footer full forward from Offaly ... The final against Frank Burke's team was like a Croke Park final. Tom Duke of St Margaret's played the fiddle on the sideline ... wonderful days.[9]

It was not all serious competition, though, and the following month the *Leinster Leader* reported on an unusual match, the 'Mutts vs Jeffs', with no indication of the players' identities:

> On Sunday last in fair weather the internees at Rath Camp

> turned out to witness a very interesting football match, organised by prominent G.A.A. men at present in Rath Camp. The contest which the prisoners have been looking forward to for some time past was between the 'Mutts' and the 'Jeffs.' The 'Mutts' measuring six feet two and over and the 'Jeffs' five feet and under. Both teams put forward a fine exhibition of football and from start to finish neither side slackened. After a long drawn out struggle, and to the great admiration of their followers, the small men romped home the victors. The captain of the 'Jeffs' team was heartily congratulated on the fine performance of his team.[10]

Tom 'The Boer' Byrne was in goal for the taller team, the Mutts. Despite the big man's best efforts, though, the Jeffs put several balls past him, leading one onlooker to remark loudly enough for Byrne to hear, 'That fellow would not stop a haystack!'[11]

Micheál Ó Laoghaire, captain of Liverpool Company, IRA, maintained that the good summer weather in 1921 contributed to the prisoners' good morale and allowed them to engage in a number of sporting pastimes:

> Practically no rain fell, with the result that the prisoners were free from early morning until 10 p.m. during the summer months to roam about, play games, such as hurling and football, train in running, jumping and weight-throwing as well as several other activities they were engaged in.[12]

Athletic competitions were also popular among the internees. The fine weather favoured a sports day held on 6 July at the Rath Camp, organised by prominent interned members of the

SPORT AND PASTIMES

GAA – Tom Burke, Tom Derrig, James J. McNamara, Joe Kenny (Dublin) and Tom Behan (Rathangan) – who formed the Rath Internment Camp Sports Committee. The unique athletic championship was carried out in 'splendid style' and 'the good weather helped greatly', the *Leinster Leader* said.[13] There were twelve championship events, the winner of each being presented with a silver medal with a gold centre, and the second in each event receiving a silver medal. As well as the championships, a 'veterans' race, a 'jifs' race and an obstacle race were held. The results were:

> 100 Yards – 1, Tom Glynn, Attymon. 2, J. J. McNamara, Dublin. 10½ secs.
> 220 Yards – 1, J. J. McNamara. 2, D. Crowley.
> 440 Yards – 1, J. J. McNamara. 2, J. J. Conaghan, Dublin.
> 880 Yards – 1, J. J. Conaghan, Dublin. 2, T. S. McCarrick, Sligo.
> 1 mile – 1, J. J. Conaghan. 2, J. O'Connor, Dublin. 4 mins 40 secs.
> 3 mile – 1, J. Kenny, Dublin. 2, J. J Conaghan.
> 120-yard hurdle – 1, T. Glynn. 2, D. Crowley.
> High jump – Tom Mullins, Castlebar, 5ft 3ins. J. O'Neill, 5ft 3ins.
> Long jump – T. Glynn, 21ft 3ins. J. Conroy, Ballinrobe, 19ft 8ins.
> Hop, step & jump – T. Glynn, 44ft 6ins. Tom Mullee, Ballyhaunis, 40ft 1in.
> 16lb shot – Peter Farrell, Lanesboro, 39ft 1in. Martin Joyce, Hollymount, 38ft 10½ ins.
> 56lb shot – William McEllin, Glasson, 22ft. Timothy Dunne, Mountmellick, 21ft 10½ ins.
> Veterans Race, over 45 – O'Callaghan, 1; O'Connor, 2; O'Grady, 3.
> 'Jifs' Race – B. Hynes, 1; James Nohilly, 2; Kavanagh, 3.
> Obstacle Race – Kevin O'Carroll, 1; McCarrick, 2. In this event Nohilly was first, but was disqualified.[14]

The judges were John J. Walsh, TD, Dr Cusack, TD, Fr Smith and Tom Behan. The presentation of the prizes was by John F. 'Jack' Shouldice, a former football player with London and Dublin, and secretary of the Leinster Council of the GAA (1917–26). An officer in the 1st Battalion, Dublin Brigade and an Easter Week veteran, Jack Shouldice had been imprisoned after the Rising until June 1917. On his release, he was appointed an organiser for the IRB and the Volunteers in his native Mayo. Arrested and jailed in 1918, he made a dramatic escape from Usk Prison in South Wales in January 1919. Operating from his Leinster GAA Council office at 68 O'Connell Street, he acted as liaison between the Dublin Brigade and the Prisoners Dependents' Fund, and organised the challenge match between Dublin and Tipperary which witnessed the attack by crown forces on 'Bloody Sunday'. Shouldice remained free until December 1920, when he was again arrested and jailed.[15]

Representing the press as 'sports correspondents' were interned newspapermen Patrick J. Lynch, *Irish Independent*, and Michael O'Kelly, *Leinster Leader*. The magazine *Ireland's Own* reported:

> Certainly, never has such an event taken place under more peculiar, or, should I write, more historic conditions. A peculiar feature is the excellent times and distances in each of the events. The boys may not have much facility for training, but it certainly appears to me that they did not require it. The winners must have 'been in the pink' and by no means downhearted ... I would

SPORT AND PASTIMES

suggest the readers comparing the grand performances of the Rath Internment Camp athletes with those in America, who, we may be certain, trained for their events under the most scientific tutors, and the most up-to-date conditions.[16]

Not too far away, the Hare Park Internment Camp sports event was held on 31 July. Hare Park continued to be used for internment purposes and at the beginning of August there were 113 prisoners held there.[17] The sporting activities represented were running, tug-of-war and a football match, and keen competition was witnessed in all events. Thomas Abbey, Rathvilly, Co. Carlow, won the 5-mile marathon and was presented with a cup donated by Coby Rigney, Esq., Kilmeague, Co. Kildare. Thirty men competed but only seven finished. A further thirty men took part in a 1-mile race, which was won by Anthony Brock, Deansgrange, Dublin. Only twelve men finished the race and the Moy Cup was presented by the camp commandant to the winner.[18] The *Leinster Leader* said:

> The weather was glorious when the Hare Park Internment Camp Sports opened on Monday last in the exercise grounds. The events in a long programme were keenly contested. Among the more notable events were:–
>
> 220 Yards Hurdle – D. Hanly, Rathvilly, 1; M. O'Neill, do., 2; W. Howe, Suncroft, 3. Nine competed. Won by 4 yards.
>
> Two Mile Flat – M. Kelly, Castle Farm, 1; W. Byrne, Kilcock, 2; Michael Galvin, Tullamore, 3. Seven competed. A close finish; won by a yard.

High Jump – Won by L. Millett; 5 feet 10 inches. Five competed. Long Jump – Won by L. Millett; 19 feet 5 inches. Fifteen competed. Won easily.[19]

A football match between a team from Huts 1 and 2 against a team from Huts 3 and 4 rounded off the sports events, with the former the winners. The evening ended with a concert and music supplied by Henry Armstrong (Maynooth) and a fellow player named Doyle. Exhibition dancing of four-hand reels, hornpipes, three-hand reels, songs and recitations were the principal items. Anthony Brock rendered in fine style the 'Hare Park Camp Song' to the air of 'Sean Bhean Bhocht'. James Scully sang 'Skibbereen', while Daniel O'Brien recited 'Fontenoy' to great applause.[20]

There were other activities at the Rath Camp besides sports, among them up to a dozen Irish classes. The teachers included Gaelic League activists Seán O'Dairdis (John Dardis, Kells), Liam Ó Briain and Seán Tuttle (Stradbally, Co. Laois) and Sligo TD Alex McCabe. Seán O'Dairdis, an Irish teacher with the Meath County Committee of Technical Instruction, taught three Irish classes every day. About 400 students attended his classes – a junior class in the morning, an intermediate one in the afternoon and a senior class at night. O'Dairdis was a brilliant scholar of Irish, holding numerous certificates and diplomas from Irish colleges. He was an enthusiastic teacher and was much admired by the men, who, towards the end of internment, presented him with a superb gold watch as a token of gratitude for his teaching efforts.[21]

SPORT AND PASTIMES

While most prisoners tried to learn or speak a few words in Gaelic, others tried to learn French. Professor Liam Ó Briain, as well as teaching Irish, conducted a French class, lecturing on the language, French history and literature. Ó Briain was a professor of Romance Languages in UCG and had been a member of the IRB since 1915, when Seán T. O'Kelly swore him in. He was later best man at O'Kelly's wedding. He helped print the Proclamation of the Republic in Liberty Hall in the days before the Rising. Ó Briain served under Michael Mallin of the Citizen Army in St Stephen's Green and the Royal College of Surgeons during the Rising, rather than with the Volunteers. After his arrest, he spent two months in Wandsworth Prison in London, and was then interned for a further six months in Frongoch. He stood for Sinn Féin in Mid-Armagh in the 1918 general election, receiving 5,689 votes against 8,431 won by the unionist candidate. His attempts to mobilise nationalists in the Armagh area to support the National Loan initiative of Michael Collins led to his arrest and to three months in prison in Belfast in 1919–20. On his release, he was appointed a judge of the republican courts in Galway. At the behest of Collins, he travelled to France and Italy to arrange arms shipments, but in November 1920 was arrested in the UCG dining room by Black and Tans and imprisoned for thirteen months, first in Galway and then in the Rath Camp.[22]

Many prisoners took to drawing, and writing poetry, songs and ballads. Filling autograph books or albums with verses and quotes as well as autographs was also very popular.

INTERNED

Many autograph books survive and offer an insight into the living conditions and personalities who inhabited the camp.

Tom Behan wrote a book of poems, published in 1923 after his death in the Civil War (he took the anti-Treaty side). One poem, entitled 'My Calico Shack in Kildare', captures the atmosphere of his arrival at the Rath Camp in the summer of 1921:

> In the year 'twenty-one my troubles began,
> As nature from sleep was awaking;
> I woke by a noise of some Houlihan boys,
> Thought all demons from hell were escaping;
> I listened to see what the devil it might be,
> When a crowd rushed the sides and the rear
> Shouting General Skinner invites you to dinner
> To a calico shack in Kildare.
>
> The leader politely told me to dress quietly,
> To pack up my kit and make haste;
> And lest I might bring any brandy or gin,
> He searched from my boots to my waist.
> Then off in a hurry, with an escort of lorry,
> And armoury to bring up the rear;
> Through the grand morning dew, o'er the hillside we flew
> To a calico shack in Kildare.
>
> On arrival, I found my new home was all bound
> With decorations so varied and strong;

Electric lamps and barbed wire in hedgerows like brier,
A sentry en route all day long.
The guests all assembled, amongst them was mingled
The heroes of Kerry and Clare,
From Mayo to Navan, from Longford and Cavan,
All to dine on the plains of Kildare.

The dinner once over, I was told by a soldier
That I should be chancy and stay,
As here every boy did fully enjoy
The wonderful pastimes and play.
At once I consented that I'd be contented
To stay where this scenery fair,
Combined with protection, disloyal correction,
In a calico shack in Kildare.[23]

Entertainment in the camps was in the form of concerts, dancing, readings and short plays. Songs, poems and plays were written by the men and performed with much enthusiasm. Anyone who could sing was expected to do so. Music halls were very popular at the time and everybody sang songs and at the very least could join in, if not lead. An Internees' Amusements Committee was set up to procure costumes, wigs and other theatrical aids for plays.

A reporter from the *Nationalist and Leinster Times* visited Hare Park Camp and gave an account of a wet evening's entertainment in one of the huts. The first item on the programme was an original song by Seán Connolly entitled

'The Hare Park Camp Huts', and was followed by a hornpipe from Seán O'Toole of Nurney, Co. Kildare. Michael Behan, one of three brothers interned from Graiguecullen, Co. Carlow, recited 'We Never Forget'. 'When Shall the Day Break in Erin', was sung by Dick Furlong from Naas, who had previously been interned in Hare Park during Easter Week 1916. Seán O'Toole's most promising dancers from the Huts Dancing Class, the brothers Behan and Art Doran (Ballymore Eustace, Co. Kildare) danced a four-hand reel. T. J. Carney of Newbridge recited Brian O'Higgins' stirring lines 'An Irish Father's Address to His Son Who Joined the Army'. Thomas Fallon from Hacketstown, Co. Carlow, recited the soulful verses of the martyred Tom Ashe's poem, 'Let Me Carry Your Cross for Ireland, Lord'. Recitations, songs, jigs and reels continued until 'The Soldier's Song', enthusiastically chorused by all present while standing, brought the programme to an end.[24]

Some prisoners continued their trades within the internment camps: doctors, butchers and carpenters were much sought after. John Murray of West Port, Ballyshannon, Co. Donegal, was a popular prisoner who acted as hairdresser to the internees. He became known as 'The Sinn Féin Barber' to the crown forces after he painted his hairdressing premises near Ballyshannon Military Barracks in green, white and orange, and the name stuck. He also inscribed Sinn Féin mottoes on the roof and flew the tricolour. Murray had previously spent some time in Derry Gaol, where he undertook a hunger strike before his release.[25]

Much to the frustration of the internees, life outside the wire continued as normal. The Curragh Racecourse could be seen in the distance, and on race days it was possible to see the horses at the start of the long-distance races. Todd Andrews said:

> However much turmoil gripped the country, the horsey men carried on business as usual. We resented their activities and anyway gambling was against the spirit of the Movement. The Turf was the preserve of the Garrison and the Anglo-Irish community and we did not see why, while we were in jail and our comrades outside were fighting, they should enjoy themselves as if normality prevailed.[26]

Nevertheless, the Curragh races were a source of enjoyment to some of the internees. Gerry McAleer and Charlie O'Neill from Dungannon, Co. Tyrone, were classmates of the medical student and IRA Volunteer Kevin Barry, who was executed in Mountjoy Gaol on 1 November 1920. The following summer, the two friends travelled to the Barry family farm at Tomeagh, Co. Carlow, to help with the hay harvest. They were caught up in a general round-up of local republicans and conveyed to the Rath Camp. However, neither of them was a member of any branch of the republican movement – in fact, local activists suspected they were spies! One day, while in the camp, McAleer asked a British officer for a loan of his field glasses so he could watch the races across the plain. Soon he was relaying the results of the races to half the camp. McAleer and O'Neill were released without charge after three weeks' internment.[27]

Prisoners were released habitually. George O'Connor, chairman of the Kells Rural District Council (RDC) was released in early June 1921 and told a reporter he could not complain of his treatment at the Rath Camp. The food in the camp, he said, was very wholesome and the internees did the cooking themselves. Fr Smith said mass every morning for the men and they were allowed two priests from Kildare to hear confessions weekly. They had, he added, fine recreation grounds, baths twice a week, and were permitted to be out until 9 p.m.[28]

In contrast, however, a colleague of O'Connor, Michael Farrelly, also a district councillor from Kells, who was released from the Rath Camp on health grounds, said that, as one who had spent eighteen [sic] months there, he was in a position to know what treatment internees got and what hardships they had to endure. Internees, he stated, were not supplied with anything to eat from four o'clock in the evening until 8.30 the following morning. The four o'clock meal consisted of eight ounces of bread, with 'very inferior tea' and margarine that was not always usable.

Farrelly also said that he wished to draw attention to:

> ... two classes who did much harm to the cause of all Irish prisoners. The first were those who, arrested in mistake, or worse still, with the intention of obtaining information from them, were detained a short time and then released; and the

second were those who were interned, appealed against their internment, signed the £50 bond, and got released. The first of those two classes were rarely badly treated, for any prisoner badly treated at first, without divulging information, was kept. The latter class, though undoubtedly having suffered, feared to mention their suffering because of their bond. Both classes on regaining their freedom left the public under the impression that we were taken away for a kind of holiday.[29]

Not only militant republicans were interned. Throughout the country, elected officials who were jailed had to resign from their positions. Matt Cardiff, interned in Hare Park, had no option but to resign from Naas No. 1 RDC and was replaced by James Scanlon, a Newbridge town commissioner. Labour Party members of the Co. Kildare Trades Council – Joseph Lee (interned); Joe Keane, Suncroft; and J. Keogh, Kildare – 'whose spirit was willing, but the opportunities not great', were also unable to attend meetings. Lee was the chairman of the Ballymore Eustace branch of the Irish Transport and General Workers' Union (ITGWU), and a prominent member of the Labour movement and of the Co. Kildare Trades Council. One popular member of the Labour Party remarked with a smile, when speaking of a spate of recent arrests, including representatives of Labour, that they should soon be able to start a good working branch of the ITGWU at Hare Park.[30]

6

TRUCE OUTSIDE, DISSENT INSIDE

Though the Rath Camp was quite full by June (holding 1,007 prisoners according to *The Freeman's Journal* of 23 June 1921), further batches of prisoners continued to arrive. The building of a second internment camp – to be known as 'B Cage' – began on the west side of the existing camp and adjoining it. In the meantime, new arrivals were housed in marquee tents pitched in the spaces between the huts. Two Carlow men, John McDonald of Clonore and Thomas McManus of Rathvilly, arrived in the Rath Camp on 1 June and were housed under canvas, where they remained until November. When it rained the tents leaked, making it very uncomfortable for the occupants.[1]

Internment powers continued to be used on a massive scale in the spring and summer of 1921, with maximum intensity of use in the month of May. From 30 April to 21 May, 684 men were arrested and interned, the highest number of any period since the powers were introduced.[2] In the countryside, internment swoops and the relentless pressure of military cordons, raids and patrols, coupled with a shortage of ammunition, continued to take its toll on the republican movement, but the impact on the IRA's capacity to conduct its campaign appears to have been negligible. The constant reassurances from senior British officers that the defeat of the IRA was imminent became increasingly muffled as their deadlines for military victory were constantly missed.[3] Todd Andrews said:

> In May rumours of peace negotiations with the British began to sweep through the camp. Naturally, it was the main topic of conversation not merely at our solo school but among all internees. The general feeling was that nothing would come of them. We were much more interested in the course of the fighting. We were always on the look out for news of activities which took place in our own particular areas … We were all thrilled by the burning of the Custom House in May, regarding it as a great triumph. It affected us internees in as much as the British stopped our parcels as a reprisal. My mother was very indignant that parcels were stopped. She wrote me a letter 'crying a plague on both your houses'. I replied that she should write to the generalissimos of both armies, not to me. I had not burned the Custom House.[4]

In the early part of 1921 the IRA decreased its activity slightly and spent its time reorganising. The old brigade structure had become cumbersome, a result of the steady increase in membership. In terms of organisation it made little sense to try to co-ordinate dozens of units from one headquarters, and the creation of divisions was intended to improve communications between GHQ and the localities, and to increase co-operation between the brigade areas and enable them to lessen pressure on areas in which the IRA was active. When the new divisional organisation came on line, tactics and emphasis shifted according to circumstances as methods of operation and targets changed. The intensity of IRA attacks increased steadily, eventually surpassing all previously reported attacks: in January 1921 there had been 1,234 republican attacks reported by the crown forces, but by the month of June reported attacks had increased to 2,256.[5]

The military situation was a huge drain on Britain's increasingly stretched martial resources, and the prospect of continuing a long and costly war with the IRA and the risk of further major political embarrassment on both the domestic and international fronts was important in convincing the British government that peace negotiations with the republican movement were necessary. The various military measures enacted by the British, including the deployment of the Black and Tans and the Auxiliaries, the imposition of martial law and instituting of official reprisals, and the policies of executing captured republicans, had all failed to halt the intensification and spread of the IRA's military campaign.[6]

At the same time, the crown forces were adapting to the new IRA tactics and having a small measure of success in combating flying columns in the countryside and countering urban foot patrols in Dublin. Nevertheless, despite the military surge, casualty rates for the crown forces soared in 1921: 119 British soldiers and policemen were killed in action or died of wounds in the months of April and May. This figure does not include soldiers who died as a result of accidents or illness. The month of June was no better for the crown forces, with another sixty-three soldiers and policemen killed.[7] The IRA was in a position of strength to negotiate, but the loss of men and materials meant it was also under pressure if it wanted to continue with the armed campaign. The British were no closer to defeating the IRA than they had been a year previously. General Macready estimated that another twenty battalions of troops would be needed to restore British authority, and as many as 100 republicans would have to be executed weekly, but he still had reservations as to whether this would work. He declared: 'It must be all out or another policy.'[8]

The militarist lobby in the British cabinet had been significantly weakened by the resignation in March of Andrew Bonar Law, the Conservative leader and an ultra-unionist. Macready and Sir Henry Wilson, MP and security adviser to the new Northern Ireland government, held a pessimistic view of the military situation, and while Winston Churchill was optimistic about the military campaign, he thought there was a case for negotiating with republicans from a position of strength. So tentative contact between Dublin Castle and Sinn Féin, which had been initiated briefly in late 1920, was resumed in June 1921.[9] The republican leadership was also interested in a settlement and relatively amenable to peace talks.

Rumours of peace were heard behind the wire of the Curragh internment camps but had no effect on escape attempts. This led to tension within the camp and, in an effort to dissuade internees from trying to escape, a warning notice was issued to the prisoners on 5 July, signed by Adjutant Vinden:

> Warning
>
> The Commandant will not be responsible for the lives of any Internees seen outside their Huts or Tents between Evening Roll Call at 9 p.m. and Morning Roll Call at 7.15 a.m.[10]

Outside, peace negotiations continued. All sides were anxious to end the war. The British prime minister, David Lloyd George, invited Éamon de Valera, and any colleagues he should choose to bring, to meet him in London. Talks led by de Valera and southern unionist leader Lord Midleton took place over the four days of 4–8 July, with a view to securing a truce. Arthur Griffith and several other prominent republicans, including Robert Barton, were released from jail to take part in the negotiations. Final agreement on the terms of a truce was reached at 8 p.m. on Friday 8 July.[11] On the following day a truce was formally signed between two members of the Dáil cabinet, Barton and Eamonn Duggan, and the British military commander in Ireland, General Macready, at the Mansion House in Dublin.[12] It was agreed that it should come into effect at noon on Monday 11 July. The Dáil publicity department issued the following statement:

> On behalf of the British Army it is agreed as follows:
>
> 1. No incoming troops, RIC, and Auxiliary Police and munitions, and no movements for military purposes of troops and munitions, except maintenance drafts.
> 2. No provocative display of forces, armed or unarmed.

3. It is understood that all provisions of this truce apply to the martial law area equally with the rest of Ireland.
4. No pursuit of Irish officers or men or war material or military stores.
5. No secret agents, noting description or movements, and no interference with the movements of Irish persons, military or civil, and no attempts to discover the haunts or habits of Irish officers and men. Note:– This supposes the abandonment of Curfew restrictions.
6. No pursuit or observance of lines of communication or connection. Note: – there are other details connected with courts martial, motor permits, and ROIR to be agreed later.

On behalf of the Irish Army it is agreed that:

a. Attacks on Crown Forces and civilians to cease.
b. No provocative displays of forces, armed or unarmed.
c. No interference with Government or private property.
d. To discountenance and prevent any action likely to cause disturbance of peace which might necessitate military interference.[13]

In agreeing to the Truce, the British government had effectively conferred 'belligerent status' on the IRA as a lawful combatant.[14]

While the negotiations were going on, the arrests in Ireland continued. On 7 July 1921 Michael Smyth, commandant of the newly formed 7th Brigade, was arrested with Lieutenant Bill Jones, near Athgarvan, the Curragh. They had just enough time to throw their pistols into a hedge before being taken on board a Crossley Tender, where the arresting Black and Tans beat them about the head with the butts of their revolvers. Some months before, Smyth had received this 'final warning' from the 'forces of law and order':

> Whereas, it has come to our knowledge that the Sinn Fein organisation of which you are a prominent official through the so-called IRA or murder gang has been committing outrages in this hitherto God-fearing and law-abiding country, this reign of terror must be stopped. You are, therefore, most earnestly warned that in the event of the continuance of those heartless and cowardly crimes you will be personally held responsible and punished in such a manner that others will be deterred from criminal course.[15]

Smyth and Jones were imprisoned in Hare Park Camp, and some months later, in October, were court-martialled for possession of ammunition and transferred to Mountjoy Gaol.[16]

On the same night as their arrests, the Army and Navy Canteen in Ballymany, Newbridge, was accidentally burned down, resulting in two fatalities. Around 3 a.m., several IRA Volunteers arrived by car, forced their way into the store and sprinkled the goods with paraffin oil to render them useless. However, the caretaker, William Doran, came down from his accommodation above to investigate the commotion, holding a lighted candle. It was thought that he let it fall and in the resulting inferno his wife, Bridget, and his fourteen-year-old son, John, sleeping upstairs, were burned to death. Before she died, Mrs Doran (34) managed to throw her ten-month-old baby from a window to her husband, who, though badly injured, caught the child safely. She then went back to rescue her stepson, but the floor gave way and both perished.

Newbridge was a garrison town with a large cavalry barracks, and the deaths were met with horror and condemnation. The charred remains of Mrs Doran and her stepson were taken to the mortuary in the military barracks.[17] Ballymany, on the edge of the town, was about 2 miles from the Curragh Camp and the incident was deeply felt there, too. A new form of reprisal was inflicted on the Curragh internees because of this attack and an order issued decreed:

INTERNEE SUPERVISOR.

Owing to the cowardly attack by rebels on the Navy and Army Canteen at NEWBRIDGE which resulted in an unfortunate [*sic*] and child being burned to death the Rebate paid by the N.A. & A.F.I., on goods sold in the Internees' Canteen[,] will not be used for the benefit of the Internees.

Under no consideration will a canteen be opened again.
(SGD) H. F. VINDEN.
Lieut. & Adjutant.[18]

Three days later, on Monday 11 July, the Truce came into effect. Relatives and friends of prisoners, and, indeed, the public, expected immediate releases from internment camps and prisons. Some internees also believed they would soon be freed. Todd Andrews was not so optimistic:

> When the Truce came in July my mother assumed that we would be released immediately, writing to inquire if I would wire to let her know what time she should send a car to pick me up. We felt no such certainty of a final settlement and release.[19]

Joe Lawless agreed with Andrews, saying that the general feeling the internees had at the time was that the Truce was most probably a temporary respite and that, when negotiations broke down, the war would begin again, with redoubled effort on both sides:

> Naturally, we discussed the situation daily amongst ourselves and occasionally attracted one or other of the British officers attached to the camp into some casual conversation on the matter. In our discussions we could not visualise the British Government consenting to any measure of freedom that would satisfy our national aspirations, while on the other hand we knew we could not and would not abate our demand for the recognition of Dáil Éireann as the only lawful government of our native land. I think the British garrison had much the same feelings about the unlikelihood of the truce eventuating in anything except a resumption of hostilities. Certainly there was no relaxation of discipline within the camp, and the adjutant, a certain Captain [sic] Vinden, who was a particularly obnoxious type, went out of his way in many matters of detail to let us see

that the truce had nothing to do with us, and that he at any rate still looked upon us as malignant enemies whom he might punish at his pleasure. I had a few passages with Vinden in my position as Internee vice-Commandant, or supervisors as they called us. I was acting commandant in the absence of Peadar McMahon who was ill on one occasion and came before Vinden in connection with an ultimatum he had delivered concerning a shortage of dinner knives. He became incensed with rage because I persisted in treating his orders and threats with an affectation of levity and we wound up the interview by a frank exchange of our opinions of each other which could hardly be described as complimentary.[20]

The days passed, but there was still no release for the internees. Public feeling began to reflect unease at the continued detention of men held without charge or trial. Press coverage, however, tended to focus on conditions in the camps and prisons. A representative of the *Evening Telegraph* made inquiries at military headquarters in Dublin about allegations that a number of prisoners in the Rath Camp were still undergoing special punishment a week after the Truce had become effective. The military authorities denied official knowledge of any complaints.[21] *The Freeman's Journal* asked on 23 July 1921:

> **Is the Truce being broken in the Curragh Camp?**
> A complaint has reached Offaly that, despite the truce that is being rigidly observed by all parties in Ireland, for some reason not yet explained prisoners interned at the Curragh Camp were,

it is alleged, put on a punishment diet of bread and water for some days.

They were, it is also alleged, compelled to sleep on the floor, bedding being removed, and communication with family and friends cut off.

When this information reached Tullamore, from which, our correspondent states, many prisoners are interned in the Rath Camp, it created surprise and disappointment.[22]

The Freeman's Journal warned that the Truce 'to be a reality must include the prison camps, and the sooner the Government take steps to extend it in this direction the sooner will they remove a dangerous source of friction'.[23]

In reality, the Truce was never extended effectively to the internment camps and prisons, and they became the places where the conditions of the struggle continued to exist. And though the prisoners had hoped the Truce would facilitate a general release, it gradually dawned on them that they would have to wait and see what the negotiations would bring.

On 14 July Éamon de Valera led a delegation to London to represent the various sections of Irish opinion. They met Lloyd George, who was eager to settle the Irish problem but was not willing to concede a republic. He warned de Valera that if the Truce had to be terminated 'the struggle would bear an entirely different character'. De Valera returned to Ireland with Lloyd George's proposal – partition and limited dominion status in the form of a treaty – to put before the Dáil cabinet, who quickly agreed that the proposals were not good enough. Cathal Brugha and Austin Stack wanted no further truck with the British and were willing to go back to war, but for the majority this was too drastic. Arthur Griffith, however, revealed a strong interest in the terms.

To enable their proposals to be put to the entire Dáil, the British cabinet agreed that it was proper to grant an amnesty to the members who were still in captivity.[24] A meeting of Dáil Éireann was summoned for 16 August to enable it to consider the British peace terms, with notices of the meeting sent to all members. Many of the notices were sent to the jails and internment camps, where thirty-eight TDs were *'fé ghlas ag Gallaibh'* – 'locked up by foreigners'. On 10 August the British government agreed to release thirty-seven TDs but would not free Seán MacEoin, TD for Longford–Westmeath, who was under a sentence of death in Mountjoy Gaol for shooting dead an RIC inspector. Michael Collins urged the Dáil cabinet to take a firm position on the matter, and MacEoin was released after Collins said there would be no meeting of Dáil Éireann unless he was freed. The elected TDs held in the Curragh and released to take part in the Second Dáil were:

Donegal – Joseph O'Doherty and Patrick J. McGoldrick
Dublin Northwest – Philip Cosgrave
Galway – Dr Brian Cusack
Kerry–Limerick West – James Crowley
Leix–Offaly – Francis Bulfin
Louth–Meath – James Murphy and Justin McKenna

> Mayo North and West – Dr John Crowley, P. J. Ruttledge, Joseph MacBride and Thomas Derrig
> Sligo–Mayo East – Dr Francis Ferran and Alexander McCabe[25]

On 15 July Desmond FitzGerald had also been released from the Curragh to take part in the peace negotiations, and he returned to his position as head of publicity and editor of the *Irish Bulletin*. Of his release, Lieutenant Vinden said:

> A call from GHQ while we were at dinner one night told me to release Desmond FitzGerald and take him immediately by car to his house in Merrion Square in Dublin. As we had not been allowed to move without armed escort, I asked a brother officer to accompany me and we set off, each with loaded revolvers in our pockets. We arrived in Merrion Square about 10 p.m. to find a welcoming party gathered to greet FitzGerald. Many of the Sinn Fein leaders were there, including Michael Collins, on whose head up to that moment there had been a price of £20,000. We were invited in and a good time was had by all.[26]

The Second Dáil was convened in Dublin's Mansion House on 16 August, able for the first time to meet in the open. De Valera was elected president of the Republic, a position that had not existed previously. Over the next few days, the proposals made by Lloyd George were debated and unanimously rejected. A protracted exchange of letters and telegrams between de Valera and Lloyd George followed, centring on the need to find some form of words on the identity of the Dáil government that would enable a full conference to begin. De Valera was unwilling to cede Irish sovereignty before the negotiations began, while Lloyd George was loath to allow the conference to start on an unconditional basis.[27]

During the weeks that followed the signing of the Truce, there was much divided debate among the internees about what would happen. One section believed the Irish delegates to London should accept no final agreement that did not include full fiscal freedom for an Irish republic. A second section argued that any disagreements over this might be injurious to the ultimate results of the London negotiations. The third section contended, from what they could glean, that the Irish delegation would compromise and accept something less than an Irish republic – a measure of freedom. Tom Behan was a very prominent spokesman for the first section, and argued that if there was any compromise with Britain, civil war in Ireland would be inevitable. Behan's prophecy came true and he died defending the Irish republic, allegedly 'shot while trying to escape' from the Curragh Camp.[28]

Despite the signing of the Truce and the peace negotiations in August, construction and extension works continued unabated in the Rath Camp. This included the building of a new style of hut in the compounds that was able to accommodate thirty men.[29] For the internees, the prospect of escape was still foremost in their minds and consumed much of their time and energy.

On 19 August James 'Jim' Staines made a daring escape

from Hare Park Camp. Jim was a brother of Alderman Michael Staines, TD, and Vincent Staines, who was being held in the Rath Camp. As a member of Fianna Éireann, he was a youthful veteran of Easter Week and had been in Hare Park since his arrest in March 1921. About 3 p.m., when Staines and some fellow internees were strolling around the camp, two military lorries drove in with a quantity of timber and other supplies. Their arrival was a mistake, as the proper destination should have been the Rath Camp. Realising their mistake, the drivers turned their lorries around and as they did so Staines and Willie Keegan of Tullamore observed that the vehicles were open at the back. Without being seen, they boarded separate lorries and concealed themselves.

The first lorry, carrying Jim Staines, drove out of the camp having been examined by the sentries, who noticed nothing unusual. When the lorry was some distance from the camp Staines dropped cautiously to the ground and took cover. His disappearance was not discovered until roll call that evening. The other prisoner, Keegan, was not so lucky; he was found in the second lorry, taken back immediately to the camp and placed in custody. (Keegan was subsequently sentenced to twelve months' hard labour and transferred to Mountjoy Gaol.)

Staines' escape caused General Nevil Macready, GOC of the British forces in Ireland, to issue an order banning further parole, which had been introduced for prisoners in the first week of August, pending Staines' return to custody. Macready's action excited much comment, with one prominent TD describing the order as 'silly and absurd'. Another TD said the order was 'amusing and childish'. How could the interned prisoners affected by the order be responsible for the return of Staines and where was the sense in penalising them?[30]

The *Irish Bulletin* pointed out that 'No parole has hitherto been permitted to internees. The reference to the "cancellation of all leave on parole" suggests that some arrangement has now been come to by which this injustice is to be remedied. The decision of the British C.-in-C. to withdraw parole immediately after it was conceded is a piece of vindictive meanness.' About the punishment of 3,000 interned men because one prisoner took the risk of escaping, it added, 'to say the least of it, the action is not sportsmanlike'.[31] Staines, of course, did not return.

Because of the escape, a lorry containing a consignment of bread for the prisoners was refused entry to the Rath Camp. The military guard threw the bread in a pile at the gate and then ordered the internees to carry it to the camp store. The prisoners refused and the guards ended up carrying the bread in themselves. The following day the guards did the same thing and again ended up carrying the loaves to the camp stores. After this the military relented and allowed further bread consignments into the camp.[32]

Alfred Cope, the assistant under-secretary for Ireland, who had worked closely with Sinn Féin during the Truce negotiations, believed that regular granting of parole would ease tensions within the prisons and camps.[33] Many men had been detained for months without charge, while others had been found innocent of charges but remained in custody. For example, Richard J. Broderick of Glenageary, Dublin, arrested with his two sons, Richard and Myles, on 26 November 1920, was not released until August 1921 despite having been acquitted at his court martial six weeks earlier. Why he was detained so long he did not know.[34]

The released prisoners told stories of ill-treatment and hardship, which the newspapers were quick to notice. The *Irish Independent* of 24 August published an account by Michael Farrelly of Kells, who had been released from the Rath Camp on medical grounds. He said that prisoners were contemplating with grave apprehension the thought of spending the autumn and winter there, and stated that there was an outbreak of German measles, which the prison medical staff were doing their best to contain given their lack of proper facilities for isolating patients.[35]

Some of the recently released TDs condemned the sanitation at the Rath Camp, others the accommodation for those interned on Bere Island in Co. Cork, and the press began to push for prisoner releases and access to the internment camps.[36] The Rath Camp quartermaster, Micheál Ó Laoghaire, recalled a visit by the British commander-in-chief, General Macready:

> To our great surprise, we were honoured one day by no less a personage than the Commander-in-Chief of the British Forces in Ireland, Sir Neville [*sic*] Macready, the Quartermaster

General and their retinue. They called and inspected the Camp. Sir Neville was in mufti. While the others were carrying out their inspection, Sir Neville made his way unaccompanied to my stores. He came in, looked around the stores and asked me if I knew who he was. I said I did not and I didn't give a damn who he was. He only smiled. He started asking questions and then asked me if I had any complaints to make. I asked him was he serious for, if so, I said, pointing to a stool in the store, I could keep him sitting there for a week before I was finished complaining. I picked up an old ledger given to me by Lieutenant Mellot [*sic*; Mallett], opened it and began quoting the complaints, the nature of the complaints and the dates they occurred. While we were thus engaged, the whole retinue had arrived. Hearing my complaints which were all about food, the D.M.S. butted in. I said to him sharply, 'I am not speaking to you. And when I did' – referring to the fish incident and the margarine – 'you certainly did nothing to put matters right!' He shrivelled up. Lieutenant Mellot, the Quartermaster, butted in also when I was speaking about weight shortages. I gave him a similar reply and he looked very small.

After having listened to my complaints for at least a quarter of an hour, Sir Neville and his party moved off, but the Camp Commandant remained and asked me to walk around the playing ground with him. He took me by the arm. He said he was an Irishman (Hannan or Hanna, I think, was the name he mentioned, from Wicklow) and although he did not agree with us, he firmly believed that we were sincere and that the complaints I had just made were genuine. He then said to me that, if I had any further trouble over the rations, I was to report immediately to his Line Officer who came in to call the roll morning and evening and that, if I did not have the matter fixed up within twenty-four hours, I was to report to him. He was the only officer who, while speaking to the Commander-in-Chief, never showed any sign of an inferiority complex. That I admired. I must say that, in my dealings with him and the M.O., I always found them perfect gentlemen who knew how to treat and respect prisoners; and the prisoners in turn respected them.[37]

Despite the cessation of hostilities, courts martial continued at the Curragh, and at the end of August more than sixty sentenced prisoners were taken from the Rath and Hare Park Camps by military convoy to Dublin for transfer to detention centres in England.[38] They included Larry O'Neill, Mick Ryan and the rest of the Carlow flying column captured in April 1921.

In early September, the new extension to the Rath Internment Camp, 'B Cage', was opened for the reception of a batch of prisoners from Kilmainham Gaol. It had been constructed by about fifty ex-soldiers, while at the same time some of the military works at the Curragh Camp, which provided much employment locally, were closed.[39] That same month, *The Freeman's Journal* was quick to report that:

> Complaint is made that men in the Cage were supplied with no dinner from Tuesday to Saturday last. On Friday they got a little fish, but on the other days, a correspondent states, they had to subsist on a breakfast of porridge, tea, bread and margarine until the evening meal, which consisted of tea, bread and margarine.

It is stated that a supply of meat was not available and that the internees had to do without dinners. To men who are confined in a camp and deprived of the ordinary freedom the lack of a substantial midday meal naturally was a great strain and indignation was expressed that steps were not taken to ensure a regular supply of food.[40]

Also in September, a conference was arranged for 11 October in London, 'with a view to ascertaining how the association of nations known as the British Empire may best be reconciled with Irish national aspirations'.[41] However, in the Rath Camp not everyone was willing to wait for the outcome of the conference. A large group of internees had decided they were leaving immediately.

7
A TUNNEL TO FREEDOM

As a result of the discovery of the earlier tunnel in May, which had been dug towards the outskirts of the wire entanglement, a trench 4 feet deep and 4 feet wide was sunk by military engineers on three sides of the Rath Camp as a deterrent against any further escape attempts. On the fourth (north) side of the camp no trench was necessary, as it adjoined the quarters of the British officers.[1]

Three weeks after the discovery of the first tunnel, the internees decided to begin a greater venture. The new tunnel was known as the 'Dublin Brigade tunnel' because it was dug mainly by men of that brigade who had managed to get themselves quartered in the same hut. The tunnel was excavated on the east side of the camp, beginning with a pit under the floor of one of the huts, and was intended to run at a depth of 8–10 feet, emerging about 100 yards clear of the outside wire in a clump of furze bushes, clear of the ring of lights that surrounded the camp at night. The soil was of a sandy nature, and bed boards and floorboards were used at intervals as props to prevent a cave-in. It was a big, ambitious project, and the tunnellers decided to make the tunnel wider than in the earlier attempt in order to get the maximum number of men out – it was intended that the camp would be cleared, according to Joe Lawless, of most, if not all, prisoners during this breakout. Lawless said:

Our thoughts were bent on escape and I think it is true to say that our prime motive in the wish to escape was that we might justify ourselves in our own eyes by striking an effective blow against the enemy who was now our captor. We felt daily the galling frustration of our bondage as we read in the newspapers the events and incidents of war, which by this stage seemed to have penetrated every corner of Ireland.[2]

At the same time, another group of prisoners had also decided to dig their own tunnel. Joe Galvin, who had been involved in the first tunnel attempt, had never given up on the idea of tunnelling. He again approached the miner Jim Brady:

I clearly remember a Sunday morning when 500 troops led by a band were marching past our huts to divine service in the Curragh church. After they had passed Brady and I called together the few who had decided to work on the first tunnel and we agreed that we would try again. The first tunnel had been propped up with sticks and boards. This was too slow. We would have to risk it without losing time on safety measures. It had to be a quick job and it was going to be difficult. After finding the first tunnel, the British had dug a four feet deep and four feet wide trench on the inside of the boundary wire, all around the compound. Strange to say I think this turned out to be to our advantage, as I believe they felt secure that it would be impossible for us to run so deep a tunnel. From our experience with the first attempt we knew we could do it. The British were also making arrangements to flood the trench. Brady and I began the tunnel in the same manner as the first one – a hole two feet square and four feet deep and then outwards and downwards.[3]

The select half-dozen involved in the Brady escape plans held daily and nightly meetings in which the major problems were tackled. First was the starting and finishing point of the proposed tunnel. It was decided that the tunnel entrance would be under the hut, as the huts rested on concrete blocks and there was a 1–2-foot crawl space beneath the floor. The huts were 70 feet from the barbed wire, so the tunnel would have to go about 20 feet beyond that. Digging tools would be needed. Because of the many plants and spies in the camp, secrecy would be a priority, but all the men in the hut were considered trustworthy. Tomás Ó Maoláin of Roemore, Breaffy, Co. Mayo, said:

> In common with the general I.R.A. policy in dealing with the pernicious enemy Intelligence System, we simply removed the kid gloves. That policy succeeded within the barbed wire, as it assuredly did outside.[4]

The arrival of a new batch of prisoners in August had led to the erection of tents between the huts, so as part of the escape plans John J. Martin, camp quartermaster, made a request to his British counterpart for a marquee tent to enable him to discharge his 'heavy duties'. The marquee was delivered and was made the headquarters of the escape committee. It was set up beside Hut 31 (some accounts say Hut 37) and all that was necessary was for the tunnellers to lift the canvas wall and crawl under the adjoining hut.[5]

Hugh Byrne succeeded in 'commandeering' from the quartermaster's stores a screwdriver that had been seized after the discovery of the first tunnel. Nevertheless, he had considerable difficulty in persuading Jim Brady to use the tool, as Brady regarded it an unlucky omen after the first unsuccessful attempt.[6]

Liam Murphy had assisted in the digging of the first tunnel, so his assistance was once again enlisted. William P. Murphy, of 35 South William Street, was a section leader with B Company, 3rd Battalion, Dublin Brigade. A member of the IRB, he was in the Boland's Mill garrison during Easter Week 1916. Two of his brothers, Richard and Jack, were also Volunteers and mobilised for the Rising: Richard was killed in action at Clanwilliam House during the Battle of Mount Street Bridge, while Jack was a dispatch carrier for the 3rd Battalion. Liam was arrested by the military in February 1921 and held in Arbour Hill before being moved to the Rath Camp. His experience in digging the first tunnel was instrumental in the success of the second tunnel.[7]

One late August night, Joe Galvin and Jim Brady slipped quietly out of their beds and crept under their hut. With primitive tools, the two men started the job of opening a shaft for a new tunnel. They lay flat on the earth beneath the hut and scooped away the first sod over the proposed shaft – making a circular hole some 30 inches in diameter. Shortly before dawn they cautiously returned to their beds, tired but contented with the results of their work – their new tunnel became known variously as 'Brady's Tunnel', the 'Tullamore Tunnel' or the 'Rabbit Burrow'.[8] Tom Byrne explained: 'Many of the tunnels made in the Irish internment camps were quite large and required the use of wooden props. Brady did not follow this method; his tunnel was quite narrow and more like a rabbit hole.'[9]

An opening for a vertical shaft was begun with a crowbar picked up from workmen in the camp. A few knives from the kitchen were forthcoming, but these quickly broke when faced with hard earth. When the tunnellers had excavated several feet, Brady used the screwdriver, a crowbar and spoons from the cookhouse. The shaft was about 10–12 feet across and the soil was distributed evenly on the remaining space under the hut. A makeshift ladder was provided to enable the workers to get up and down the shaft, and timber battens were jammed into the sides. The clay was hauled back to the entrance in strong canvas mailbags supplied by the camp postman, Andy Harrold, and pulled up with ropes that belonged to the marquee. From there, when the space under the floor had been filled, the bags of earth were carried up into the hut and stored temporarily in fire buckets, suitcases and anything else available. The soil was eventually spirited away in jacket pockets or paper bags, to be carefully and unobtrusively distributed in handfuls all over the camp so no one would notice it on the surface of the compound.

When the shaft was completed, two major problems confronted the tunnellers: direction and lighting. The tunnel was to be driven eastward for about 80–90 yards to a spot covered by a clump of furze bushes, as it was hoped that the exit among the furze would be most likely to escape observation by the sentries in the elevated posts.[10]

Tunnelling was done entirely at night after roll call, when it was unlikely that the occupants of the hut would be disturbed without warning. One factor that greatly assisted the tunnelling was the type of soil, which was favourable to the enterprise, being of a gravelly nature. Large stones were comparatively few.[11] Initially, the tunnel was about 30 inches square, barely enough to permit a man to crawl through on hands and knees. This was the first serious mistake. In time, the tunnellers learned to round off the roof into a rough arch, but only after several cave-ins, which fortunately didn't cause any casualties. To the credit of the tunnellers, not one accident resulting in injury, even of a minor nature, occurred. Jim Brady did most of the tunnelling, lying on his back or his side as he struck out over his shoulder at the tunnel face.[12] Only one man at a time could work on the tunnel face and get the earth back to the end of the shaft. Brady's tunnelling expertise in the Curragh earned him the title of 'The human ferret', so skilful and rapid was his work.[13] He worked tirelessly in the tunnel and also oversaw the work of others.

Brady chipped his way through the earth grimly, helped by Joe Galvin, enduring the foetid smell of damp earth and their own sweat for the most part of eleven days until they were almost completely exhausted.[14] They were relieved by Joe Rochford, Joe Shaughnessy and Patrick 'Scottie' Regan (Keadue, Co. Roscommon) for short spells. A lookout system was devised to warn the tunnellers of the approach of guards. As the work proceeded, every prisoner in the hut who could do so lent a willing hand, though only a few were able to manage working in the tunnel.[15] The task was exhausting, with extreme restriction of movement as all the work had to be done in a supine position. Light was supplied by candles – which were scrounged, bartered for and plundered – and when they were not available, supplemented by makeshift candles made of grease and string. Candles gave necessary light, but they also devoured the limited supply of oxygen. The air in the tunnel was foul, and a stage was reached when a lighted candle at the face of the shaft would not remain alight because of the lack of oxygen. The only ventilation was through the entrance and, consequently, the air at the shaft face was rank. Rochford and Shaughnessy lasted only an hour on their first attempt, after which they emerged choking and gasping for breath.

When Brady had excavated about 50 feet, he said he could go no further without an air shaft. He went into the tunnel again and, with the crowbar, dug an outlet upwards, in the shape of a cone, to the surface 8 feet overhead, so the poisonous gases could escape. Outside, anxious watchers waited to see where the crowbar would come through the surface. It came through – right in No Man's Land! The air quality in the tunnel then became tolerable. There was little danger of the tiny vent being noticed by the guards, as it was concealed by grass. As Brady continued his excavations, he added several more air holes.[16]

Tomás Ó Maoláin (Thomas Mullen) was an organiser on the escape committee and was also involved in the tunnel escapes. He was a national schoolteacher from an energetic republican family. He became active after the 1916 Rising, and his two brothers, Michael and Edward, were also prominent in the fight for freedom, while their sister, Mary, was a Cumann na mBan leader in Mayo.[17] Ó Maoláin described the back-breaking work in the rival tunnel, mainly using a sharp-tipped iron bar:

> Vainly, we had searched for even a pocket compass and without it we had to rely upon a couple of right-angled contrivances made from stray strips of timber, and held vertically in the shaft to enable us at least, to strike off approximately in the desired direction, as we shaped and scooped out the first few inches of the mouth of the tunnel.
>
> What was its shape and size? About 30 inches square, or barely large enough to permit a man to crawl through on hands and knees. Usually, the worker – so often the hardworking Heery from, I think, North Meath – lay on his back or side, and struck over his shoulder at the tunnel face.
>
> 'Boring' is an apt description of endless scraping at a tunnel face which at times becomes just solid rock. When this happened we veered to the right … these digressions – in our tunnel – made the problem of our underground direction more difficult still and lacking the mechanical aid of a compass, we would probably have described a circle, instead of an exit from the Camp, were it not for those vents which we had bored to the surface every few yards. At the surface they were no more than a couple of inches in diameter, but it was possible to push a stick upwards through each vent and a Scrutineer at a hut window was able to get visual evidence of the direction the tunnel was

taking. Inevitably, the tendency to veer to the right had to be corrected after each check-up.

So we strove – the tunneller on his back and striking at the wall of clay and stone; forging ahead inch by inch, hoping for the best in the matter of direction, continually devising ways and means to solve the countless problems that arose, daily and nightly.[18]

Despite the difficulties, work on the tunnels proceeded at an amazingly rapid pace. Inside a fortnight Brady and his comrades had arrived below the inner barbed-wire entanglements and after they had tunnelled about 75 feet Brady began to dig upwards.[19] While the two groups of tunnellers were unaware of each other's schemes, both tunnels were designed to come up under the outer barbed-wire entanglements at a point parallel with Row D. Though many of the men in camp knew of the tunnels, none spoke about them for fear of British spies learning about the projects.[20]

In the space of only eighteen days, Jim Brady had reached the outside wire and reported to Liam Murphy that the job was completed and, except for the outer barbed-wire barrier, the escape was ready to go. For that barrier he had secured a wire cutter.[21] However, a major problem then arose.

On Monday 5 September troops of the East Sussex Regiment began unloading stores – baulks of timber and barbed wire – outside the outer entanglements along the side of the camp where both tunnels were to break the surface. The Royal Engineers then began to erect a new compound for prisoners on the spot where the tunnel exit was planned. Sappers also began deepening the trench with which they had found the first tunnel, and it was probable that in a short time they would unearth the new tunnel. It was likely that the trench would also fill up with water when the weather changed. The decision to escape before all this happened became paramount.[22] Tom Byrne said:

> The British, as if they had smelt a rat, had started to deepen their trench by a further four feet and it didn't take us long to reckon that they were working right towards our tunnel.[23]

Tomás Ó Maoláin was hoping to escape from the Dublin Brigade tunnel as matters came to a head:

> As the tunnel approached the barbed wire entanglements, reports began to pour in from our I.Os. [Intelligence Officers] of enemy precautions against tunnelling and soon, we saw for ourselves the Corps of Army Engineers digging a huge trench, many feet deeper than our tunnel, all around the Camp … Luckily for us in D Line, trenching operations had begun at the opposite end of the Camp outside A Line. So our job had now become a grim race against time.
>
> Next, an I.O. came along with a further piece of startling news – that another tunnel was in progress from a hut further along our own D Line. Soon we knew the facts. It was only too true that their tunnel was a better proposition than ours, their route was shorter, their course easier and they were nearer the goal than we. So the situation was indeed a delicate one for us.[24]

Ó Maoláin approached some men he knew in the hut above the Brady tunnel, but nobody there would tell him about their escape plans. According to Ó Maoláin, a 'passive form of Civil War' existed between the two tunnel groups, but time was ticking away and there was the added danger that 'plants' in the camp might find out about the tunnels. Just as a showdown seemed inevitable, negotiations began when Todd Andrews suggested the two groups combine their escape efforts.[25]

Tom Byrne was just getting over the appearance of the British sappers when he heard the news:

> Another surprise was in store for us. We discovered that another working party of prisoners had started a tunnel of their own a few huts away from ours and that they had been working on it before Brady had started his.
>
> There was a tremendous mutual astonishment. We joined forces and a council of war was held at which it was agreed that all the workers on the other tunnel should abandon their own and get a chance to escape the Brady way.[26]

In Hut 9, D Line, section leader Tommy Brabazon from Lower Dorset Street, Dublin, knew of the Dublin Brigade tunnel and was kept informed about its progress. His companions in Hut 9 – Richard 'Dick' Molloy from Belvedere Place, Dublin, Matthew and James Cullen from Laois, and a man called Brophy from Galway – were also well informed about the Brady tunnel. All were tense, but they did not discuss the tunnel even among themselves, though they were fully satisfied as to each other's republican credentials. 'There were too many strangers in the hut,' Tommy Brabazon said, 'and whom you didn't know you didn't trust. There were many in the camp who were not IRA men, and there were a few "stool-pigeons" planted by the British.'[27]

A decision needed to be made and it was agreed that one of the tunnels should be finished and used without delay. The Brady tunnel was chosen because it was the more advanced. On Wednesday 7 September, eighteen days after the work had started, Brady and Galvin calculated they had reached a point clear of the outer entanglements. They were ready to go that night, but as an extra precaution Brady was asked to push a marker upwards to make sure the tunnel went far enough.[28] However, when they tentatively pushed an old fencing foil with a piece of white paper on its tip through the top soil, observers were dismayed to see that it appeared in the corridor between the two entanglements. Tom Byrne said, 'This was serious as we were working against time, because the new camp ... was likely to be occupied at any time, and was all complete, including arc lights.'[29] With renewed energy, the tunnellers pressed on with their work, though progress was slow. Despite this, the decision was taken that the escape should be made at night on Friday 9 September.[30]

Certain officers were to be given priority in the escape attempt. Despite the Truce and peace negotiations, the IRA was preparing for the worst and the escape of experienced men interned in the Curragh was important. Tom Byrne was one of those earmarked to escape and he was looking forward to getting home again. Byrne was commandant of 1st Battalion, Dublin Brigade, and at the time he was arrested in February 1920 his wife, Lucy, tragically lost their first child.[31] Byrne said:

> I was informed that Brady's tunnel was completed and I was given the opportunity to escape … I then asked them to allow another man to escape with me, and when I told them it was their own line captain, Joe Vize, and that he was an important Headquarters man, they agreed.[32]

It was never envisaged that the Brady tunnel, which was a small-escape project, would be used by all who were now included in the escape plans, so it became clear that many men would have to remain in the camp. Fifty were selected and there was disappointment all around. In Hut 9 Tommy Brabazon, Dick Molloy, the Cullens and Brophy endured the disappointment as best they could. They knew they would not be getting out this time but satisfied themselves that there was still a chance with the other tunnel.[33]

The plan was that those chosen were to go in two batches of twenty-five, with a two-hour interval between each batch, so that if anything went wrong at least some men would have a chance to get away. The grandstand on the Curragh Racecourse was the rendezvous point where they would meet and strike out in select groups in different directions. The strategy was to get onto the railway behind it and follow it until daylight.

It was a foggy night as the first twenty-five prisoners arrived to take up their position in the tunnel. Hugh Byrne recalled, 'While we were waiting for the signal to go on the night of the escape, all the lights in the new camp were turned on, and our hopes seemed dashed. After some anxious moments they were turned off. They were only testing.'[34] At midnight, Liam Murphy told the men their places in the queue. Meanwhile, the next twenty-five men quietly occupied the marquee tent next to the escape hut to await their turn.[35]

Jim Brady and Joe Galvin went first. Their work was not complete and they still had important jobs to accomplish as they were to open the tunnel into the outer entanglements and then lead the way. Joe Galvin said:

> At 11.30 p.m. Brady and myself slid into the tunnel and asked to be given an hour and a quarter to open the outer end and to cut the wire. We were given assurance that there would be complete silence and nothing would occur which would arouse any suspicions. After our friends said goodbye and wished us good luck, we crawled to the outer end of the tunnel …[36]

Scurrying on hands and knees as fast as they could along the narrow passage, within minutes they were at the end of the tunnel that had taken nineteen days of hard labour to complete. They hacked anxiously at the roof as loose earth rained down on them, quickly opening a hole large enough to get through comfortably. Helped by Brady, Galvin got his head and shoulders above ground. After the black darkness of the tunnel, he was nearly blinded by the glare of the searchlight. On regaining his composure, Galvin was immediately filled with despair. They had seriously miscalculated the opening: the new shaft opened about 20 yards short of the objective, between two lines of entanglements. However, the point reached was outside the area covered by the arc of light surrounding the barbed-wire fence, and in the darkness was not easily observed by the sentries in the elevated posts, so they quickly recovered from this crushing discovery.

Outside the barbed-wire fence, the Rath No. 2 Internment Camp was now complete but not occupied. A very thick barbed-wire entanglement ran right through the centre of this camp and a way had to be cut through this before the escapers could get to the camp gate, which was also heavily wired. Therefore, a great deal depended on the two leading men going ahead and blazing a trail with the wire cutters.

Brady and Galvin had brought a ball of twine and some wooden pegs with them and Brady drove a peg into the ground at the exit of the tunnel, to which he tied one end of the twine. The two men crawled in the direction of the outer entanglement, flattening themselves against the grass as apprehensive eyes watched from the darkened interior of the internees' huts, with Brady unravelling the twine behind him as he went. When he reached the first wire barrier, he managed to cut through it unnoticed.

Suddenly, a chilling challenge ripped the silence of the night: 'Halt! Who goes there?' The challenge was immediately followed by the more ominous metallic sound of

A TUNNEL TO FREEDOM

a weapon being cocked in the nearest of the observation towers. A tense few seconds passed, as Brady and Galvin lay motionless, hoping that the sentry had not seen them. The two escapers knew that the guards had orders to shoot anyone seen approaching the barbed wire. They steadied themselves for the worst but were greatly relieved when they heard the answer to the guard's challenge – 'Visiting Rounds' – which came from the side of the tower distant from where they lay. By an extraordinary twist of fate, the military patrol was approaching the tower just as the two escapers were cutting their way through the outer barbed-wire entanglements. The officer thought the challenge was directed at his patrol, and the sentry obviously thought that the noise he had heard was that of the approaching military. Suspecting nothing, the patrol moved on.[37]

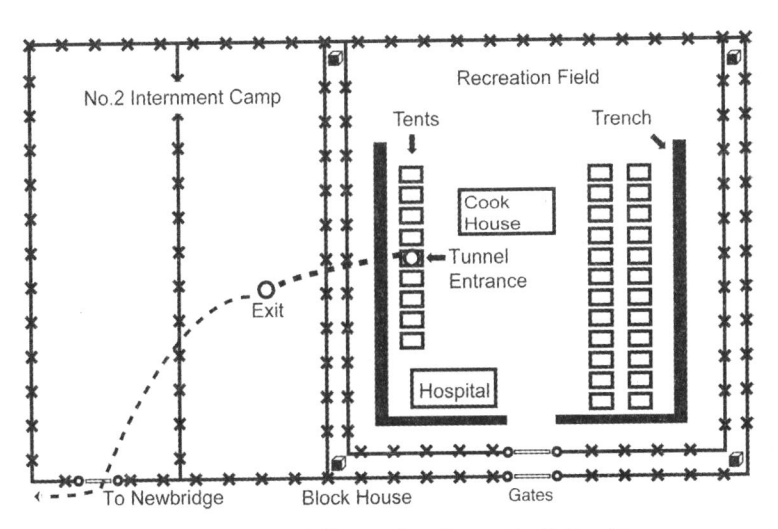

The escape route on 9 September. Image by Brian Durney.

Still trailing the twine, Brady reached the second wire barrier at the gate 15 yards further away and cut a gap in that. Using the twine as a guide in the dark, he made his way back and gave the all clear.[38] Brady turned and, with Galvin, headed for the plains of the Curragh. Despite the thick fog, their sense of direction was good and they found themselves on the Newbridge road. Galvin said:

> We passed through Newbridge and were heading for Naas when we decided to get off the main road. Hardly had we turned down a bye-road when two lorries of Tans and military passed by. We learned afterwards that they were on the lookout for escapees. We then agreed to part company and, after making arrangements to meet later, I went to one house and Brady went to another. I went to Kennedy's in the Naas district. They were very friendly and very helpful people and they arranged how we could get to Dublin. I rejoined Brady and arrived safely in Dublin and there we had the address of one of our prisoner pals, Martin's of Heytesbury Street. The Martin family got us to a camp in the Dublin mountains and I remained there for a few days before getting home safely.[39]

8
THE FOGGY DEW

Before midnight, Hugh Byrne and Liam Murphy led the first batch of sixteen men into the tunnel. Following Byrne and Murphy, the men moved at short intervals to prevent congestion in the tunnel towards the exit. Boots and shoes were not worn to avoid making any noise. Each man had instructions to wait at the exit until he heard the sentry pass. The escapers then started to leave at three- to five-minute intervals. By following the guiding twine laid down by Brady, the escaping prisoners had no difficulty locating the gaps in the barriers.[1]

It was well after midnight when the first of the remaining internees got clear of the camp. Once they were outside the barbed wire, they set off in small groups towards the racecourse, but the thick ground fog enveloping the Curragh made a rendezvous impossible. Selected Dublin prisoners were the first group out, followed by internees from the west. At the tunnel entrance, Liam Murphy and Hugh Byrne directed their batch of escapers in the order of their going. When they were finished they handed over to another party led by Walter O'Brien, and advised him of the procedure.[2]

Tom Byrne was informed that his turn and that of Joe Vize would be about 12.30 a.m., and they made their way from their hut to the other end of the camp at about

12.15 a.m. They failed in sneaking away unnoticed, however. Charlie Byrne from Dublin followed Tom Byrne and Vize and told them that he was not going to be left behind. Charlie succeeded in getting into the tunnel and away to freedom. His brother, Bernard, also escaped.[3] Tom Byrne and Vize made their way to the mouth of the tunnel by crawling under the hut. Both were tall, well-built men, and they had to 'make progress much the same as a caterpillar'. The tunnel was 3 feet wide and 2 feet high, and they found some twelve to fifteen men lying under the ground, head to toe in something that was a very close imitation of a rabbit burrow. Byrne later gave two accounts of the escape:

> I was told to go through with Joe Vize at about 12.30 a.m. When our time came we made our way from the other end of the camp sticking close to the shadows of the buildings on our way. It was a foggy night and we were hoping and praying for luck. When we got to the tent we were told to wait in an adjoining hut until our turn came, as the tent could only hold a few men. At last we got the signal and we went into the tent, lifted the flap, crawled under the hut and then we went into the tunnel.
>
> For about 7 or 8 feet we went at an angle of about 45 degrees, and then made a complete dive as we knew we were about to go under the trench. The tunnel then gradually worked up … Brady's tunnel was indeed a narrow one, each man had to fight his way through, panting and wrestling with the walls. The hole was round and Vize and I, being big men, had to lever ourselves along on our elbows. The whole length of the tunnel was full of men, all screwing themselves onward in the darkness. Sometimes

all movement would stop like a traffic block and we'd lie there wondering what was happening at the front. We couldn't go forward and we couldn't go back.

Just when we'd begun to think we were stuck there forever – or until we were caught and hauled out ignominiously – the movement would start again and we'd all wriggle forward another few yards. It was only later I learned the reason for the numerous halts. The lads at the exit couldn't go out until the sentry had passed on in the other direction to No Man's Land. Every time the sentry would turn his back a fresh batch would dodge out and away.[4]

When I emerged there was no sign of any guiding cord, but I had a fair knowledge of where the wire was to be cut, and though the night was foggy, I arrived within 6 or 7 yards of it. By creeping along the ground my friend and I discovered it; the gate presented no difficulty and we were at last in the clear. We found another man waiting for company, and the three of us proceeded across the road that ran along the Camp from the town of Kildare to the Curragh barracks.[5]

From the time when the decision was taken to go, until it was time to set off, Todd Andrews was in a state of tension that increased hourly. He discussed with his friend Myles Ford what direction they would take if they succeeded in getting away. They had no maps but agreed they would make for Dublin, with the racecourse grandstand on their left indicating the direction of the capital. Andrews did not know what towns, villages or landmarks lay between the Curragh and Dublin:

This was a measure of the ignorance of Dubliners of our time about rural Ireland or indeed of the geography of Ireland in general.

At midnight the breakout began. Murphy arranged that we should leave in groups of two or three at three-minute intervals. He allocated us our groups and our place in the queue. Myles Ford, Jack Knowthe [Noud] and myself were to go together in the sixth group. As we heard no sign of commotion from the groups that preceded us we knew that they had got away safely. We got no directions from Murphy as to what route to take once clear of the tunnel. That was left to ourselves. Our only instructions were that we should not get off our bellies until we judged we had got out of the possible view of the sentries in the watch towers of camp.

After three months' internment, a prisoner was entitled to 'procure' a new suit of clothes from the British. I claimed mine. The suit was of the type issued to soldiers on demobilisation. It was known variously as a 'Martin-Henry' after the manufacturers (who were reputed to have made millions on the supply) or a 'Hamar' (after the Chief Secretary) or a 'bum-freezer' (because the coat had no vent at the back and was very short). It was made of the shoddiest material dyed a blue colour which would run in a shower of rain. I had intended to keep it to be worn on my release. I decided to wear it for the escape.

We were not allowed to wear boots in the tunnel but there was no objection to taking them strung around your neck. I very wisely did this. Myles Ford and Knowthe unfortunately did not. The tensions of the day mounted to their peak as I slipped out of the hut and under Hut 31 to the mouth of the tunnel. After the first few yards I was seized by a fit of terror. I had no idea that the passage was so small. It was about three feet wide and rather less than two feet high. As I wriggled along, my shoulders touched the sides. Occasionally, if I failed to keep absolutely flat, I touched the roof. I was afraid that at any minute the roof would collapse, suffocating me. My body was pouring sweat. Once a boot got caught under my armpit, requiring me momentarily to stop wriggling to dislodge it. The pause of a second or two felt like hours. At last when, after a quarter of an hour or so, I reached the end of the tunnel and got into the open air and on to the green grass my whole instinct was to get up and run. With a great effort I resisted temptation, continuing to wriggle to the fence, the bottom wire of which Brady had cut. I could hear the sentry in the watch tower call out his routine report 'No. 1 Post and all is well'. By this time I was calmer and, thanks to the wet grass and a light ground mist, cooler. Here I found Myles Ford and Jack Knowthe waiting for me as we had arranged. We still had to wriggle several hundred yards, crossing the dirt tracks before we reached the main Curragh Road.[6]

The trip through the confined space of the tunnel was daunting for many of the men, and their arrival on the outside no less so, as they still had a distance to go before relative safety was reached:

The painful drag of one's body through such a tunnel is a test even of exuberant youthful fitness … My personal shock came not in the earthy darkness to which I was accustomed, but when I peeped from the exit into the myriad scintillating arclights

– magnified, of course, in contrast with the blackness through which I had crawled into a brilliancy that positively lit up the surroundings, so that I could distinguish every blade of grass.

The sentries pacing the 'Death-Walk' a few yards away, were clearly distinguishable in every feature. This situation had been foreseen and discussed in detail for weeks beforehand, and we had banked upon the theory that the lighting system was so extremely brilliant in the vicinity of the barbed wire defences, that sentries operating within the focus of that light would be blind to objects in the comparative shade just outside its ambit.

Our theory was justified completely that night, as we 'wormed' our way, inch by inch, from that hell-fired barbed wire. When we had covered 100 yards or so, we lay still, breathing in gulps the noiseless night air disturbed only by the bawling of a sentry:

'No. 1 Post and all's well!'

'Swell,' thought I, 'until Reveille.'[7]

Tomás Ó Maoláin recalled that he entered the tunnel after Todd Andrews. He was accompanied by Seán Barry and Seán Doody, both from Tullamore. Ó Maoláin heard Barry whispering to Doody, 'We're making history tonight, Seán,' to which the reply came: 'Blast history! It's geography I want to make just now!'

The trio headed towards the Curragh Racecourse but got lost in the fog. They wandered around in the 'pea-souper' until they found themselves back at the wire of the camp and heard a sentry muttering a challenge. In panic, they turned and headed back the way they came. Lost again, Doody theorised that the cold and clammy wind was coming from the east, and if they felt the icy sensation on their right cheek they should be heading off in a northerly direction, which would bring them away from the camp. This observation was correct, as the trio then crashed into a railing of the racecourse. Ducking under the railing, they soon arrived at the grandstand and subsequently the railway line. At daybreak they reached a friendly cottage in the Bog of Allen, several miles from the Curragh Camp.[8]

Hugh Byrne recalled heading for the rendezvous point of the Curragh Racecourse Stand, but only himself, Liam Murphy, Éamonn Flynn (Kinnegad, Co. Westmeath) and a man named O'Dwyer arrived together.[9] Some of the escaped prisoners wandered around for hours in the fog. Like Ó Maoláin, Barry and Doody, others, having lost their bearings, found themselves back at the outer barbed-wire entanglements, where the searchlights and arc lamps glowed away through the fog. One such group was Tom Byrne and his comrades, who lost all sense of direction:

> We headed for the grandstand of the race course which would give us our bearings. The fog held and as we melted into it we laughed as we heard behind us the sentries from the blockhouse chanting out their 'All's Well.' All was well for us – so far. But the fog which helped us at the start was nearly our undoing at the end for we managed to get lost in it. And instead of making the grandstand we stumbled around the Curragh falling over whin bushes, utterly lost.

> After a good half hour of this we got the fright of our lives …[10]

After going around several large clumps of furze, they ended up back in the glare of the lights of the camp. At a crucial point, just in time, they saw a sentry appear out of the fog only 4 yards away. After he was gone, Byrne said to Vize:

> 'We are at sea now, and you as an old sailor ought to be able to navigate us successfully.' Joe, who had sailed all the seas as a qualified engineer, was not in a joking mood and we kept going.
>
> We turned our backs to the glare of the arc lights and after some time found the road which led direct from Kildare to Newbridge. We made for the latter place and took the road from there to Sallins, which we reached around dawn. Seeing some lights in a railway shed we entered. The men there received us very well, took us to their homes and gave us breakfast and a much-needed rest for a few hours, as well as a wash to take the gravel from our hair. They then completed their kindness by making arrangements for us to travel to Dublin, which we reached later.[11]

Todd Andrews and his two companions, Myles Ford and Jack Noud, soon made it as far as the racecourse rendezvous point. Andrews had boots, but the other two wore only stockings:

> Myles, who was by far the calmest of us, took the lead until we at last reached the racecourse. Here we were able to crawl

rather than wriggle. After a few hundred yards we felt justified in getting to our feet. We ran to the racecourse stand where we paused for breath and to take counsel. I put on my boots. Neither Myles nor Jack had ever been even as far as Bodenstown for the Wolfe Tone Memorial celebrations but I had. I knew that Bodenstown was near Sallins and since in getting there we had never crossed the Curragh I reckoned that Sallins must be north of the Curragh. But we did not know that Newbridge and Naas lay between us and Sallins. The obvious route for us to take seemed to be along the railway line, but we felt that progress would be dangerously slow, stepping from sleeper to sleeper while the stone ballast between the sleepers would make walking impossible for Myles and Jack in their stocking-feet.

We decided to use the side roads keeping as near to the railway as possible. We considered knocking up some household, throwing ourselves on their mercy and asking for help, but rejected the idea because it was fairly certain that anyone living in the vicinity of the Curragh would be in some way connected with the military or, what was the same in our estimation, the gentlemen of the Turf. It was now between 1 and 2 a.m. The night was calm and soundless and the ground mist had gone. We had walked four or five miles when we heard a motor car or lorry coming towards us. We jumped into a ditch, landing in a bed of nettles. The nettle stings were a substantial addition to our growing discomfort. Myles' and Jack's feet began to give them trouble but we pushed on. After walking for a couple of hours we found ourselves in the middle of what seemed a large town. There was neither a soul nor a light to be seen. We did not know where we were but we hurried through it as quickly as possible. In fact it was Newbridge, a large military centre. As

Newbridge is only three miles from the Curragh, we must have been walking around in circles before we blundered into it. We met nobody.

When we got through the town we abandoned the main road, continuing to walk blindly in the direction, we hoped but were not sure, of Dublin. My companions' feet began to give out completely when we found ourselves on what was obviously the outskirts of another town. This town was Naas, but we did not know that. We decided that Myles and Jack would rest while I went into the town to explore the possibility of getting help. I found the place, like Newbridge, deserted. There was no light showing in any house, nor of course were there any street lamps in those days.

I knew we could not go on much further. I thought there must be a priest somewhere at hand who, even if he was not sympathetic, would neither give us away nor turn us away. He might even put us in touch with the local IRA. I saw the church. There was a small house near it. I knocked. After a long pause, a window opened. A voice asked gruffly and nervously what I wanted. I told him that there had been an accident and I was looking for a priest. With reluctance the voice directed me to a house which was easy to find as it was situated at the junction of the street we were standing in and the main road. I approached and knocked at the door. A window in the upper storey opened after some delay. A man appeared to enquire what was the matter. I repeated the story about wanting a priest to tend to some people involved in an accident. He told me he was the priest. After being interrogated as to who I was, what I was doing out at that hour of night, what accident had happened and so on, I began to realise that my efforts at persuasion were wasted. With the state of my nerves and bodily exhaustion [*sic*] I was not prepared to conduct any further conversation at the top of my voice with this unhelpful priest. I got very angry with him, told him in four letter words what he could do with himself and went off to rejoin the others. When I calmed down, I was very conscience stricken about having spoken to a priest in that way.

As it happened the priest – Father Flavin I think was his name – was most sympathetic to the Movement. Had he known we were escaped prisoners, he would have taken us into his house and looked after us. But unfortunately I did not know that at the time.

There was nothing for us to do but trudge on although by this time Myles' and Jack's feet were in ribbons. They were finding it so difficult to get along that we felt we had no choice but to waken some household and look for help. We were considering this when after walking a couple of miles we came to another village. Here we saw a light and made straight for it. It turned out to be Sallins Railway Station and the light came from the office of the night porter. We pushed open the door to find the porter reading a newspaper before a bright fire. To us it was a comforting scene. I told the porter that we were three IRA men who had escaped from the Curragh and wanted to be put in touch with the local IRA. His face lit up. 'Bejaysus', said he, 'I'm the local quartermaster'. We were safe! He sat us down and gave us some strong tea and some bread and butter while we told him of our adventures and our need to get to Dublin. He assured us that there would be no difficulty in fixing that. A goods train to Dublin would be coming through in a couple of hours and it would drop us off anywhere we wanted along the line.

INTERNED

We were a dismal sight. Dusty, wet, sore footed, nettle stung. While having tea we were given a basin of hot water to bathe the battered feet of Myles and Jack. When daylight came we went outside to collect dock leaves, of which there was an abundance, to treat our nettle stings which were still painful.

Before getting on the train the porter gave us half a crown each. The money, he explained, was from the funds of the local IRA Company. When the train arrived he signalled it to a halt, explained our problem to the guard and driver. It was decided that they would drop us off just beyond Clondalkin at Bluebell. From there we cut across the fields to a garage on the main road where Myles Ford knew that a taxi could be obtained. With the seven and sixpence we got from the porter at Sallins we hired a taxi to take us to the house of Ford's relatives at Templeogue.[12]

Most of the delegated men had escaped by 4 a.m., but not all the men who intended to escape did break out. John J. Gavigan, a member of Coole District Council, was only told about the tunnel on the morning of the escape. He had only been in the camp for nine days and was one of the last four men delegated to go. He went to the tent beside the hut that concealed the tunnel. According to Gavigan the three men detailed to leave with him were Connolly from Columbkille, Co. Kilkenny, Patrick Hopkins from Ballymahon, Co. Longford, and another man he did not know from Longford:

> I was waiting for the Longford man to get through. I was second to go in … It was very difficult to get through the tunnel,

especially in the case of a big stout man, but they got through with difficulty. When I came to the mouth of the tunnel, I remarked there were boots in the tunnel.

There was a sentry 2½ yards from me. He could hear the noise and saw the last four going out. I was waiting to give the fellow before me a chance. The next thing I heard was a call of 'Halt there,' and a shot was fired. The sentry shouted for the guard to come out, but they did not believe there was anything the matter and did not come out. The sentry went down and we heard him shout, 'If you don't come quick, there won't be a "Shinner" in the camp, they are going out like rabbits.' And so they were, but I was fated not to succeed on this occasion and had to go back.[13]

Tom Moran was one of a group of Roscommon men who escaped. He was from Crossna, Co. Roscommon, and was OC Crossna Company and subsequently OC 4th Battalion, North Roscommon Brigade, the position he held when he was arrested on 1 February 1921. Moran was held at Boyle and Athlone Military Barracks before being transferred to the Rath Camp.[14] Not long after Tom's arrest, his brother Paddy was executed for his part in the Bloody Sunday attacks on British forces.

The heavy fog was nearly the undoing of Moran's group of twelve escapers. When they thought they were well clear of the camp, they found themselves back at the wire. They turned and walked in the opposite direction and soon accepted they were lost. In desperation, they knelt and recited the Rosary. As they finished praying, they heard rooks cawing in trees nearby. Knowing that the only trees near the camp were at the back of the grandstand of the Curragh Racecourse, they used the cawing of the rooks as a guide.

The men had abandoned their boots and in stocking feet found it hard to make haste, but they walked, then ran and then walked again. They decided to take a chance when they reached a group of houses near the Hill of Allen about 10 miles from the Curragh Camp. More luck was on the side of the escapers. The house where they called was that of a friendly family and they were fed and then taken across fields to the home of Fr Smith in Rathangan. He was the local curate and, more importantly, a republican sympathiser. The group of Roscommon men found two other escapers also enjoying the priest's hospitality. They all rested there during the day, and that evening local Volunteers brought fresh clothes and footwear along with horses and traps to Fr Smith's house and conveyed the escapers to Carbury, on the border with Co. Offaly, where they were treated to excellent hospitality by the proprietor of Weyme's Hotel. The proprietor put his Leyland car at their disposal and asked the driver to take them where they wanted to go. From there, the men were driven to a rendezvous near Athlone as they decided that the large car might arouse suspicion in the strongly garrisoned town.

Mick Murphy had worked on the railway in Athlone and he made his way to a friend, Bernard Fitzpatrick of Connaught Street, who provided them with a small lorry. Mick Murphy and Dick Mee were dropped off at Kiltoom. The lorry went on to Pat Tennant's home at Knockcroghery, where the remaining nine men, including Jim Farrell, Pat McNamara, Tom Moran, Paddy Barry, Pat Beirne and Henry Compton, rested while a messenger was sent to the South Roscommon IRA Brigade staff. Pat Madden and Frank Simons arrived with two cars and drove the men to Strokestown. There they met Paddy Duffy, who provided the final car to complete their journeys to their homes.[15] Tom Moran did not go straight to his house, but went to Crossna Hibernian Hall, where he met his youngest brother, Joe. He sent his brother home ahead of him to break the news to his parents in case his sudden appearance gave them a frightful shock.[16] He later wrote to his sister Cissie:

> We left the camp about 2.30 a.m. on Friday and arrived home on Sat. night about 9 p.m. ... When [Paddy] Barry and myself came to the hall on Saturday night there were a few of the youngsters in it, our Joe among them. We walked in and stood in the centre of the floor, and for about five minutes they could not speak a word, you would think it was two ghosts that appeared to them.[17]

Tom Moran's joyful homecoming was tinged with sadness, though, because his brother, Paddy, never returned home.

Locals in Kildare reported seeing a group of bareheaded escapers at Rathangan, but before they travelled any further they had obtained hats or caps. Some of the escapers seen in the Robertstown district were said to have shown evidence of having suffered badly in getting through the barbed wire entanglements.[18] There were places in the locality where the escapers could find help. Round Tower House, in Kildare town, was a safe house and meeting place for local republicans. The owners, Michael and Elizabeth Cunningham, were responsible for the smuggling of maps and other equipment to potential escapers in the Rath and Hare Park Camps. They supplied clothing to one of the escapers and transported him to Dublin.[19]

Escapers made their way in batches to various parts of the country. Because of the order that no boots were to be worn in the tunnel, Hugh Byrne and his party were among those who struggled painfully along the roads in stockings or bare feet. At dawn the four men went into a field and slept fitfully for a short period. They then located a friendly farmer's house, where arrangements were made with local Volunteers for the completion of their journey by car to Dublin.[20]

David Daly of Faheran, Moate, Co. Westmeath, was probably one of these men. He said:

> I made my way back to Moate and then someone informed me that I would have to report back to the Rath Camp – that my escape was a breach of the Truce. I reported to Seán MacEoin who was now in charge of the Midland Division which had been organised in my absence and he instructed me to go to the Brigade Training Camp at Benown and remain there and this I did.[21]

Tomás Ó Maoláin and his two companions met up with several other escapers – Kieran Temple, Jack Killeavy, Paddy

Darcy and Joe Robinson – at the cottage in the Bog of Allen. Before his arrest Ó Maoláin had been living and working in the capital and decided to head to Dublin with Darcy and Robinson, while Doody, Barry, Killeavy and Temple made their way to their home areas. A friendly bakery van, Byrne's of Kildare, carried the trio to Lucan and from there they caught a tram to Dublin. On crossing O'Connell Bridge the three escapers were confronted by a British sergeant major who had conducted head counts in the Rath Camp. Ó Maoláin said, 'Recognition was mutual and as our hands sprung to our pockets in search of guns – that were not there – the "Major" made himself scarce, even more quickly than we.' The three men proceeded across the city to Dalkey Hill, where they found food and shelter. 'Replenished and at ease,' Ó Maoláin said, 'we slept the sleep of the tired – and free.'[22]

When he reached Templeogue, in Dublin, Todd Andrews wrote his mother a letter, which was delivered by Myles Ford's sister:

My dearest Mother,
I do not want you to express any surprise or amazement that you should hear from me from the above address so soon. The fact is I was one of a number to make a somewhat sensational escape from the Curragh last night about 12.30. By dint of crawling, walking, riding on a train, begging, and a motorcar I arrived safely here at 12.45 this morning feeling dead tired and absolutely filthy dirty but safe and sound …[23]

On their liberation, Éamonn Flynn and some of his hut companions, unfamiliar with the area, set out east towards Dublin. They, too, were barefoot and found the going extremely tough. At Greenhills, near Kill village on the main Naas to Dublin road, they met a farmer named Patrick Dunne. He was a relative of the Fenian leader John Devoy – who was born at Greenhills – and was also OC Kill Company, IRA. He arranged billets for the escapers in the area and subsequently their safe return to their home counties.[24]

The exact number of prisoners who escaped from the Rath Camp on that night has never been verified, but the accepted figure was about fifty. Republican propaganda claimed 100 men escaped, but this was later rounded down to seventy. (A list of those known to have escaped on 9 September 1921 is given in Appendix III.) The *Leinster Leader*, quoting from a 'reliable source', said upwards of sixty men, later rounded off to seventy men, escaped. *The Irish Times* claimed forty-nine men escaped.[25] The *Leinster Leader* also claimed that a concert had been arranged to help stifle any potential noise the escapers might have made, but as there was mass secrecy regarding the escape and tunnel this is unlikely. Despite this, other newspapers followed up on the concert story, with the *Belfast Newsletter* adding that the audience included 'members of the guard'.[26]

The *Donegal Democrat* reported that one youthful prisoner became caught up in the barbed-wire entanglements and lost a lot of blood, but when he realised he was imperilling the rest of the escapers, quietly crawled back to his hut where

The cookhouse, Rath Camp; note the tents adjacent on the right side.
(Courtesy of Fr Peter Clancy Collection)

Drawing by Richard McDermott, Athenry, Co. Galway.
(Courtesy of Áine Delahunt)

The 'Sinn Féin Barber' John Murray and some of his clients, Rath Camp. (Courtesy of Fr Peter Clancy Collection)

Above: Internee Sylvester Delahunt, Straffan, Co. Kildare. (Courtesy of Áine Delahunt)

Left: Fr Patrick Smith, the internees' revered chaplain. (Courtesy of Jim Doyle)

A group of internees with a guard tower in the background, Rath Camp. (Courtesy of Áine Delahunt)

Volunteer internees from the North Kildare Battalion pose for a photo in the Rath Camp. (Courtesy of Áine Delahunt)

The cook and his staff at the Rath Camp. James Miller, Mountrath, Co. Laois, is sitting centre front. (Author's Collection)

A group of prisoners in the Rath Camp. (Author's Collection)

A watercolour painting of the tunnel escape by internee Frank Purcell from Kilcock, Co. Kildare. (Courtesy of Áine Delahunt)

Prisoners exercising and socialising on the sports ground in the Rath Camp. (Courtesy of Fr Peter Clancy Collection)

Hare Park Camp under construction.
(Courtesy of Kildare Local Studies, Genealogy and Archives Dept,
Newbridge Library)

A drawing by Seán Jordan of Ballyhaunis, Co. Mayo. (Courtesy of Áine Delahunt)

Above: (*left to right*) Peter Traynor, Kill, Co. Kildare; Thomas McGiveny, Dromahair, Co. Leitrim; Andy Farrell, Beggars End, Naas, and John Traynor, Kill, outside Hut 1062, Rath Camp. (Courtesy of Paul Traynor)

Right: Tom 'The Boer' Byrne, one of the tunnel escapees. (Courtesy of Irish Life & Lore)

A guard tower and barbed wire at the Rath Camp. (Author's Collection)

The Rath Internment Camp, the Curragh.
(Courtesy of Local Studies, Genealogy and Archives Dept, Newbridge Library)

he was found the following morning with a badly injured foot.[27] Another report said guards fired at this prisoner, while other reports said they fired at prisoners emerging from the tunnel. But despite reports in many newspapers that the military guard had fired shots at escaping prisoners, and John Gavigan's statement also mentioning being shot at by a sentry, it seems that it was not until the following morning that the camp guard realised a mass escape had taken place.

Most of the internees were completely unaware of what was happening. Edward Flanagan, of Stradbally, Co. Laois, wrote in his diary on the day of the escape:

Friday, Sept. 9 1921

Changed from Tent 5 D. Coy. To back of cook-house.
Pouring rain all evening.
Pitched tent on pool of water. We had to raid Dining Hall for forms to put our beds on. Water was flowing under us.[28]

It was at morning roll call that most prisoners in the Rath Camp learned of the mass breakout. Joe Lawless said:

[T]he first we knew of the matter was when about six o'clock next morning armed troops poured into the camp and surrounded all the huts. The prisoners were held within the huts for two or three hours while they were counted, recounted and names checked, and until a thorough search for further tunnels had been carried out.

A more detailed check of the names and identities of the prisoners who had escaped was carried out later that day when every prisoner left in camp, except those confined to hospital beds, was paraded on the football field and held there for some hours while the identity of each man was checked against a list. We were also informed that privileges in the way of letters and parcels would be curtailed or withdrawn on account of the escape, and on the following day or so a party of sappers began the digging of a ten-foot deep trench around the camp inside the wire. This was intended to cut through any undiscovered tunnels and to discourage any further effort in this line.[29]

Westmeath prisoner Michael McCoy agreed:

The military spent four days in an effort to check the number and names of prisoners who had escaped. The prisoners left behind added to the confusion by giving wrong names and moving around from place to place, with the result that the military could not arrive at the same count at any attempt.[30]

Those who knew of the escape had great pleasure in answering the roll call with 'Gone through the tunnel', when an escaped prisoner's name was called out. No one could resist the humour at the frequent repetition of this phrase.[31] None of the escapers were ever recaptured and all of them reported back for duty to the republican movement.

A large-scale search was mounted as soon as the breakout was discovered. Military and police in the area began searching for the escapers, which included checking the Newbridge and Kildare railway stations, but none of them were discovered. An exhaustive search of the camp was instituted, which resulted in the discovery of the escape tunnel and the unfinished Dublin Brigade tunnel. The escape was of considerable embarrassment to the British authorities and they refused to issue an official statement. Rumours of the mass escape continued to circulate, and the Press Association enquired of both the Curragh Camp and British Military GHQ, Dublin, but no statement was forthcoming. The Irish newspapers carried the simple facts of the story on Saturday 10 September, but reported that British GHQ had told them that any statement must come from the Curragh Command, who, when contacted, told them to seek information from GHQ. Republican sources, however, provided the full details and, on Monday 12 September, the complete story of the tunnel and the escape was published in *The Freeman's Journal* and delighted the heart of pro-independence Ireland.[32]

The nearest newspaper with access to the Curragh Camp, the *Leinster Leader*, found it hard to contain its exhilaration. The paper's reporter, not even disguising his nationalist outlook, wrote gleefully:

> It is scarcely necessary to say that excitement was at its height in the Curragh Camp and in the adjoining centres on Friday morning when it was known that a great number of the boys who were being interned at the Curragh had succeeded in an attempt to break camp. It was evident that the spirit of the men

> soared some little bit over the height of the entanglements and in this instance, at all events, the iron bars were not sufficiently moulded to complete the cage which their captors had hoped for. When I was first told of the escapes of some prisoners I was rather inclined to think there was no foundation, but soon it was ascertained at the Curragh Camp that something had occurred very much out of the ordinary, and the military police, as well as the Constabulary, were busy. Reticence was observed to a very great degree and it indeed sensed to be the wish of the military and the government forces generally, not to give any information even of the slightest kind, which would tend to throw any light on the situation which was being so keenly discussed.[33]

Back in the camp, the internees had their privileges withdrawn in retaliation for the escape, but they did not mind, as many of their comrades were now free. Not everyone was happy, however. Summing it up, Tommy Brabazon said optimistically:

> If the bigger Dublin Brigade Tunnel had been finished, we could have emptied the camp. But it wasn't to be. The fog, too, could have proved the undoing of the lot that got out. Yet, ironically enough, four days later, by which time it was estimated the big tunnel would have been completed, rain poured down all night and kept the guards under cover. We'd have got a thousand out that night instead of fifty.[34]

Michael Collins, TD, congratulated the escapers from the Rath Camp at an Aeridheacht at St Enda's, Rathfarnham, held a few days after the breakout. He expressed his delight of the men regaining their freedom and stated that the prisoners had escaped with no outside help, which would have been a breach of the Truce. Collins also made allegations of ill-treatment of political prisoners in jails and camps throughout the country and in Britain, saying that there were about 5,500 prisoners interned, including 1,500 men and over forty women serving sentences. The sentenced prisoners of the Irish Volunteers should receive prisoner-of-war status, he said, while the political-civilian class should receive political status. Several had become insane from their ill-treatment and there were many who, because of their experience in jail, would never be the same again. What, he asked, was the excuse for keeping these men and women in jail? These people were only obeying orders and it was only proper that they should be released. Collins asked for a joint impartial body from the British and Irish governments to investigate whether the prisoners were treated in accordance with the status they deserved.[35]

The mass breakout of prisoners and the discovery of the tunnel in which they made their escape did not deter the remaining Curragh internees from devising other tunnels. Edward Flanagan wrote:

> There will not be a man in this camp by Xmas even if they do [are] not up for the treaty, for there is about 7 or 8 tunnels just ready. One is big enough to carry a suit-case through. They cannot hold us because all the lads are determined to be home by Xmas. There is over 1,500 men here.[36]

Micheál Ó Laoghaire was also aware of other tunnels in the process of construction:

> This was not the only tunnel operating at the time. Captain Manus O'Boyle was operating one from Hut 20, B Line, but this was never completed. Another was operating from the hospital. There were others as well that I am not acquainted with.[37]

Edward Flanagan recorded the discovery of a tunnel in his prison diary. He wrote:

> Sept 12 1921
> Tunnel found under No. 12 B Line. Six fellows placed under arrest, including JH.[38] [Probably fellow Laois man Joseph Hyland, of Wolfhill.]

Michael McCoy said the final attempt at constructing a tunnel was started at the corner of the last hut in A Line. The tunnel was sunk to go under the deep trench around the camp, under a blockhouse and eventually under the outer wire barricade and to come out in the floor of a horse stable outside. Men from each brigade were detailed to make the escape attempt:

> I was one of the men so detailed. A very heavy rainfall upset our plans. The rain flooded the trench; from there it soaked through and flooded the tunnel, rendering it impassable. After a week, and just when the tunnel was drying up, the camp guards carried out one of their periodical searches in the camp. They

lifted all floor boards but found nothing. As they were replacing the boards in the hut, under which the entrance was located, they heard something fall underneath. This noise was caused by a gravel rake, which was used to rake the sand and clay over the tunnel mouth covering and was hidden along the floor joist, becoming dislodged. The floor was again lifted and this time the tunnel was discovered.[39]

The discovery of these tunnels was the end of tunnelling from the camps for a while, but not the end of escape attempts, successful and unsuccessful. Less than three weeks after the mass escape, four men escaped in another audacious prison break.

9

PRISON BREAKS

There was no obligation on captured or interned prisoners to attempt to escape. Republicans could make as much of a nuisance of themselves behind the wire of captivity as they did outside it. Many internees had little or no interest in escaping and regarded escape activities with caution, happy enough to remain as prisoners with no wish to risk their lives. Others felt they lacked the necessary escape skills or simple physical ability – some were just too old – and that their time could be better spent studying or improving themselves. Moreover, official prisoners who tried to escape forfeited their protected status and risked being shot. As early as July 1921, British Camp Adjutant Vinden had issued a warning that internees seen outside their huts after designated hours were putting their lives at risk. The shooting of a prisoner making an escape attempt was not necessarily deemed a war crime, though warnings had to be issued before opening fire.

The mass breakout on 9 September 1921 resulted in at least fifty-four prisoners making their way out of the Rath Camp. This was not the end of escapes, but rather the beginning of a torrent of escape attempts, and by the end of the following month a further eighteen prisoners had bolted.

On 30 September 1921 four men successfully escaped from the top-security 'cage'. In July, after the discovery of an escape tunnel, twelve men were selected as most likely to have been involved and they were detained in the specially constructed secure unit. This cage was built as a punishment centre and garrisoned by some of the toughest military guards, who would stand no nonsense. It was made of corrugated iron and its position in the corner furthest away from the main road meant that its inhabitants had no interaction with the rest of the camp internees. The detention hut was surrounded by a 10-foot corrugated-iron fence and guarded by a blockhouse. Two armed men were positioned at the top of the blockhouse, while five more soldiers were garrisoned in the basement. In addition, the cage was surrounded by a substantial amount of barbed-wire entanglements.

Despite all these deterrents, five internees plotted an escape from this cage: Michael Carolan of Belfast, Peadar Bracken and Harry Feehan of Tullamore, Patrick Traynor of Dublin and another, unnamed, prisoner. For two days prior to their escape attempt, these men were busy making a new exit from the cage. On Friday night, 30 September, the occupants were locked up as usual by the officer in charge. Some hours later, the five escapers exited the cage in their stockinged feet into the open area through the latrine. A corrugated-iron sheet had been removed from the latrine wall, the nails having previously been loosened. It was a calm and bright starry night as the men began to crawl along the ground towards the barbed wire, keeping in the shadow cast by the corrugated fence.

One of the men got lost and did not continue with the

escape attempt. The remaining four, having crawled several yards, then had to cross a grassy space of about 3 yards in full light. Managing to accomplish this part of the perilous journey without attracting the attention of the sentries, the four came to the first barbed-wire entanglement erected among the high grass. One of the men, armed with a wire-cutter, cut a passage through this wire, about 10 yards from the sentries, and the men got through the opening. The process of crawling then resumed directly towards the blockhouse of the sentries and parallel with a strip known as 'the Death Trap', a space brightly lit and within view of two sentry blockhouses. The sentries had orders to shoot on sight any internees seen in this area. Those found among the barbed-wire entanglements were to be challenged.

When the men reached the second line of entanglements they were directly under one of the blockhouses, but hidden from view by the building's shadow. It took about forty-five minutes to cut through the wire as the remaining men lay flat on the ground listening to the sentries calling their posts every fifteen minutes: 'All's well'. At this point Harry Feehan reportedly lost sight of his comrades but still made his own way to freedom (although it has never been revealed how this happened).[1] The three remaining men – Carolan, Traynor and Bracken – succeeded in cutting their way through without attracting the attention of the sentries. The little party continued on, passing by the door of the blockhouse and beneath a window. They crawled safely past an exercise area until they came to another barbed-wire entanglement.

This obstacle was successfully overcome and the trio found themselves on a road outside the camp. They were still within the area swept by powerful searchlights, though, and had to occasionally take cover in patches of furze until they eventually passed beyond the range of the lights.

At 7 a.m. they found themselves about 9 miles from the camp, having walked from the time they left without meeting a single person. The three escapers kept to the fields heading north, and only paused after they had walked about 19 miles, stopping near Carbury, Co. Kildare.[2] They sat down to rest in a potato field but fell into an exhausted sleep. A friendly farmer found them and took them to safety.[3] Michael Carolan travelled to Dublin, where he subsequently gave an interview to *The Freeman's Journal* detailing the events of the escape.[4] Carolan had been arrested in Galway in 1921. He worked as a national schoolteacher in Belfast and was an unsuccessful Sinn Féin candidate in that city, and had been interned in Frongoch after the 1916 Rising. At the time of his arrest, he was OC 2nd Battalion, Belfast Brigade.[5] Peadar Bracken, an Easter Week veteran, had been a GHQ organiser for Offaly, East Kildare and North Tipperary when he was arrested in March 1921. Following his escape, he helped to organise republican courts in Westmeath, Offaly, Meath and Kildare.[6]

Joe Lawless and Tom Glennon, having observed for some time the method of removal of the cookhouse swill from the camp, formulated another plan of escape. The swill was removed daily by two young boys using a donkey and cart. On arrival at the gate, the boys would hand over the cart to a member of the guard, and this was then taken to the cookhouse, loaded by prisoners, returned to the gate and handed back to the boys. Glennon had ascertained the willingness of one of the military guards to accept a bribe for his help.[7] (Glennon was the son of an IRB man from a nationalist enclave in South Belfast and had been an organising officer for Antrim when he was arrested in April 1921.)[8] Lawless knew that the prisoners' chaplain, Fr Paddy Smith, held some money that was available for escape projects and he asked Fr Smith to 'loan' him £10 to bribe the soldier. Plans were then set in motion and Lawless and Glennon appropriated two large canvas mail sacks from the post office censor's hut. On 2 October, after Sunday mass, Lawless spent the time disposing of his spare clothing and other belongings. He then waited anxiously for the swill cart to arrive after the prisoners had eaten dinner, at about 6 o'clock. Glennon had arranged that two other prisoners, who were members of the cookhouse staff, would handle the actual financial arrangements with the soldier in such a way as to keep some hold over him until Lawless and Glennon had escaped. They paid the soldier £5 when he agreed to help, with the remaining £5 to be paid when the prisoners were safely outside the gate. The arrangement with the soldier took only a few minutes while he was enjoying his 'usual cup of tea inside the cookhouse, and the loading of the cart was delayed by a lot of shovelling of swill from one container to another until the pre-arranged signal was given from inside the cookhouse'.[9]

Lawless and Glennon were nervous that something would go wrong at the last minute, despite quite a large group of prisoners collecting around the cookhouse door to watch and give what help they could, if only by concealing the movements around the swill cart with their bodies. Meanwhile, the two internees climbed into the mail sacks and curled up on the floor of the cart while their comrades began to empty barrels of swill on top of them. The thick canvas mail sacks kept the slush from their clothes and allowed them to breathe, but the limited air supply and weight of the swill pressing down on them began to take its toll. Lawless said:

> … I began to wonder if we would be able to survive long enough to get through the gate. Glennon apparently had the same thought. I heard him groaning once or twice and, though feeling no better myself, I mumbled to him to be quiet. He said that he could not stand it, and was about to get out of the cart when it at last began to move as the soldier took the donkey by the head. The slight movement of the cart improved our air supply somewhat, and, with a last appeal to Glennon to be quiet and stick it out, I gave my attention to systematic breathing while listening for sounds that would enable me to identify what was going on around us.

> The progress of the donkey seemed terribly slow but at least we could now breathe more easily until at last we were halted and we heard our soldier shouting 'Gate'. Other footsteps, with a great rattling of keys, indicated the opening of the double gate by the sergeant of the guard, and, being halted, the breathing problem had again become difficult. The system required the sergeant of the guard to lock one gate before opening the other, which meant that he had first to open the outer gate and lock it again when he came inside. Then he had to open the inner gate,

admit the donkey cart with its load and escort it between the gates, lock the inner gate again before opening the outer gate to allow himself, the soldier and the donkey cart out on to the road, after which, of course he locked the outer gate from the outside. To our keyed-up nerves the seemingly excessive delay was almost more than we could stand. Knowing that the cart was now under the immediate eye of the sergeant and possibly other members of the guard we dared not make the slightest move nor make the slightest sound in our efforts to breathe.

I imagine that the soldier's nerves were also rather taut at this point as, if we were discovered, he would certainly suffer a heavy punishment. With a loud 'Giddap' and a tug at the donkey's bridle, he tried to move the cart quickly as the outer gate opened, but the donkey's feet slipped as he tried to start the heavily laden cart and he was almost on his knees when the soldier, grasping the point of the shaft, helped him to his feet. That was a bad moment for both the soldier and ourselves, but it was quickly over and in another minute, we heard the soldier say to the two small boys who waited on the roadside: 'Hi, you nippers. Take your bleeding donkey and 'op it.' We were outside the wire and on our way, but what a slow and tedious way it was, as the donkey ambled along and the two youngsters chattered to each other as they walked beside the cart. Suddenly one of the boys exclaimed: 'Where's the shovel, it's been left behind'. The other boy climbed up on the load of swill and began walking around on it, apparently searching for the missing shovel and incidentally treading on our prone bodies underneath. He must have recognised that the lumps he could feel under his feet were rather unusual for he got down suddenly and, having whispered something to the other, they were both silent for a minute or so.

We could hear a heavy footstep with measured tread coming

along the road behind us and gradually overhauling the slow-moving donkey. This sound was ominous enough, but when the donkey was suddenly halted as one of the boys announced to the other: 'We will have to go back for the shovel', it seemed the last straw. Poking my head carefully up through the cabbage leaves I said, with as much menace as I could put into the words: 'Drive on and not a word out of you'. The boy I spoke to looked at me in open-mouthed amazement, but the other one who apparently was the one who had walked over us, addressing his pal, said: 'Now, I told you there was someone in it'. The boy I had spoken to was at the donkey's head and, quickly recovering from his astonishment, he said quietly to me: 'There is an officer coming along the road behind us'. It was his footsteps we had been listening to for some minutes and the footsteps were now within fifteen or twenty yards of the cart. I repeated the order to drive on and ducked back into my cover of cabbage leaves where I listened anxiously for the footsteps to overhaul and pass the cart as the donkey ambled slowly along.

The boys acted like men, now that they felt they had a part to play. They chattered away gaily to each other as the footsteps of the officer closed upon us, passed us out and faded away ahead. Apparently, he was not interested in boys or swill carts for he spoke no word to the boys as he passed and they never stopped their chatter to each other.

In the darkness of our hiding place we had no idea where we were, or where the cart was heading for. My quick look at the boy leading the donkey was insufficient to orient myself further than to know that the buildings and barracks of the Curragh Camp lay ahead. We travelled on for a while like this, until the cart stopped abruptly and one of the boys coming close to where my head was said: 'I'm afraid to bring you any further'. Raising my head cautiously, I inquired where we were and he told me we were at the western boundary of the Curragh Camp which he had to pass through to his home.

Taking a quick look round I saw no one in sight and, as Glennon also emerged from his cabbage leaves, proposed that we leave the cart at this point and make our way on foot across the open plain. We climbed out of our bags easily enough, but some of the more messy element of the swill, boiled potatoes, pieces of fat meat and suchlike had got into our hair and around our necks and faces and we found it necessary, therefore, to make ourselves a little more presentable on the spot. While we were thus engaged – the swill cart had passed on into the camp – a dispatch rider on a motor cycle came towards us from the Curragh Camp, but as we stood close in to a wooden fence, he passed without seeing us. His passing warned us to cut short our toilet however, so, not waiting to put on the collars and ties which with some foresight we had carried in our pockets, we started off in the general direction of the Curragh Racecourse, the grand stand of which acted as our landmark.

I could hardly restrain Glennon who wanted to run, in order to put as much distance as quickly as possible between us and the internment camp. Realising, however, that two figures running across the open plain would appear much more suspicious to any casual observer than two people strolling quietly along, we walked until we reached the main road which crosses the plain between the towns of Kildare and Newbridge. Once on the road we walked faster as we headed for Newbridge, meeting no one until we left the plain at Ballymany crossroads. Here we began to meet soldiers and N.C.Os. in twos and threes returning off local leave pass to Newbridge, and with something of a shock I recognised two N.C.Os. who belonged to the staff of the Rath

Camp. Fortunately, however, they were slightly inebriated and never even glanced at us as they passed, but we decided that it was high time to improve our appearance by washing off the traces of swill and putting on our collars and ties. We climbed over a fence near Moorefield crossroads at a place now occupied by a row of cottages and, using the long wet grass to clean each other, fitted the collars and ties. Feeling less remarkable we then walked unconcernedly through the town of Newbridge and entered the Central Hotel to which we had been directed before we left the camp by a fellow prisoner …[10]

The day after he escaped, Joe Lawless gave an interview to a Dublin *Evening Herald* reporter, though he would not give the details of his actual escape:

We were of the opinion they [the camp authorities] would not imagine we had taken the public thoroughfare in broad daylight. Without conceiving any plan as to where we might finally reach, we set off. Some distance from the camp, we discovered that the road was cut off by barbed wire, and that a side road diverted all traffic. We soon, however, made a way through and eventually reached Newbridge. From Newbridge we got a vehicle and reached Dublin about 10 o'clock the same night …[11]

In his BMH witness statement, he recalled his first impressions of freedom:

The feelings of joy in regaining my freedom; of reunion with my loved one, and the rejoicing of my friends was, in itself, overwhelming, so that my memory of those first days of freedom is confused and sketchy; to make it more confusing still, there was the strange atmosphere of the Truce which took me some time to grasp. To learn of these conditions from the newspapers, as we had done in the Rath Camp, was one thing, but to experience them was another. The mental habits of years cannot adapt themselves to a new orientation overnight, and it took me some days to accustom myself to going around with a feeling of assured safety while publicly acknowledging my identification with the national revolutionary movement.[12]

Both Volunteers returned to duty with the IRA. Lawless was billeted in Drumcondra, while Glennon was posted to the 1st Northern Division as divisional adjutant in November 1921.[13]

The successful escape of Lawless and Glennon gave other Volunteers the impetus to abscond. Henry Vincent Staines, whose brother Jim had escaped from Hare Park Camp, tried the swill cart method again, only to be injured by the thrusts of a bayonet from a camp guard. As a youthful member of Fianna Éireann he had served alongside his brother Jim in the Four Courts garrison in Easter Week. He evaded capture after the surrender and in 1917 transferred to D Company, 1st Battalion. Vincent, as he was known, was arrested on 29 April 1921 in Dublin and brought to the Rath Camp.[14] Fellow internee Frank Dooley said that Staines' identity was unknown to the camp authorities at the time, and that he was arrested using a false name. He referred to Vincent Staines as 'Hunt', while Staines' brother, Michael, said he was using the name 'Harry McCann'. Dooley said:

We had at the time a patient/prisoner named Hunt whose real identity was unknown to the British – he was really a man for whom the British were still looking! It was imperative that he should be got out before his identity became known.

The camp itself was surrounded by what became known as the 'Death Walk'. It consisted of two barbed wire fences with a space between. This space was controlled by machine gun watchtowers placed at each corner of the perimeter. All supply vehicles were searched in the 'Death Walk' before entering the camp.

The escape plan was initiated by Doctors O'Farrell and Feehily [sic] and the vehicle selected was the swill cart – a flat horse-drawn vehicle designed to carry the floating mass of swill out from the camp. Dr [Michael] O'Farrell designed and made an air tube through which a person lying underneath the swill could breathe. It consisted of a length of surgical tubing interspersed with a length of glass tubing to hold it erect. There were two armed sentries allotted to escort the vehicle in and out of the camp.

A diversion was caused at the rear of the hospital by a mock fight staged by other prisoners and during which Hunt was smuggled underneath the floating disgusting mass of swill equipped with his improvised breathing apparatus. The operation was thus far successful, and we watched through the Dispensary windows as the vehicle proceeded in to the 'Death Walk' on its way to the dump outside the Camp. This particular vehicle was usually exempt from search as it was not thought possible that a human being could remain concealed underneath such a load.

As we watched with bated breath we saw to our horror that a young soldier had mounted the cart by standing on the wheel and, reversing his rifle, proceeded to probe the contents of the cart with his bayonet! Hunt suddenly stood up to the cheers and jeers of the soldiers – he was bleeding profusely from his neck and shoulder and was removed by ambulance to the Military Hospital at the Curragh. We never saw him again though I am happy to record that he survived his ordeal and was eventually released at the General Amnesty.[15]

Michael McCoy recalled that a military corporal had spotted Staines climbing into the swill cart through a hole in the wooden guard hut and called out the guard with fixed bayonets. They were ordered to prod the swill and the would-be escaper was given four jabs of a bayonet before he shouted out. After his wounds were dressed, he was removed to Mountjoy Gaol, where he was charged with attempted escape and held until December 1921.[16] His brother, Alderman Michael Staines, TD, as a member of the Internment Camps Inquiry Commission, visited the Curragh a few days later. Michael Staines was a staff officer from IRA GHQ and a member of the IRB, and had been released from captivity in August 1921 after the signing of the Truce:[17]

> Vincent was there under the name Harry McCann and had been bayoneted a few days before when trying to escape in a refuse cart. The English representative did not know that 'Harry McCann' was my brother and strongly objected to the length of time I stayed with him, but I said I could stay as long as I liked with any prisoner.[18]

A successful group escape took place on Sunday 9 October, when three unnamed prisoners from Ballinalee absconded.

(There were five men from Ballinalee interned: James Baxter, Joseph Connolly, Hugh and Michael Donohue, and James Early.) An internees' strike – when the men refused to stand to attention for roll call – provided an opportunity to escape. The three men succeeded in getting through the wire and gaining their liberty.[19]

Two nights later, inspired by the successful escape of the three Ballinalee prisoners, three more internees fled. James Lillis from Tullow, Co. Carlow, Jack Rooney from Dublin, and Henry John Coan from Belfast used the confusion around the internees' strike to make their bid for freedom:

> We were afraid that their escape would be discovered, but owing to a strike by the prisoners against the practice of holding 'roll-calls' twice daily, which were really arranged for the benefit of the British intelligence officers[,] and the fact that they had refused to answer their names, the camp authorities did not become aware of the escape by Tuesday night. We then decided that we would follow the example of our friends and make a dash for it.[20]

Around four o'clock on Monday evening, Lillis, Rooney and Coan hid in an isolated hut used as a store. They stayed concealed for ten hours until 2 a.m. the next morning, spending their time lying down and saying prayers. There was a small broken window in the hut, through which they squeezed and dropped to the ground. The three prisoners then proceeded to crawl towards the barbed-wire entanglements. It took each man about twenty minutes to get through the barbed wire.

Having scrambled through the first entanglement, they found themselves in the military compound with two sentries dangerously close. However, what they were mostly afraid of was that the camp pet terriers, which were constantly running around, might hear them and start barking. Luckily, it began to rain heavily, shrouding the place in a mist and helping to conceal their movements. The three men crawled in and out among the military tents. They were so close to the tents they could hear the snores of the sleeping soldiers. A sentry began to walk straight towards them and, aware that he had seen some movement, called out 'Halt! Halt!' They lay as flat as they could in the mud and remained there for several minutes.[21]

The sentry did not open fire, 'probably because he was afraid he would be held responsible for a false alarm', Jim Lillis said.[22] After a momentary pause, the sentry turned on his heel and continued his beat up and down the line of huts. The escapers resumed their journey, eventually reaching the outskirts of the military encampment, and worked their way through the remaining barbed wire. They then crawled about half a mile further to keep out of sight of the camp and the roving searchlight.[23] In the murky weather, the three made off across open country and headed for the home of the principal of Brownstown National School, where they were given sanctuary. Lillis was taken to Carlow by car, while Rooney and Coan were taken to Dublin. Lillis had joined the Irish Volunteers in 1918 and was a member of 6th Battalion, Carlow Brigade when he was arrested in April 1921. After his escape he reverted to his role as Carlow Brigade adjutant.[24]

His fellow escapers gave interviews to *The Freeman's Journal*, where Coan described the Rath Camp as no better than a 'slough … a dirty, muddy, waterlogged lairage'.[25] Rooney added that the discontent which prevailed in the camp made every man so desperate that the slightest chance that presented itself was used by the prisoners to escape their surroundings.[26]

One of those who failed to escape in the September tunnel breakout, John J. Gavigan, decided he was going to use the isolation hut in his bid for freedom. Joseph Duffy, of Milltownpass, Mullingar, was to accompany him. Having gained his freedom, Gavigan subsequently gave an interview to the *Roscommon Herald*:

> I noticed that the officers and sentry did not search this isolation hut and the idea struck me that when the sentries would have their backs turned, I could get through without any wire cutters. Having determined to make the attempt on this Sunday evening, I got two fellows to answer our names. We hid an hour before roll-call. I got hid back in a corner and Joe Duffy under an old bench. Our comrades handed us in tea which we took. After we were about an hour in this position an officer looked in on the window. At the time we did not know whether he saw us or not. We left our hiding places about 11 o'clock and remained at the window until half-past three. Up to that there was an eclipse of the moon and the sentries were very watchful. About three the moon began to get bright and soon it was shining very clear and bright and the sentries were not going up and down as often. So I got out of the top window out of the hut and Joe followed me. We crept through the wire which was about a perch [16ft 6in] in width.

INTERNED

My clothes were well torn by the barbed wire. When I got outside I lay down. There was a military policeman's hut quite close and the door was open. I crept on up the field north-west. When Joe came out of hiding he tripped and fell over two sentries who were asleep but they never awoke. There was a search-light from the military station and we had to lie down and keep out at the back of the officers' quarters until I got to a place called Brownstown. Joe Duffy went in a different direction. I met Joe Duffy next day in Rathangan. We left our boots in the hut. From Rathangan we went to Edenderry and on to Mullingar and Castlepollard until we got into one of the Longford camps.[27]

Internee Michael McCoy recalled another successful escape:

A prisoner named Christopher Dunne from either Kildare or Offaly had been detailed to assist in the fumigation of blankets etc., each time the fumigator was brought into the camp. He had worked at the job on several occasions when suddenly it occurred to him that the fumigator might provide a means of escape. That evening, when the work on fumigating was finished and the machine was about to be taken out of the camp, he hopped inside and escaped without detection.[28]

Within days of these successful escapes, a mass breakout was foiled. Lurgan Battalion OC Michael Murney, from Killowen, Co. Down, was arrested in March 1921, along with the battalion quartermaster and battalion adjutant, after a list of officers' names was seized in a raid on a GHQ office in Dublin. Murney was imprisoned in Belfast's Crumlin Road Gaol and later in the Curragh:

About forty-nine to fifty of us were brought by the train to the Rath Camp in the Curragh, and by lorry also, and we were kept the whole day without food. We spent the summer in that camp and at the end of the summer we had about one thousand prisoners, so they had to open a number two camp, which had five hundred in it.

... About the end of September [18 October], we tried to escape from the isolation camp ... about eleven of us. The O/C camp knew of the attempt and GHQ sanctioned it and there were eleven men picked, [including] Dave [*sic*] Gibbons from Armagh City; Seámus O'Kelly, Offaly; Donoghue, Carlow; Hyland, Laois; Seán Graham, Kildare; McCarrick, Sligo.

We were in number two and we were to escape from the one hut. It was arranged that my bed would be made up for the check so that would pass. We were in the isolation [hut] waiting to cut through the wires that night and we had pliers. We sheltered in a vegetable shed and we intended to move out between 11.30 and 12.00. At about ten o'clock we must have been given away by fellows who were afterwards known to be spies. The British gave us a good hiding and dumped us in the clink. We were held by a Major [*sic*] Vinden, the adjutant of the camp, in this beating up. We were taken two-by-two up to the clink by men with crash helmets and we were beaten with rifle butts and truncheons on the way up. Then we were taken to Keane Barracks in the Curragh where we were sentenced to twelve months' imprisonment by a field court-martial.[29]

Along with Michael Murney were Joe O'Connor, Dublin; Daniel Gibbons, Armagh city; Seámus O'Kelly (James Kelly), Tullamore; William 'Bill' Donohue, Hacketstown, Co.

Carlow; Tom Hyland, Portarlington, Co. Laois; Seán 'Jack' Graham, Kildare town; Tommy McCarrick, Tubbercurry, Co. Sligo; and Tom Leonard, Athlone.[30] After being court-martialled and sentenced, the would-be escapers were transferred to Kilkenny Gaol. McCarrick was only a few days in Kilkenny when he proposed to the prisoners' OC, Martin Kealey, that they should tunnel their way out, as the Curragh internees had. On 21 November 1921, Murney, McCarrick, Hyland, Leonard, Gibbons, O'Connor and thirty-seven other prisoners successfully escaped from Kilkenny having burrowed a tunnel out of the prison with a table knife and sharpened spoons.[31]

In the Rath Camp, the constant escapes heightened the tension, and in a further effort to deter them a mock shooting was enacted by the British guards of a man dressed as an internee. Lieutenant Vinden said:

> On several occasions, the patrol which went round the inside of the cage after lights out had found an internee hiding in the exercise cage, either in a latrine or against a pole carrying an electric light, which was rather sketchily encased in a sheet of corrugated iron. I took six of my brother officers into the cage one night about 10 p.m., we went into the exercise cage and after some minutes I fired my revolver into the ground and one of the officers then 'groaning' as if in agony. We immediately called stretcher bearers as in the trenches in France. These arrived – they were Suffolk soldiers – and an officer got onto the stretcher and we threw a blanket to cover him completely and he was carried out through the main gate of the camp. Of

course, the internees heard the shots and were all looking out of the window and the padre, also an internee, demanded his right to give last unction. The internees were quite convinced that one of their number had been killed or wounded. We had a list of the internees, but the hut leaders were supposed to keep lists of those sleeping in their huts. They were lax about keeping their lists up to date and as people sometimes moved from one hut to another, they were unable to discover who had been killed or wounded. We foxed them and had no more cases of hiding before lights out.[32]

The internees were for a time convinced that one of their comrades had been brutally killed by the military guards. They were told that the internee who was wounded subsequently died and that the military were preparing an inquiry. (At least two prisoners were prepared to attest on oath to witnessing the shooting.) It was also reported that Dr Fehilly and Fr Smith were refused access to the wounded man. Subsequently, there was considerable tension in the camp and, to avoid a repetition of a recent riot that had wrecked Spike Island Internment Camp in Co. Cork, the prisoners' commandant, Peadar McMahon, sought an interview with the British commandant. The latter obviously realised the seriousness of the situation and assured McMahon that no prisoner had been fired at or wounded.

This only aroused further speculation and rumour. That evening, matters were brought to a head when Colonel Hanna declared that the shooting was a 'practical joke' on the part of two officers, designed to frighten prisoners from making any further escape attempts; and for a short time it seemed to have worked.[33] However, Lieutenant Vinden had his suspicions that there was continuing escape activity, and on 7 November 1921 he visited the gate of A Cage:

> We were free of trouble for some time, but we later had a series of disappearances of one internee at a time. Gave much thought to discovering the method. One afternoon, I went down to the guard room at the main gate to see the officer on duty for an idle chat. I was looking out the window of the guard room still half-thinking about the escapes and saw a working party of Royal Engineers marching out. There were about twenty soldiers under a sergeant. Working parties were almost permanently in the camp patching roofs of the huts which leaked or other maintenance jobs. I went out to the gate as the party was passing through and ordered the sergeant to march them into an empty hut on the opposite side of the road. I followed and was then at a loss to know why on earth I had given such an order. However, inspiration made me tell the sergeant to ground tools and when this was done, I said: 'I am going to search you.' This I did, making each man turn out all his pockets. From the pockets of the sergeant and four men I found letters from internees addressed locally telling the recipient to give the bearer five pounds for which he would bring into the cage a uniform in which the internee would dress and march out with a working party. They were tried by court martial and sentenced to five [sic] years' imprisonment.[34]

Three sappers of the Royal Engineers subsequently went on trial charged with 'treacherously holding communications with the enemy'. They were Sappers John Scuffil, Alfred Lintott and John Manfredi of 17th Field Company, Royal Engineers. Scuffil had three letters in his breast pocket, while Manfredi had three letters wrapped in a newspaper from internees in A Cage. Lintott had twenty letters on him. Manfredi said he did not think he was doing wrong in taking the letters from the camp since they were only personal communications. The three were convicted and each sentenced to ten years' imprisonment, three of which were remitted.[35]

Dublin-born John J. Scuffil (32) had eleven years of service in the British Army, including time spent at the war front. He had married during the war, in 1915, and had a certain sympathy with his fellow countrymen. His comrades were Englishmen – Manfredi (20) was born in Chester and Lintott (24) was born in Hampshire.[36] All three were transported to Chatham Prison in England to serve their sentences, but soon a campaign to free them began in both Ireland and England. The *Leinster Leader* asked that the three be pardoned, saying that their sentence was 'unduly harsh' as there was nothing important in the letters, which merely related to family matters. Popular opinion was strongly in favour of these men being included in the amnesty proclaimed for republican prisoners.[37]

Scuffil's father, Albert, a Dublin painter, wrote a letter, which was published in *The Freeman's Journal* on 25 January 1922:

A Case for Amnesty.

Sir, – On reading the sentence passed on soldiers in London, to my mind the old saying, 'It's as good to be hanged for stealing a sheep as for stealing a lamb,' not only still holds good, but has improved; or is it a matter of time and place?

Now my son, Sapper John J. Scuffil, R.F. with two others, tried by G.C.M. on the Curragh for conveying three simple letters from Rath Camp to post for the internees, receives the vindictive sentence of ten years (three commuted), and is sent off to an English convict prison – first to Liverpool, and now moved to Maidstone.

This is his reward for over eleven years' service, and while the war lasted all the time in France. Where he gained a medal for distinguished conduct on the field, with a future recommendation for six months' continual bravery by his officer in command. He is Dublin-born of Dublin parents, but his companions in misfortune are Scotch and Welsh. Can there be nothing done to forward on their release, as to the ordinary person their offence does not warrant such a sentence, especially as the internees were released about a week after? The only plea I have seen for them came from the 'Limerick Leader.' Surely, they should come under the amnesty, as the so-called crimes were committed in Ireland.

– Yours respectfully, Albert J. Scuffil,
4 St Michael's Terrace, Belleville, S.G.R., Dublin. Jan. 23.

The campaign paid off, as all three men were discharged on 29 March 1922. Scuffil returned to Dublin, where he picked up his father's trade as a painter. He died in Mercer's Hospital, Dublin, in 1959, aged seventy.[38]

18

FÉ GHLAS AG GALLAIBH – LOCKED UP BY FOREIGNERS

As autumn turned towards winter, the conditions in the internment camps deteriorated. A report in the *Leinster Leader* said that the huts in Hare Park had not been repaired since they were built in 1915, while those in the Rath Camp were of the 'felt hut class' and 'the necessary patent tarring has not been used as far as the huts are concerned for some years, with the result that they are all in a very bad condition'. When the Royal Engineers sought to hire men from Naas for building work on the camp, at the rate of £3 1s 8d a week, there were no takers. According to the *Leinster Leader*, the men refused as they did not want 'to put the wire round our comrades in the Rath Camp'.[1]

By October the camp grounds had turned into mud, often knee-deep, and in addition to these difficult conditions there were further complaints of the prisoners going hungry because food parcels were not being distributed as a result of the many escape attempts. John Flanagan, Fontstown, Athy, wrote in his friend's autograph book:

We're getting dam [*sic*] little to eat or drink
We're getting dam little to wear

> We're all living wild now here in the clink
> On the Plains of Kildare
> The margarine question is being discussed
> And our quarter of bread is now dry
> If it is not soon settled our rifles will rust
> And then sure I'm damd we must die.[2]

One of the September escapers, Peter Feeney of Kinvara, set out the prisoners' daily diet in a letter to the newspapers:

> Breakfast – (1) Bread, insufficient and half baked. (2) Tea. (3) Margarine – unpleasant and unpalatable.
>
> Dinner – Beef: 'horsehide' would be the more applicable term; 6 ozs; rejected by our interned doctors about twice a week as unfit; a solitary potato; a tablespoon of beans or peas; and for dessert a cigarette between 20 internees is considered a luxury.
>
> Tea and Supper a repetition of breakfast.

Feeney added that the milkman was regularly late, resulting in black tea for the internees. He said the men were 'actually starving' and urged the public to organise a food committee in every county to supply the internees with bread, tea, bacon, cigarettes, tobacco, matches, stamps and stationery, and that 'wholesome food, no matter how plain, will be accepted with gratitude'.[3] However, the republican prisoners in the Rath Camp disapproved of outside appeals to charity for funds to send parcels to the internees, adding that they would prefer to see any money collected on their behalf handed over to the Irish Volunteer Dependents' Fund.[4]

The atmosphere in the camp was not good, with frequent accusations by the prisoners of brutality. The military claimed that the internees engaged in obstruction, which took the form of refusing to answer roll call, refusing to obey orders given by British officers, 'destruction of government property, and incessant clamour and complaint. The obvious and only remedy for such a course of action was to enforce obedience and good behaviour by physical violence, but such a course was not permitted by the regulations governing the treatment of internees.' *The History of the 5th Division* was prepared to admit, in what was probably an understatement, that 'a few isolated cases took place of harassed officers and men treating internees with some roughness'.[5]

A letter to *The Freeman's Journal* from the Rath Camp and signed 'Measles' alleged that:

> While watching, in the distance, the finish of an exciting race at the last Curragh meeting, and although standing four yards off the wire, a number of internees were charged by a British private with a fixed bayonet. As a result of the bayonetting, seven men were treated in the hospital, while some had to be detained there.
>
> Our huts are raided repeatedly and personal property is scattered broadcast on the floors, while we are kept standing outside. Our lives are threatened several times a day, and, I fear, if the slightest provocation is given, the threats will be put into operation.

> We are confined to our huts now at 6 p.m., and no matter how urgent the necessity, we cannot go outside after that hour, without the risk of being shot. Repeatedly we are prevented from sleeping, by the armed sentries who patrol the camp during the night.[6]

New measures were introduced to enforce discipline: the military camp commandant called general parades if all prisoners were not present at hut inspections, while lock-up was set at 6 p.m. The internees claimed these measures deprived them of hours set aside for classes and other useful work. A hut leader who refused to co-operate was placed under arrest, and the military further declared a stoppage of all parcels and letters to the camp, leaving the prisoners to depend on the inadequate camp food supply. The internees retaliated by refusing to take any notice of hut inspections by military line captains or the camp commandant, or to answer any roll call.[7]

In response, 200 additional troops were marched into the Rath Camp to coerce the men to give their names and answer roll call. The internees were first driven into their huts. In each hut, the occupants were subsequently pushed into a corner and a head count was taken by an army officer. The troops were then withdrawn, nothing having been accomplished beyond a count of heads.[8] Tension within the Rath Camp was at an all-time high. The alarms and searches at all hours of the night were very trying for the internees. It was hard for them to imagine that a truce was in progress and negotiations to end the conflict were continuing on the outside. For the men behind the wire there was little sign of it, although it was reported that the men's spirit 'is as usual'.⁹

However, the Irish and some of the British press began to call for change. On 4 October *The Freeman's Journal* launched a formal campaign insisting that British reluctance to release the internees could be overcome if the Dáil applied enough pressure. In the succeeding weeks, the paper published messages of support from prominent individuals, while local representative bodies all over the country responded with motions calling for the immediate release of the internees. Galway County Council passed a motion calling 'on the Ministry of Dáil Éireann to suspend all and further negotiations with the English Government until such time as the Irish Political Prisoners are released'.¹⁰

Throughout Ireland, empathic resolutions were adopted by county councils and others calling for a release of untried political prisoners. Mayo County Council adopted a resolution calling on President de Valera to withdraw the Irish plenipotentiaries unless all political prisoners were released unconditionally. Cork Corporation passed a similar motion. Galway Urban District Council (UDC) proposed a resolution demanding the release of tried and untried prisoners, saying they had as much right to be free as the men who were negotiating with Lloyd George, and there could be no spirit of peace in the country if these men remained in jails and camps. Similar resolutions were passed by Tyrone County Council, with no opposition from unionist members; Listowel UDC;

Tullamore UDC; Callan Town Council (TC); Mohill Board of Guardians; and Athlone TC.[11]

The military authorities responded by giving three English reporters permission to visit the Rath Camp. This effort to counter the allegations about conditions in the camps coincided with the arrival of the Irish delegation in London for the opening of formal talks. The visit was not simply a guided tour conducted by the military. Former prisoner Desmond FitzGerald had given the journalists a letter of introduction to the internees' commandant, Peadar McMahon, enabling them to talk to the prisoners personally. Donald Boyd of the *Manchester Guardian* was one of the visiting journalists. The liberal *Manchester Guardian* had been consistently condemnatory of the British government's repressive policies in Ireland, and Boyd's uncensored report on activities within the camp was published in the Irish and British press under several headlines:[12]

CAMP CONDITIONS

English Pressman's Visit to Rath

Appalling Monotony

A special correspondent of the Press Association in Dublin furnishes an account of his visit, with other English journalists, to Rath Internment Camp, Curragh, and bears out in some detail the truth of charges as to the conditions under which internees exist.

He shows that applications for release on behalf of men who are dangerously ill have, against medical advice, gone without reply; that food is bad; that some of the men are in rags, and that many of them are unkempt and unshaven.

It may be mentioned that an application by the 'Weekly Independent' for permission to investigate conditions in the internment camps was refused.

A DÁIL INTRODUCTION
Wretched Conditions

In view of the public demand being raised in Ireland for the release of interned prisoners and the allegations made from time to time of the prison conditions of internees, I obtained, says the correspondent, permission from the military authorities to visit Rath Internment Camp at the Curragh in company with 2 other English journalists.

The camp has gained celebrity recently through a number of successful escapes by internees. It contains 1,300 prisoners, none of whom has been tried, many not charged, but all suspected of complicity in the revolutionary movement. Our visit, although made, necessarily, under the discretion of the military authorities, was entirely free from special preparation or surveillance. The Commandant was not warned until a few minutes before our arrival. Neither was there any form of obstruction.

We carried with us a letter of introduction from a Minister of Dáil Éireann, and were permitted to use the document and talk freely with the internees.

ATTITUDE OF INTERNEES
Judged by the standards of a military camp, they leave much to be desired, and one found that even this was not seriously disputed by the military authorities. There are, however,

complicating factors in the case, not the least important of which is the attitude of the internees. They are, for the most part, bitterly resentful, which is, under the circumstances, by no means unnatural. This state of mind is made manifest in a spirit of passive resistance against their internment.

They are required, as far as practicable to look after themselves, but quite evidently some of them decline to do so, and the result is not good for their conditions. To cite an illustration of this, many windows in the huts, which are of usual army type, were shattered. The military alleged that they were broken deliberately by internees. The explanation of the prisoners, while admitting that the military statement might be true to a small extent, was that many windows were broken when they arrived, and that others had been broken by soldiers throwing stones. The military authorities provided glass, and told the internees to mend their own windows. They refused, saying they would not repair their own prison. The military say they have no labour to spare, and the internees reply by pointing out that they had plenty of labour to dig trenches to prevent them from escaping. There the matter stands, and the windows remain broken.

MEN WHO SHOULD BE RELEASED

The camp hospital was interesting. Under the general supervision of a military doctor, it is run by qualified medical men who are amongst the interned. This is done at the election of prisoners and appears to work satisfactorily.

The interned doctors explained bitterly that 8 men who were consumptive were being slowly murdered through their detention. Two of the men, at any rate, had the appearance of being dangerously ill.

The military doctor agreed that upon medical grounds the

men should be released. The application was first made nearly 2 months ago, and has been forwarded to the authorities. It has been renewed several times, without result. The men are stated, in the meantime, to have become dangerously worse. Complaint was made of some of the sanitary arrangements in the hospital, but the medical facilities provided were admitted to be good.

BAD FOOD

So far as food is concerned, one learned that rationing was on the same basis as in the army. The cookhouse is run entirely by internees. Facilities were declared good, but there were complaints of shortage. On the day of our visit something had clearly gone wrong.

It was a fish day, and the whole supply had had to be returned as unfit to eat. The result one learned would be a dinner eked out on potatoes and rice, and some hard words were used towards the contractor. The potatoes also were partially bad, a fact which was admitted and deplored by the military.

PARCELS AND CLOTHES

Proceeding, the correspondent reports that many of the huts leak, and the military explanation was the same as that concerning the windows. The tents are merely temporary accommodation. A system had been adopted which is proof against theft of parcels.

The prisoners' clothes are, on the whole bad. Some of them are literally rags. There is a military allowance for replacements, but some of the men refused to wear the military issue; on the other hand, the men alleged that they have to be in an entirely ragged condition before clothes can be obtained.

The only work required of the prisoners is to keep the camp

in order; they can play games at any hour of the day, but in spite of efforts towards instructional classes amongst themselves the appalling monotony of their lives would be difficult to convey. Discipline is conducted more or less upon a military basis. Many of the prisoners were unkempt and unshaven. Mostly they lounged round the huts, listless and despondent.[13]

Boyd's report on the Rath Camp was critical, but only moderately, implying that the conditions were far from horrifying. Frank Gallagher, who provided much of the content of the *Irish Bulletin*, was irate and published a raging dismissal of Boyd's report. Desmond FitzGerald, the *Bulletin*'s editor, then wrote from London censuring Gallagher's dismissal. He believed Boyd to be sincere and to have genuinely reported what he saw. FitzGerald further informed Gallagher, 'I know the Camp and am satisfied that he wrote honestly.'[14]

On 11 October a strong Irish delegation arrived in London to meet a formidable British group. The Irish deputation carried a letter of accreditation, carefully worded to empower them as 'Envoys Plenipotentiary from the elected Government of the Republic of Ireland to negotiate and conclude … a Treaty or Treaties of Settlement, Association and Accommodation between Ireland and the community of nations known as the British Commonwealth'.[15]

There was great hope in Ireland for a negotiated settlement of independence. At the annual meeting of the Irish Catholic hierarchy in Maynooth, Cardinal J. M. Logue appealed for the cordial continued observance of the Truce and, as an important factor towards peace, urged the immediate liberation of the internees 'whose prolonged confinement, in most cases without charge or trial, is, to say the least, a cruel hardship and exasperating cause of resentment and ill-will'.[16]

On the first day of negotiations, Michael Collins raised the question of 'prisoners and camps' and suggested a joint visiting committee. Lloyd George did not dismiss the idea, intimating that while releases were not an option, they were 'most anxious' to do their best 'in the matter of treatment'. The conference established a sub-committee to discuss means of ensuring 'better observance of the truce' and to address 'the treatment of prisoners'.[17]

In the House of Commons, Sir Hamar Greenwood, Chief Secretary for Ireland, in replying to Liberal MP Lieutenant-Commander J. M. Kenworthy, said that complaints made as to the conditions and treatment of prisoners in the internment camps had been taken up with the Irish representatives in London, and a system of joint visits to prisons and camps had been arranged. Kenworthy, a vocal opposition figure, asked for an assurance that if the complaints were found to be based on fact the commandants in charge of the camps would be dealt with suitably.

Greenwood said he did not want to prejudice the decision, but Kenworthy persisted, repeated his request for an assurance, and asked if there was one law for the English and another for the Germans during the First World War. In reply, Greenwood said he did not accept the statement that the prisoners were ill-treated.[18]

On 15 October it was announced that a 'joint investigation committee representing the republican party and the crown government' had been set up and was to visit the Rath Camp at the end of the month.[19] Six days later, a meeting was held at General Macready's house in Kilmainham, Dublin, between Commandant Fintan Murphy, acting chief liaison officer Commandant Michael Staines and representatives of the British Army and the Irish Office to discuss the inspection of internment camps and prisons. Staines was nominated to represent the IRA; Colonel T. A. Andrus was nominated to represent the British military, while Inspector Horatio John Chippindall was to represent the General Prisons Board of Ireland. The members of the Internment Camps Inquiry Commission, also known as the Prisons and Camps Inspection Committee, were to visit camps and prisons in rotation. Inspections began on 22 October, when Commandant Staines and Inspector Chippindall visited Mountjoy Gaol.[20]

Michael Staines had been appointed in September as liaison officer for jails and internment as a result of a British request. It was a job he did not relish, and he told Éamon de Valera so, but Staines was told 'someone had to do it and it was an order'. Staines said:

> ... that the prisoners had been kept in all the time since the beginning of the Truce, and that they would think it impertinence on my part to go visiting them with a representative of the British Government. Some of them did object and I was not

too favourably received. The fact was that our people wanted to keep the lads in jail quiet while the peace negotiations were proceeding and that was the object of my visit. I impressed on them that there was nothing to prevent them escaping and, in fact, there were several escapes during that time. As a matter of fact, the British authorities asked me to hand up my own brother who escaped during that time but I refused, saying that he was perfectly entitled to escape.[21]

This resentment was understandable among men who were still behind bars or barbed wire, and in the words of Colonel Andrus, 'were not enamoured of their brothers in arms who were getting all the good jobs outside'. Andrus believed that prison protests were orchestrated from the outside, but by working with Staines came to believe the protests 'were neither ordered nor came from his headquarters'.[22]

On All Saints Day, 1 November, a tunnel in No. 10 Hut was found by the military in the Rath Camp. The thirty-one occupants of the hut were arrested, deemed guilty of conspiracy and taken out of the encampment.[23] An internee released a week later said, 'Batches of soldiers were going about probing the ground in search of tunnels, tearing up planks, and creating a great noise amongst the internees. Huts were visited and the flooring torn up. The men's bedding and clothing, and everything found inside the huts were pitched out in the mud and snow, despite the protestations of our comrades.'[24]

To cut down on escapes by tunnelling, the ditch that had been constructed around the camp was filled with stagnant water, a development which 'produced vehement protest from medical authorities and much activity on the part of the local fire engine'. Consignments of barbed wire arrived by road and rail for more entanglements to be added to those already existing, as well as for intended extensions.[25]

A letter from an internee in the Rath Camp, published in the *Irish Independent* on 7 November 1921, said:

> In wet weather here you could swim or boat not alone in the exercise ground, but in most huts and tents. It is a good thing for them to have such notice of the joint commission, as they are travelling at breakneck pace to get things ship-shape for it. You should see the pretence they are making at patching the huts – but they will look repaired, and they will cover a multitude of sins …

On 11 November the members of the Internment Camps Inquiry Commission – Alderman Staines, Colonel Andrus and H. J. Chippindall – visited the Rath Camp to investigate the conditions. They interviewed the military staff and the internees' camp commandant, and inspected the cookhouse, hospital, post office and a number of the huts.[26] The internees had many complaints: the inadequate food supply – 1lb of bread per man was not enough, the meat was so bad it could only be used in stew, and the ovens could not be used for roasting on account of them having been continually exposed to the air. The issue of blankets and clothing was another complaint: each man received only one shirt and one set of drawers, which could not be changed or washed because of the cold and wet; moreover, one blanket per man was not enough. The visiting committee agreed that these supplies were not sufficient and promised rectification.[27] As a result of their 'visits to the camps drastic changes were to be made in the conditions and general treatment of the interned men'.[28]

A new system of liberalised parole was introduced, whereby men were released for a specified time – usually ten days – and had to return on a certain date. It was estimated that on any given day 5 per cent of all internees, or approximately 800 a month, could be given temporary release under this scheme. Those who had been interned the longest, those who had business reasons, and those who sought parole on compassionate grounds would be given priority. Despite Commandant Fintan Murphy's refusal to give guarantees as to future behaviour in the camps, the military authorities proceeded with the proposal. *The Freeman's Journal* begrudgingly described the improvements as 'tardy and incomplete', and noted that convicted prisoners were not included, but many relatives and no doubt prisoners themselves were happy.[29]

Five prisoners were immediately released unconditionally from the Rath Camp because of ill health: Laurence O'Callaghan, Naas; Jim Hunt, Leitrim; Frank Murphy, Moyhill, Co. Leitrim; Michael Horan, Mullingar; and Tom Cotter, St Andrew's Road, Drumcondra. The authorities usually provided transport – described as an old, creaking lorry – from the camp to the railway station.[30]

Further releases were included when the authorities embarked on a process whereby the evidence against internees was reviewed. As a result, in early November, small numbers of internees were released unconditionally each day. *The Freeman's Journal* was scornful of the insignificant numbers freed, but in the first week fifty-three men were released, including three from the Curragh. A week later, a further ten men were freed from the Rath Camp.[31]

Releases were going well until a British sentry shot dead internee Tadhg Barry in Ballykinlar Internment Camp on 15 November. Barry had been saying goodbye to a group of internees and was shot through the heart when returning to his quarters. The young sentry claimed he thought Barry was about to make a dash out the gate, but the sight of the internee celebrating the release of his fellow prisoners probably enraged him. There was the usual cover-up, but the fall-out nearly derailed the peace talks. Michael Collins broke from the negotiations in London to attend the funeral, one of the biggest ever seen in Barry's native city of Cork.[32]

Donal O'Callaghan, lord mayor of Cork, immediately announced that he would support a motion calling for the suspension of talks until 'the prisoners tried and untried were released'. Within days, Kilkenny County Council and Wexford County Council passed motions to this effect. The *Manchester Guardian* warned that the incident had excited 'more popular feeling than anything which has happened since the truce' and that Tadhg Barry was viewed 'as the representative of all those unknown who are still being supervised at the point of the bayonet and exposed to the chances of a loaded rifle'. However, the Dáil had never pressed for prisoner releases during the Treaty negotiations, or as a condition of these negotiations, and the moment passed.[33]

Meanwhile, the remaining internees grew more despondent and resentful. They had seen the release of senior politicians and key leaders immediately after the Truce, when they were expecting a general release of prisoners, or improved conditions at least, but circumstances got worse. The change in weather caused increased hardship, with frost, wind and considerable rain. Blankets for the men were damp and often wet, and there was not enough room to dry them. The tents were constantly leaking, the ground so wet and soft that tent pegs slipped and the tents were constantly collapsing. Some huts lacked windows and the roofs often leaked too. It was unnecessary to wake the internees in the morning because they claimed it was impossible to get proper sleep because of the cold from insufficient and damp bed covers.

A recently released internee spoke to a reporter from *The Freeman's Journal* and said that conditions were bad enough as they were, but that the military was also engaging in 'cruel jokes' on the prisoners. He said certain groups of men were told by camp guards that they were to get ready for release. When the eager prisoners had packed up their belongings and had 'fallen in', an officer would announce that the prisoners' release had been revoked. Another internee, Patrick O'Brien from Knock, Co. Mayo, said there were forty-one huts, each holding 25–30 men, but some had one or two more than that, and about 100 men were in the hospital, many of them suffering from colds and pneumonia from the poor conditions.

Complaints were also made that telegrams announcing the death or illness of relatives were purposely delayed. O'Brien also expressed indignation that the arrival of *The Freeman's Journal* was irregular. (According to *The Freeman's Journal,* they posted over 100 copies of the newspaper to the Rath Camp every morning.) 'We don't get it regularly and we draw our own conclusions,' O'Brien said. He also added that orders had been issued prohibiting the use of cameras by internees and threatening confiscation, with the result that those who possessed cameras sent them home.[34]

As Christmas approached, morale was plummeting. A recently released internee, Thomas McSherry of Dublin, told the *Irish Independent* that prisoners were suffering severely from the cold and that, in addition to the bad food, leaking tents and mud-sodden compound, the exercise area had been shortened. He said that when the tents were blown down during high winds, the prisoners were liable to be shot if they attempted to put them back up at night. The internees also complained that the military were tampering with their food parcels.[35] Another released internee said that the prisoners were locked up at 6 p.m. and were forbidden to leave the huts or tents after that time under any circumstances. The quality of the food, restricted exercise, leaking and uncomfortable quarters, and the attitude of the guards were frequent sources of trouble.[36]

To boost morale, the Internees' Amusements Committee appealed to the public through the media, in particular to 'those interested in amateur or professional theatricals', to 'send along any "fit-ups," viz. – paints, wigs, whiskers, old costumes (ladies and gents), or anything they might think useful to assist in the indoor amusements. As Christmas is approaching fast, the Committee would be grateful for prompt attention to the above matter.' Parcels were to be addressed to Richard J. McDermott (Athenry) or Thomas P. Smith (Dublin).[37]

Clearly, the internees were expecting to stay behind barbed wire for the foreseeable future. Nevertheless, as negotiations on the outside were coming to a head, some prisoners were not prepared to take the chance and await a favourable outcome. John J. Byrne of Kilkelly, Co. Mayo, made a sensational escape from the Rath Camp on the evening of 21 November. Byrne reported back after sixteen days' leave on parole and, having handed over his parole papers to an NCO, he was taken to the guardroom. The NCO left to find an officer to search the prisoner. After some time, Byrne went to the door to see if the officer was coming and, seeing no one about but a sentry, decided to make a dash for freedom. He made it over a 6-foot-high barbed-wire fence with much difficulty and had run about 20 yards when a shot rang out. Byrne threw himself to the ground and, aided by the darkness, crept along for some distance and succeeded in getting away.[38]

After the escape was publicised in the newspapers, British GHQ issued an official statement:

Recent Rath Escape
An Official Contradiction to the Editor 'Irish Independent.'

Sir, – I am directed to draw your attention to a paragraph in your issue of 22nd inst., headed 'Sensational Rath Escape,' and to inform you that the account is a complete fabrication. J. J. Beirne [sic] did not at any time return into Rath Camp, but he has broken his parole, with the result that, pending his return, or such other period as may be decided upon, the privilege of parole is being withheld from certain internees at Rath Camp.

I should be glad if you would give the true facts of the case the same prominence as you gave to the paragraph referred to above.

R. I. Marians (Major, General Staff),
General Headquarters. Ireland Parkgate Dublin,
24/11/21.[39]

Some weeks later, Byrne, who had been hospitalised for two weeks, made his reply via the news media with a letter headed 'An escape that was denied':

To the Editor 'Irish Independent'

Sir – Referring to my escape from the Rath Camp on 21st ult., which the military authorities afterwards contradicted, I wish to state that after entering the guard-room and handing in my papers I succeeded in gaining my freedom. In crossing the outer wires I sustained serious injuries, which necessitated my remaining in hospital for 15 days, during which I had to undergo an operation.

It was during my term in hospital that the military contradiction appeared in your paper, and for that reason I was unable to define my position earlier. Now, in order to clear myself of the accusation of having broken my parole, I hereby demand a public inquiry into the matter.

J. J. Byrne (Kilkelly, Mayo.)[40]

By this stage, the Anglo-Irish Treaty had been signed and most republican prisoners, including all held in the Curragh internment camps, had been released. There was no appetite for a public inquiry and frankly no need for one. Whatever way he had gained his freedom from the Rath Camp, J. J. Byrne was free and remained at liberty.

11

AND THE GATES FLEW OPEN

At 2.10 a.m. on 6 December 1921, the Anglo-Irish Treaty was signed in London by representatives of the Irish and British governments. It was officially described as a 'Treaty between Great Britain and Ireland'.[1] As the teams negotiating the Treaty argued among themselves, the plight of the prisoners again came to the forefront. The British cabinet agreed that the king 'should not be advised to release the internees until after Dáil Éireann had ratified the Articles of Agreement'. When the Irish delegation heard this, there was consternation. On 7 December the British cabinet considered 'strong representation' from the Irish delegates for the immediate release of internees to help secure acceptance of the Treaty by the Dáil. General Macready, who was present, said that the military had no objection to the immediate release of around 4,000 internees. He admitted that conditions in the camps were unsatisfactory, though he blamed the internees themselves for much of the trouble. It was decided to advise King George to act at once, as 'it would be more difficult for the Irish Parliament to reject the Articles of Agreement if the internees had been released as an act of clemency immediately after the signature of those Articles'. The question of convicted political prisoners or those awaiting trial, as distinct from those held without trial, was put back pending the negotiation of a mutual amnesty.[2] An announcement was issued from Downing Street:

> In view of the agreement signed between the representatives of the British government and the Irish Delegation of Plenipotentiaries, his Majesty has approved of the release forthwith of all persons interned under the Regulation of Order in Ireland Act. It is understood that this decision was arrived at by the Cabinet on Wednesday morning, and was approved by the King at the meeting of the Privy Council.[3]

The next day, 8 December, the release of interned republicans began. Around 500 prisoners – from Dublin and Kildare – were released from the Rath Camp. The remaining 700 were to be freed the following day, apart from four who had been court-martialled and sentenced to terms of imprisonment for attempting to escape: Leo Close and William Murphy of Belfast, Patrick Dyer of Sligo and Martin Thompson of Galway. These men were removed from the camp under an armed escort to join other convicted prisoners in England.[4]

When an *Irish Independent* reporter visited the camp at eleven o'clock, a small group of people were waiting for the prisoners' release outside the barbed wire. They were exchanging greetings with those inside. According to the *Leinster Leader*, 'The internees looked in very good health despite their long rigorous incarceration, and were in the highest spirits.' The men were standing without overcoats or hats with their backs to the huts, the newspaper said, and they had not received the news of their release until that morning.

A camp official admitted to the reporters that the place was cheerless and miserable, for them as much as for the prisoners. 'The only thing,' he added, 'is that we are paid for being here; they aren't.' An officer confessed that they were as pleased at the prisoners leaving the camp as the prisoners themselves were.[5]

At 2.30 p.m. the gates opened, and two lorries carrying the internees' belongings drove out of the camp amid a scene of great rejoicing. Groups of prisoners then emerged, receiving great cheers from a large gathering of locals, sympathisers and relatives. As they walked out of the camp, the prisoners received a salute from a group of soldiers who had congregated in the compound. 'Good-bye Shinner, see you on the Christmas tree', was the parting salute from one soldier. He stood to attention as the unkempt hundreds poured out onto the roadway.[6]

The prisoners marched four-deep to the railway station at Kildare town to travel on the 4.25 p.m. train to Dublin, receiving enthusiastic cheers from the townspeople who came out to applaud them. At the railway station, local republicans and members of Cumann na mBan provided the men with tea. Arrangements for their departure to Dublin and other areas were provided by Colonel Hanna and Commandant McMahon: the military provided train vouchers and special carriages were laid on. The *Irish Independent* said: 'They all looked in good health notwithstanding their long imprisonment, but their clothing in many cases presented a wretched appearance, and in some instances the men's knees protruded through their trousers. A big percentage of them wore no headgear.'

A large and enthusiastic crowd saw off the ex-prisoners. A number of military personnel on a train drawn up at the station also joined in the celebrations. Furze fires were lit on various parts of the Curragh plain and fires were lit at all stations en route to Kingsbridge Station in Dublin. There, huge crowds assembled to greet the freed prisoners.[7]

The Co. Kildare prisoners left by motors for their respective homes and were loudly cheered en route; on arrival, bonfires and tar barrels burned as large crowds warmly greeted the ex-internees. Many cars passed through Naas conveying homewards numbers of men from the vicinity of the town, and Kill, Rathmore and Ballymore Eustace. In Naas itself, the arrival of cars with local and other internees generated enthusiastic scenes, and bonfires blazed in several parts of the town. That night the streets of Naas were ablaze with tar barrels as considerable revelry took place.[8] Camp quartermaster Micheál Ó Laoghaire explained the logistics of the end game:

> When the Camp was about to close, I sent an order to Wallace's, Carriers, Newbridge, asking them to send two G.S. wagons and to report to me the following morning at 8 a.m. I signed an order for their admission. When they arrived the next morning at the gate, the Camp Commandant began loading them up with the internees' belongings for the Kildare railway station. I arrived

at the gate about this time and asked the Camp Commandant what he meant by confiscating my two G.S. wagons. He said he wanted them in order to remove the luggage to the station. He asked me what I wanted them for. I told him, 'To remove my rations.' 'What?' he shouted, 'A soldier does not sell his rations.' I said for the first time he recognised us as soldiers. After some further arguments, the G.S. wagons went into the Camp, were loaded up with the rations and went away. They came back again for two more loads which completed the job. These rations were handed over to Miss Kearns and the late Miss Wallace, Newbridge Cumann na mBan, who disposed of the margarine to the local bakeries and gave the tea to the St. Vincent de Paul Society in Newbridge. The remainder they passed on to the White Cross, Dublin, for disposal.[9]

The remaining prisoners were released on 9 December, and processions of hackney cars came to the camp to transport the released men to the railway station at Kildare where more special trains were laid on to take them to their home destinations. Around seventy Westmeath men arrived at Mullingar, including Michael McCoy, vice-chairman of Mullingar RDC. Those not from the town, around sixty men, were taken to various parts of Westmeath in cars decorated with tricolours.

Carrick-on-Shannon Brass and Reed Band, joined by Croghan Fife and Drum Band and headed by torch-bearers, took part in a huge demonstration of welcome for the prisoners from the district who had been released from the Rath and Ballykinlar camps. Andrew Lavin, TD for Leitrim–Roscommon North, delivered a brief address.

Scenes of remarkable enthusiasm were witnessed in Castlebar, Co. Mayo, on the arrival of the ex-prisoners from the Rath Camp. There was a large crowd at the railway station and the local band struck up 'The Soldier's Song', the unofficial anthem of the Republic, as the train drew up to the platform. A torchlight procession through the town followed.

Loughrea, Co. Galway, was bright with bonfires to welcome the liberated prisoners. The tricolour was noticeable as a large procession led by local bands accompanied the released men from the railway station. The ex-internees arriving in Clifden were escorted through the town by a band and a torchlight procession. Tar barrels were lit in various parts of the town and tricolour flags flew from vantage points.

An interesting arrival among the internees who returned to Tullamore, Co. Offaly, was William Mooney, an ex-British soldier who had served on the Western Front from the Battle of Mons in August 1914 to the Armistice in 1918. He was awarded the Distinguished Conduct Medal and, before his release from the Rath Camp, the British military authorities had forwarded a further medal to his mother's address, at Crow Street, Tullamore. Another Tullamore internee was James Longworth of O'Connell Street, also an ex-soldier who had served through the First World War with distinction.

Ten prisoners from Liverpool, including Micheál Ó Laoghaire and seven others from the Rath Camp, sailed on the Irish Sea ferry to their home city on 10 December. A crowd several thousand strong awaited their arrival. A procession was formed, led by tricolour flags and a pipe band,

and made its way to St Joseph's Hall, where the liberated men were joined by other released prisoners and entertained to tea and other refreshments.[10]

The Hare Park internees were also released and published a letter in the *Leinster Leader* thanking the 'ladies of the Newbridge, Naas and Kildare Cumann na mBan' for the 'many kindnesses shown to them during the period of their internment at the Curragh'. The prisoners, the letter continued, were 'deeply grateful for all the kind and thoughtful action taken on their behalf by these ladies'.[11]

Micheál Ó Laoghaire later described the evacuation of the Rath Camp, though the date he gave was 7 December, instead of 8 or 9 December:

> When the Camp was actually evacuated and only a few of our officers left behind, including Peadar McMahon, Tom Kerr, Mick McHugh and myself, the British Camp Commandant had word sent to us to say that he would like to meet us at No. 1 Hut (known as the internees' Officers' Mess). When we arrived, he welcomed us and produced a bottle of wine. We all sat down around the ordinary soldiers' table – victors and vanquished – and drank from the cup of peace. (Tom Kerr did not partake as he was a lifelong pioneer). The Commandant wished us well and we thanked him. He was glad the fight was over and the whole trouble ended. Was the long fight of 750 years over? And was the whole trouble ended? That was the question. We had only to wait and see. The treaty our plenipotentiaries brought back from London had first to be ratified by Dáil Éireann and then endorsed by the people of Ireland. On this we could offer

no opinion. We stood up, shook hands and parted with the Commandant on the plains of Kildare on the evening of the 7th December, 1921.[12]

By the release of the internees, an escape, on a grand scale, was averted. A tunnel 7 feet beneath the surface and over 170 feet in length had just been completed, and all was ready for another dash for freedom to rival the 'Great Escape' of 9 September. The opening of the tunnel was made in the floor of the kitchen in B Cage, near the cooking range. A boiler cover was used to camouflage the opening when the military were on the premises. An electric battery provided light, and saws, hammers and trench tools had made the sophisticated tunnel possible. The tunnel had been dug during the day and around forty tons of clay had been removed and deposited about the surrounding area.[13]

The day after the Rath Camp was evacuated, Major General Jeudwine, commanding the 5th Division at the Curragh, was given information about the withdrawal of troops from the country, and the proposed concentration of units on the Curragh before the final evacuation from Ireland via Dublin.[14]

On the narrow approval of the Treaty by the Dáil on 7 January 1922, the machinery for the departure of the British Army was immediately put into operation. Arrangements were made to dispose by local sale of the huts and contents of the Rath Camp. Robert J. Goff and Co., Auctioneers and Valuers of Newbridge and Kildare, advertised in local and national newspapers the sale of 250 wooden huts, kitchen ranges, boilers and galvanised sheeting from the Hare Park and Rath camps.[15] Catalogues were available at 7d, post free. Local farmers and businessmen bought up the items, but several weeks later Goff's were still advertising sales, including:

100ft. x 28ft. Wooden Hut, Boarded and Felt Roof,
90ft. x 20ft.,   "   "   "   "   "
60ft x 30ft.,   "   "   "   "   "
60ft x 20ft.,   "   "   "   "   "
80ft. x 8ft, Iron Shed.
40ft. x 15ft, Iron Roofed Shed.
A large quantity of Barbed Wire in convenient lots.
1000 Iron Fencing Posts, 6ft.
1000 Iron Posts, 4ft.
1000   "   "   2ft.
For full particulars and Price apply to –
Mr. T. J. O'Neill, Highfield, Kilmainham, Dublin. Robert J. Goff and Co., Newbridge and Kildare.[16]

On 17 May 1922 the British Army evacuated the Curragh Camp, but by then the Rath Camp was no more. Within a year of its erection, practically all traces of the camp, once home to up to 1,500 men, had disappeared from the Curragh plains, but the fencing posts and barbed wire of the camp continued to be used by local farmers for many years after. The only visible signs now of the camp are a few concrete foundations facing the Curragh Racecourse grandstand. Hare Park Camp continued to be used in the next round of the Irish revolution.

The Rath Internment Camp had lasted barely ten months, and while it had a reputation for brutality and repression, the regime was no more oppressive than that of any prisoner-of-war facility during the First World War. Despite republican propaganda, the Rath Camp was not on a par with Ballykinlar in Co. Down, where three prisoners were shot dead and several more died of ill-treatment. There were no deaths in the Rath Camp and very little concrete evidence of severe ill-treatment. Micheál Ó Laoghaire summed up the reasons:

> In spite of all this [the conditions and overcrowding], however, the health conditions were excellent and continued to remain so until our release. In my opinion, the conditions must be attributed in the first place to the good weather conditions that prevailed during the spring, summer and the late autumn of 1921. Practically no rain fell, with the result that the prisoners were free from early morning until 10 p.m. during the summer months to roam about, play games, such as, hurling and football, train in running, jumping and weight-throwing as well as several other activities they were engaged in. Besides all this, there was no dearth of medical doctors and students and there was at least one prisoner M.O. for every 100 men.[17]

The Curragh internment camps were crowded, and the conditions difficult, but the internees had much greater freedom in running their lives than was typical of inmates of convict prisons. When the Curragh internees were released in December 1921, they were in high spirits and good health. They had spent their incarceration well – with education and sport to the forefront. The many successful escapes, IRA successes and the Truce and Treaty negotiations also lifted their morale. But the divisions that appeared in the republican movement during the Treaty debates were also found in the internment camps and prisons. The republican leadership gave the impression of addressing prison conditions via inspections and parole, but the conflict between the prisoners and their leaders on the outside was part of an emerging dissent within the republican movement. Throughout the republican struggle, the prisoners and their supporters had sustained the potential to destabilise negotiations, and in 1921 this was a real possibility.

As the internees left the Rath Camp, few thought that within six months many of them would be back behind the wire at the Curragh, guarded by their former comrades.

APPENDIX I
LIST OF INTERNEES, HARE PARK CAMP 1921

Some internees held in Hare Park Camp were subsequently transferred to the Rath Camp and Ballykinlar Camp, or, if convicted of a political offence, sent to penal institutions to serve their sentences. (Consequently, some men held in Hare Park may also appear on the Rath Camp list.) Where full names or home towns are not given, these are not known.

Carlow
Abbey, J., Rathvilly
Abbey, Thomas, Rathvilly
Behan, Michael, Graiguecullen
Behan, Seamus (James), Graiguecullen
Behan, Thomas, Graiguecullen
Bennett, E., Hacketstown
Bennett, Thomas, Hacketstown
Black, John, Hacketstown
Brennan, L., Hacketstown
Byrne, D., Rathvilly
Carpenter, Michael, Raheen
Carty, P., Clonmore
Condron, E., Clonmore
Condron, Martin, Brown's Hill Road, Carlow
Dolan, Patrick, Clonmore
Doyle, T., Rathvilly
Dyland, James, Hacketstown
Fallon, Thomas, Bridge Street, Hacketstown
Fitzpatrick, Patrick, Leighlinbridge

INTERNED

Foley, Pat, Hacketstown
Furlong, D., Clonmore
Furlong, P., Clonmore
Gaffney, Patrick, Killeshin
Hanly, D., Rathvilly
Hickey, William, Clonegal
Hyland, J., Hacketstown
Kearns, Patrick, Rathvilly
Kelly, Myles, Gormona, Bagenalstown
Kelly, P. J., Clonmore
Kenny, Harry, Hacketstown
Nolan, M., Rathvilly
McKenna, William, Carlow
Millet, Laurence, Bagenalstown
Murphy, William, Hacketstown
O'Brien, James, Hacketstown
O'Neill, Laurence, Graiguecullen
Roche, Thomas, Carlow
Ryan, Michael, Carlow
Sheehan, Thomas, Barrack Street, Carlow

Dublin
Brock, Anthony, Deansgrange, Co. Dublin
O'Brien, Daniel
Staines, James, 63 Murtagh Road, Arbour Hill

Galway
Connolly, Seán

Kildare
Allen, Peter, Kilcock
Armstrong, Henry, Maynooth
Byrne, W., Kilcock
Carney, T. J., Newbridge
Colgan, Patrick, Maynooth

APPENDIX 1

Cooney, John/Seán, Naas
Doolan, 'Lunch', Carna, Suncroft
Doran, Art, Ballymore Eustace
Dunne, Michael, Grangehiggin
Dunney, Charles, Grangehiggin
Farrell, Andy, Eadestown
Fitzgerald, Richard, Seven Stars
Flood, Laurence, Grangehiggin
Flynn, Peter, Newtown, Kilcock
Foley, Patrick, Knockbounce, Kilcullen
Furlong, Dick, Naas
Grehan, Seán, Naas
Heavy, Martin, Grangehiggin
Herbert, Frank, Allen
Howe, William, Suncroft
Ledwige, Joseph, Maynooth
Lee, John, Broadleas, Ballymore Eustace
Magee, Padraig, Ballymore Eustace
Murray, Michael, Kilcock
O'Brien, James, Moyvalley
O'Brien, Thomas, Kilcock
O'Callaghan, Laurence, Naas
O'Keefe, Joseph, Kilcock
O'Kelly, Michael, Gleann na Griene, Naas
O'Reilly, Daniel, The Square, Kilcock
O'Toole, Seán, Nurney
Simms, John, Kilcock
Smyth, Michael, Athgarvan
Ward, Joseph, Grangehiggin
Williams, Thomas J., Naas

Kerry
Lyston, T.

INTERNED

Laois
Dunne, Patrick, Stradbally
Fitzpatrick, Francis, Springhill, Borris-in-Ossory
O'Riordan, Denis, Borris-in-Ossory

Meath
Byrne, James
Kelly, Peter, Killbrush, Enfield
Kenne, A., Enfield
Smith, Patrick, Kilskyre, Kells

Offaly
Bulfin, Francis, Birr (transferred from the Rath Camp)
Feehan, Harry, Tullamore
Galvin, John, Ardan, Tullamore
Galvin, Michael, Ardan, Tullamore
Grogan, P., Tullamore
Keegan, Willie, Tullamore
Molloy, A.

Wicklow
Byrne, Robert 'Bob', Kilquiggan
Curran, Richard, Snugborough, Donard
Deering, Joseph, Milltown, Dunlavin
Doyle, James, Knockroe
Doyle, Peter, Knockendarra, Donard
Hayden (Headon), John, Ballyleonard, Donard
Lawler, P., Dunlavin
Neill, Michael, Kilbaylet, Donard
Neill, Thomas

No confirmed address
Kelly, M., Castle Farm
Nolan, D.
Redmond, M.

APPENDIX II
LIST OF INTERNEES, THE RATH CAMP 1921

Spellings of names and places may not be correct but are as they appeared in the original British internment lists and newspaper accounts, or as they were spelled at the time. Some place names may no longer exist. Internees names were largely recorded in their anglicised versions.

At times, internment orders to be served on a prisoner arrived from General Headquarters at Parkgate Street, Dublin, only for it to be found that the interned prisoner had been released or was in a different camp or prison. Prisoners were also moved from Hare Park Camp to the Rath Camp and occasionally vice versa. Again, where full names or home towns are not given, these are not known.

Antrim
Dillon, Joseph, Cloughmills
Dillon, Robert, Cloughmills
Kelly, John, Dunloy
McKeegan, Malcolm, Cushendall
Murray, John, Ballybrack, Cushendall
Shiels, James, Dunloy

Armagh
Boyd, Frank, Clea, Keady
Carroll, Patrick, Carrickasticken
Corrigan, Patrick, Chapel Lane, Armagh
Fegan, John, Lagan, Keady

INTERNED

Gibbons, Daniel, Bambrookhill, Armagh
Hughes, John Thomas, Mullyard, Keady
McCann, Michael, Ballykeel, Mullaghbawn
Mourney, Michael, Aghacommon
Murphy, Bernard, Maphoner, Mullaghbawn, Armagh
O'Callaghan, John, Carrickabolie
Rafferty, Bernard, Lagan, Keady
Short, John, Lower Irish Street, Armagh

Belfast
Allen, Thomas, 23 Cavendish Street
Carolan, Michael, 80 Chief Street
Close, Leo, 507 Falls Road
Coan, Henry John, 28 Frederick Lane
Davidson, James, 3 Scotland Place
Downey, Hugh, 10 Irish Street, Belfast & 2 Hendrick Street, Dublin
Gallagher, James, 119 Cullentree Road
Gilmore, Edward, 345 Crumlin Road
Glennon, Thomas
Harvey, John, Hillman Street
Loughran, William, 35 Welsley Avenue
Murphy, William, 33 Hamill Street
O'Boyle, Manus, 10 Foundry Street
O'Brien, William, 37 East Street
Ryan, Philip, St Paul's Terrace, Belfast

Carlow
Bennett, John, Hacketstown
Bolger, Edward, Rathvilly
Bolger, Peter, Cappagh, Ballon
Brophy, Michael, Aradattin, Tullow
Byrne, Joseph, Nimveud, Clonmore, Hacketstown
Byrne, Michael, Knockagarry
Byrne, Peter, Clonmore
Clark, Michael, Williamstown

Condron, Martin, Rownshill Road, Carlow town
Cullen, John, Monavoth, Rathvilly
Donohue, William P., Clonmore, Hacketstown
Dundon, Edward, Borris
Dundon, J., Borris
Fallon, Thomas, Bridge Street, Hacketstown
Ferris, William, Ballinakill, Tobinstown
Gorman, Charles, Grange, Maganey
Hanley, Matthew, Williamstown
Haughney, Martin, Carlow town
Howe, John, Leighlinbridge
Kane, Eugene, Kilmeany, Tinryland
Kelly, Martin, Borris
Lillis, James, Tullow
Maher, Michael, Leighlinbridge
McDonald, John, Clonmore
McManus, Thomas, Rathvilly
Millett, Laurence, Bagnelstown
Monaghan, John, The Bridge, Tullow
Murphy, William, Grange, Tullow
Nolan, Con, Hacketstown
Nolan, John, Tullow
Nolan, Michael, Tullow
O'Leary, William, Tullow
O'Neill, Michael, Tullow
O'Toole, Laurence, Carlow
Pender, Dan, Springhill
Quinn, Michael, Ardoyne, Tullow
Roche, Thomas, Ballyshane, Clonmore
Sheppard, Patrick, Tullow

Cavan
Baxter, Patrick, Templeport, Bawnboy
Bennett, Patrick, Fertagh

INTERNED

Boylan, Matthew, Toneylion, Kineleek
Boylan, Michael, Battleneagh, Virginia Road
Boylan, Patrick, Battleneagh, Virginia Road
Brady, James, Bailieboro
Brennan, John, Shercock
Carrolan, Patrick, Nevigna
Cassidy, Joseph, Annafarney, Shercock
Coyle, Bernard, Lecks, Shercock
Coyle, John Joseph, Letnadronagh, Kilnaleck
Donegan, James, Lecks, Shercock
Kiernan, Owen, Carrickarnon, Shercock
Lynch, John, Kimeagh, Baileboro, Drumagh
McBreen, Frank, Drummamuck, Bailieboro
McCauley, James, Swanlinbar
McKenna, Justin, Mullagh
O'Connor, Anthony, Kingscourt
O'Connor, Frederick, Pauls Street, Kingscourt
O'Reilly, Patrick, Corlattycarroll, Bailieboro
O'Reilly, Peter, Shercock

Clare
Considine, John, Feakle
Doyle, Edmond, Leccarow, Feakle
Gleeson, Michael, Bodyke
Rochford, James, Feakle
Tuohy, Michael, Leccarow, Feakle
Tuohy, Patrick, Leccarow, Feakle

Cork
Byrne, James, Kiltankin, Kilbehney
Byrne, Patrick, Kiltankin, Kilbehney
Cronin, William, Midleton
Fehilly, Eugene, Ballineen, Bandon
Hogan, John J., Longueville, Ballynoe
Murphy, Timothy, Friars Walk, Cork city

APPENDIX II

Derry
Hurl, Patrick, Derrygarve, Castledawson
McGuiness, Hugh, 9 Sackville Street, Derry city
O'Doherty, Joseph, Little Diamond, Derry city
Shiels, Francis, 2 Philips Street, Derry city
Taylor, James, 26 Barry Street, Derry city

Donegal
Bonar, Patrick, Glenties
Breslin, Patrick, Ardara
Cannon, Peter, Glencolumbkille
Carey, Edward, Glencolumbkille
Conway, Patrick, Ballybofey
Cunningham, Denis, Straleel, Carrick
Doherty, Charles, Main Street, Ballybofey
Doogan, Francis, Glenties
Gallagher, Charles, Ardara
Gallagher, John, Ardara
Green, Hugh
Harley, John, Frosses
Hirrell, William, Mallow Street, Carndonagh
Ireland, Patrick, Ardore
Judge, John, Bundoran
Lafferty, Leo, Carrowreagh, Carndonagh
Lanagan, Frank, Cardonagh
Lanagan, James, Cardonagh
McCahill, Patrick, Castletown
McGoldrick, Patrick J., Buncrana
McGowan, James, Navenny, Ballybofey
McLean, Hugh, Navenny, Ballybofey
McLoon, Francis, Glenties
Murray, John, Westport, Ballyshannon
O'Doherty, William, Dungloe
O'Flaherty, John, Castlefinn East

INTERNED

Queenan, Michael, Dooballagh, Clonlough

Down
Campbell, Arthur, Bornmeehan
McKinley, John, Clarkhill
McNamara, Edward, Broclough, Loughinisland
Murney, Michael, Killowen
Murphy, James, Kilteel
Murray, Eugene, Warrenpoint
Murray, Francis, Slieveinsky, Castlewellan
Reavey, Patrick, Corgary, Newry
Smyth, James, Corgary, Newry

Dublin
Adams, Thomas, 9 Bessboro Avenue, North Strand
Adamson, Joseph, 11 Upper Abbey Street
Andrews, Christopher S., Terenure
Arthur, Michael, 4 North Wall
Baker, John, 18 Crampton Buildings
Baxter, William, 44 Sitric Road
Beaumont, Seán, 1 Clare Street
Behan, Michael, 21 Thomas Street
Beirne, John, 7 Carrick Terrace, South Circular Road
Boyce, James, 11 Aungier Street
Boyle, Andrew
Brabazon, Thomas, 96 Lower Dorset Street
Bradshaw, John, 18 Little Mary Street
Brennan, Michael, Pembroke Cottages
Brien, John, 9th Lock, Clondalkin, Co. Dublin
Brien, Michael, 9th Lock, Clondalkin, Co. Dublin
Brien, Patrick, 9th Lock, Clondalkin, Co. Dublin
Broderick, Myles, Ardcuaine, Glenageary
Broderick, Richard, Ardcuaine, Glenageary
Broderick, Richard J., Ardcuaine, Glenageary
Burke, Michael, Ardmeen, Newtown Park Avenue, Blackrock

APPENDIX II

Byrne, Bernard C., 24 Manor Place
Byrne, Charles, 24 Manor Place
Byrne, Denis, 42 Railway Avenue, Inchicore
Byrne, John, 59 Kings Street
Byrne, John Joseph, 3 Great Longford Street
Byrne, Patrick, 32 Kennedy's Villas, James Street
Byrne, Peter Joseph, The Lodge, St Joseph's Common, Ranelagh
Byrne, Robert, Portmahon Lodge, South Circular Road
Byrne, Thomas, Shamrock Cottage, Dalkey Hill, Co. Dublin
Byrne, William, Shamrock Cottage, Dalkey Hill, Co. Dublin
Cannon, Edward, Ballyedmonduff, Sandyford, Co. Dublin
Carloss, John, Bridge Inn, Chapelizod, Co. Dublin
Carthy, Edward, Dundrum, Co. Dublin
Carton, Owen, 7 Temple Street
Casey, Thomas, 25 Ardee Street
Cassells, John, 5 Colberts Hole, St James's Walk
Claffey, Joseph, 40 Great Western Villas, Phibsboro
Clark, James, 2 Blackhall Street
Clark, Michael, 24 Mount Temple Street
Conaghan, James J., Seaforth Avenue, Pembroke
Connolly, John, 97 Upper Dorset Street
Connolly, Patrick, 97 Upper Dorset Street
Conroy, Isaiah
Cooney, Richard, Edwards Grocery Store, Ballybrack, Co. Dublin
Corlass, Patrick, 38 De Courcy Square
Cosgrave, Philip B., James's Street
Costello, Michael, Tower Road, Clondalkin, Co. Dublin
Cotter, John P., 2 Belvedere Place
Cotter, Thomas, St Andrew's Road, Drumcondra
Courtney, Hugh, 37 Talbot Street
Crilly, Nicholas, 38 James's Street
Cullen, Patrick, 23 North Strand
Cummins, John, 10 Lombard Street
Daly, James, Carmelite Priory, Aungier Street

INTERNED

Daly, John K., 9 Vance's Buildings, Bishop Street
Darcy, Patrick, Dalkey Hill, Co. Dublin
Delaney, P., Dalkey, Co. Dublin
Dempsey, William, Grace View, Donabate, Co. Dublin
Dennis, John, Lusk, Co. Dublin
Denny, Malachy, 27 Fingal Place, Prussia Street
Dooley, Frank, 95 Upper Dorset Street
Dowdall, Michael, 81 Tirconnell Road, Inchicore
Downey, Edward, 2 Rathfarnham, Co. Dublin
Doyle, Andrew, 1 Grants Row, Lower Mount Street
Duke, Thomas, St Margaret's, Co. Dublin
Dunne, John, 5 St Joseph's Terrace
Dunne, William, 3 McGuinness Avenue
Earle, Daniel Hubert, Harolds Cross
Ennis, Christopher, Beach Hill Lodge, Donnybrook
Eustace, Richard, 27 Warren Street
Faber, Fritz, 47 Upper Garden Street
Farrell, John, 42 Queen's Square
FitzGerald, Desmond
Fitzgerald, Thomas, 90 Harcourt Street
Fitzpatrick, John, 37 Victoria Buildings, Blackrock
Fitzpatrick, Michael, 11 Upper Exchange Street
Fitzpatrick, S., Little Mary Street
Fitzwilliam, James, 191 Great Brunswick Street
Foley, Michael Patrick, Nelson Street
Ford, Myles, Rathgar Road, Rathmines
Fox, Joseph, 7 Sandyford Avenue
Freeman, Maurice, 8 Ballsbridge
Furey, James, 2 Hendrick Street
Gaffney, Thomas, Camden Court
Gannon, John, Bluebell, Inchicore
Gartland, Michael, 8 Corporation Buildings, Bride Street
Geraghty, Thomas, Moureen Lodge, Dundrum, Co. Dublin
Gibson, Andrew, 115 James Street

Gileenan, Andrew, Naul, Co. Dublin
Golding, John Joe, 6 Vincent Street
Goodwin, Robert, Kilmacud Road, Stillorgan, Co. Dublin
Griffen, Thomas, 124 Deansgrange, Co. Dublin
Griffin, M., Queen Street
Griffiths, Gabriel, 54 Eccles Street
Griffiths, Michael, 54 Eccles Street
Grimes, Christopher, 4 Pleasant Place, Camden Street
Grogan, Laurence, 2 Croydon Cottages
Guinan, Frank, 37 Talbot Street
Hanlon, Bernard, 52 Mountjoy Street
Harmon, Thomas, 62 Lower Dominic Street
Hart, Michael, 15 St Patrick's Road
Hart, William, 16 Upper Exchange Street
Hickey, Peter, 20 [Hetsberg] Street
Hill, Valentine, 23 Stoneybatter
Hurley, Patrick, Mountainview, Ballybrack, Co. Dublin
Hyland, John, Dodderview Cottage, Co. Dublin
Joyce, John, North Circular Road
Kane, G., Fitzwilliam Street
Kavanagh, Charles, 30 Aungier Street
Kavanagh, John, 37 Convent Road
Kavanagh, John, 207 Parnell Street
Keane, George J., 7 & 8 Buckingham Street
Keating, Michael, 51 East Arran Street
Keenan, Eugene, 5 Mountbrown
Keenan, Thomas, 74 Marrowbone Lane
Kehoe, William, 81 Lower Georges Street
Kelly, John, 47 Lower Dominick Street
Kelly, Joseph, The Green, Lusk, Co. Dublin
Kelly, Joseph Patrick, Corduff, Finglas Hospital, Balrothery, Co. Dublin
Kelly, William, 11 Donohue Street
Kennedy, Patrick J., 58 Great Charles Street
Kenny, Joseph, 10 Eglington Street

INTERNED

Kerwick, Patrick, Parliament Street
King, Edward, 4 Gulistan Terrace, Rathmines
King, Patrick, 4 Gulistan Terrace, Rathmines
Kinsella, Frank, 19 Tyrconnell Street, Inchicore
Kirwan, Edward, 14 Old Camden Street
Kirwan, Laurence, Cornelscourt, Foxrock, Co. Dublin
Lane, H., Shanganagh, Co. Dublin
Larkin, Hugh, 27 Lower Erin Street
Lawler, William, 40 York Street
Lawless, James, 20 First Avenue, Saville Place
Lawless, Joseph, Saucerstown, Fingal, Co. Dublin
Lawlor, Michael, Bluebell, Inchicore
Leddy, William, 17 North Terrace, Inchicore
Ledwidge, Simon, 2 Erne Terrace, Upper Brunswick Street
Lee, Hugh, 29 St Patrick's Cottages, Rathfarnham
Lemass, Noel, 2 Capel Street
Long, Andrew, 12 Enfield Cottages
Lucas, William, 23 Upper Mount Street
Lynch, John, Mountain View, Ballybrack, Co. Dublin
Lynch, Patrick J., 32 Rathgar Road
Lyons, Vincent, 76 Aungier Street
MacNeill, Dermot John
Magee, Robert, Maddens Cottages, Ballybrack, Co. Dublin
Magee, William, Maddens Cottages, Ballybrack, Co. Dublin
Mahon, Arthur, 4 Bishops Street
Mallin, James, 107 Summerhill
Markey, John, 48 Thomas Street
Martin, Edward, 157 Oxmantown Road
Martin, John J., Heytesbury Street
Martin, Thomas, Westview, Monkstown, Co. Dublin
Mason, George, 4 Lower Dominick Street
McCann, Henry, 21 Oxmantown Road
McCann, John, Cornelscourt, Cabinteely, Co. Dublin
McCann, Patrick, 22 Doris Street, Ringsend

APPENDIX II

McEvoy, James, 22 South Erin Street
McEvoy, John, 2 Ashbrook Terrace, Leeson Park
McGarry, Michael, Hawthorn House, Shankill, Co. Dublin
McGlynn, John, 4 Portobello Harbour
McGrath, Laurence, 55 Belgrave Square, Rathmines
McGrath, Patrick, 3 Upper Northbrook Avenue, North Strand
McGrath, William, 14 Henrietta Street
McGuiness, John, 55 Leinster Avenue
McGurk, Patrick, 108 Leeson Street
McLoughlin, Thomas, 29 South [Clones] Street
McNamara, James J., 11 Elm Park Avenue
McSherry, T. A. V., 21 East Essex Street
Minihan, John, Clondalkin, Co. Dublin
Molloy, Richard, Belvedere Place
Mooney, Patrick, Red Cottages, Dalkey Hill, Co. Dublin
Moore, Thomas, Killiney Hill Cottages, Co. Dublin
Moore, William, 8 Moore Street
Morrissey, Thomas, 7 Gulistan Terrace, Rathmines
Mulhall, Donald, 7 Stream Street
Mullarney, John, 131 Northampton Road
Mullett, William, 37 Talbot Street
Mulvaney, Thomas, 4 Granite Terrace, Inchicore
Murphy, Charles, 20 Shamrock Cottages, North Strand
Murphy, James, 36 Great Eastern Street
Murphy, Laurence, 20 Arbutus Place, South Circular Road
Murphy, Stephen, 71 North Brunswick Street
Murphy, William, 35 Aberdeen Street
Murphy, William P., 35 South William Street
Newman, John P., 5 Marino Avenue, Fairview
Nolan, Patrick, Grove Park, Rathmines
Nolan, Thomas, 90 Audia Street
Noud, John, Kimmage Road
Nunan, Ernest, 5 Cambridge Avenue
Nunan, Michael, 17 Clonmore Terrace

INTERNED

O'Brien, Stephen, 16 Upper Exchange Street
O'Brien, Vincent, 1 Marina Terrace, Clontarf
O'Brien, Walter
O'Brien, William, 4 Adelaide Place
O'Brien, William, 16 Upper Exchange Street
O'Brien, William, 1 Philipsburgh Avenue, Fairview Strand
O'Carroll, Kevin, Washington House, Rathfarnham
O'Carroll, William, 92 Manor Street
O'Connor, Brian, 12 Appian Way, Ranelagh
O'Connor, John, 46 Nash Street, Inchicore
O'Connor, John, 29 Thomas Street
O'Connor, John Joe, 6 Barret Street, Dún Laoghaire, Co. Dublin
O'Connor, Joseph, 140 Terenure Road
O'Connor, Rory, Kildare Street
O'Connor, Thomas, 21 Prussia Street
O'Connor, William, 14 Adelaide Road, Dún Laoghaire, Co. Dublin
O'Farrell, Dr Michael, 32 Blessington Street
O'Hanlon, Bernard, Prebend Street, Broadstone
O'Hogan, Eamon, 7 Prince Arthur's Terrace
O'Keefe, John, Newtown Park, Blackrock
O'Leary, David, 10 Belgrave Road
O'Loughlin, John, 172 James Street
O'Moore, Patrick, 6 Lower Columbus Road, Drumcondra
O'Neill, Andrew, 69 Marlboro Street
O'Neill, Edward, 12 Cuff Lane
O'Neill, Edward, 50A New Street
O'Neill, Edward, 14 Rings Street, Inchicore
O'Neill, Fergus, 6 Montague Street
O'Neill, Thomas, 10 Ellesmere Avenue, Cabra
O'Reilly, Edward, 122 Upper Church Street
O'Reilly, Edward, 37 St Mary's Road
O'Reilly, William Joseph, 10 Rialto Street
O'Toole, Andrew, Cabinteely, Co. Dublin
O'Toole, Laurence, Spratstown, Inchicore

APPENDIX II

Pollard, Charles, 21 Lower Wellington Street
Purtell, John, Newcomen Avenue, North Strand
Quigley, Patrick, Cornelscourt, Foxrock, Co. Dublin
Quinn, Laurence, 4 Benburb Street
Quinn, William, 8 Temple Street
Redmond, Patrick, 27 Turners Cottage, Shelbourne Road
Reynolds, William, Foxrock, Co. Dublin
Rice, Matthew, 90 Benburb Street
Robinson, Joseph, Dartry Road, Rathfarnham
Rochford, Joseph, 11 Elm Park Avenue, Ranelagh
Rooney, John
Rowley, James, 25 Grattan Street
Ryan, Daniel
Ryan, Nicholas, 4 Nicholas Avenue, Church Street
Ryan, Patrick, 13 Upper Cumberland Street
Scanlon, Michael, Ringsend Park
Schweppe, Frederick, Usher's Quay
Seville, James, Findlater Place
Sexton, James, 21 Summerhill
Sheridan, Henry William, 49 Harrington Road
Sheridan, Peter, 27 Gardiner Place
Sheridan, Thomas, Gardiner Place
Sillott, Mark, Cabinteely, Co. Dublin
Smith, Thomas Patrick, 1 East James Place
Soye, James, 32 Inchicore Road, Kilmainham
Staines, Vincent, 63 Murtagh Road, Arbour Hill
Stapleton, Michael, 1 Mountjoy Place
Sweeney, Edward, 9 Haymarket
Sweetman, John, 1 Deansgrange
Talbot, John, 129 Emmett's Road, Inchicore
Thornton, James, O'Brien's Cottages, Bray Road, Co. Dublin
Tisdale, Thomas, Brittas, Co. Dublin
Tonge, Joseph Leo, St Mary's Avenue, Rathfarnham
Trahy, Richard, 135 Summerhill

INTERNED

Traynor, Patrick
Treston, Joseph, Emal, Harbour Road, Dalkey, Co. Dublin
Troy, W., Clanbrassil Street
Troy, William, 9 St Francis Terrace
Vaughan, Thomas, 9 Mountain View, Templeogue
Walsh, Bernard, 32 Blessington Street
Walsh, John, 16 Addison Road
Ward, Anthony, 33 Blackhall Place
Ward, George, 15 Werburgh Street
Whelan, Jeremiah, 10 Kirwan Street
Williams, Arthur, Balbriggan, Co. Dublin
Williams, Charles, 5 Sorrento Road, Dalkey, Co. Dublin
Wilson, William, Balheavy, Swords, Co. Dublin
Woods, Anthony J., 131 Morehampton Road

Galway
Brophy, —
Brown, Daniel, Knocknagarra
Burke, Laurence, Kilnadeema, Loughrea
Burke, Martin, Clifden
Burke, Patrick, Loughinwadda, Peterswell
Burke, Thomas, Ballydoogan, Loughrea
Byrne, Patrick J., Cappataggle, Ballinasloe
Carroll, Michael, Castleblakeney, Ballinasloe
Caughlin, John, Ballygar
Clarke, Charles, Gurtymadden, Ballinasloe
Cloherty, John J., Roundstone, Gort
Cloonan, Patrick, Killenoen, Craughwell
Coen, Michael, Clontusker
Cone, Michael, Ballinasloe
Collins, Patrick, Menlough, Ballinasloe
Concannon, Thomas, Briarfield, Ballinasloe
Connors, Richard, Craughwell, Athenry
Conroy, Michael, Ballinrobe

APPENDIX II

Courtney, Hugh, George's Street, Gort
Coyne, Charles, Abbeytown, Tuam
Crehan, Michael, Ballyvoneen, Castlefrench
Cusack, Brian, North Galway
Daniels, Martin, Loughrea
Donohue, Joseph, Currygrave, Ballinasloe
Dowd, James, Kilconnelly, Tuam
Fahy, Thomas, Dunmore, Tuam
Fahy, Thomas, Coolfin, Ardrahan
Fallon, B., Loughrea
Fallon, John, Loughrea
Farragher, Patrick, Ballinrobe
Feeney, Peter C., Kinvara
Finn, John, Carrakeel
Fitzgerald, Michael, Gort
Fitzgerald, Thomas, Ballinlough
Fleming, Michael, Clarenbridge
Fleming, Patrick, Clarenbridge
Flynn, James, Loughrea
Fogarty, Michael, Barrack Street, Tuam
Gallagher, Michael, Curran, Achill
Garvey, Laurence, Mullagh, Loughrea
Geraghty, Patrick, Caltra, Ballinasloe
Glennon, Patrick J., Coolagh, Killimore
Glynn, Thomas, Attymon
Hargrove, Michael J., Gort
Hargrove, Patrick, Gort
Healy, Thomas, Skehanagh, Peterswell
Higgins, Alex, Clifden
Higgins, Thomas, Moylough, Aughrim
Hobbins, Patrick, Kiltomagh, Ballinasloe
Kelly, John, Kilclare, Ballinasloe
Kilcommins, John, Caltra, Ballinasloe
Killeen, Timothy, Abbeylands, Eyrecourt

INTERNED

Kyne, Charles, Abbeytown, Tuam
Lally, Michael, Loughrea
Lally, Patrick, Loughrea
Leahy, Patrick, Kilmacreagh, Newtowndaly
Lennon, Michael, 3 Castles
Lowry, Thomas, Killimore, Ballinasloe
Lynch, William, Abbey, Loughrea
Mannion (Manning), John, Dangan, Ballinasloe
McDermott, Richard J., Athenry
McGrath, Martin, Cloon, Gort
McQuade, Michael, Kelly Street, Loughrea
Monahan, John, Barnaderg
Monoghan, John, Kilshandy, Tuam
Mulvey, Patrick, Feigh West, Ballyglunin
Nohilly, James, Dublin Road, Tuam
O'Brien, Charles, Brackagh, Tuam
O'Brien, William, University College Galway
O'Connor, Patrick, Ryehill
O'Farrell, Michael, Craughwell
O'Reilly, William, Headford
Patton, Joseph, Lawrencetown
Power, Michael, Kilnadeema, Loughrea
Quinn, Joseph, Tuam
Rafferty, John, Cahir, Loughrea
Reidy, Michael, The Square, Gort
Reilly, James, Kiltomagh, Ballinasloe
Roseingrave, Joseph, Tubber
Roseingrave, Michael, Tubber
Ruane, John J., Gort
Rush, James, Dunmore
Schley, John, Ardrahan
Thompson, Martin, Ardrahan
Tully, John, Barrack Street, Athenry
Tully, Patrick, Ballinamore Bridge, Ballinasloe

APPENDIX II

Tully, Patrick, Riversdale
Turner, Michael, Milltown, Clonbur
Varley, Thomas, Ardclare, Clonbur
Waldron, Peter, Bekan, Cong
Walsh, Charlie, Tuam
Walsh, Martin, Oldcastle Chapel, Oughterard
Walsh, Patrick, Clifden
Ward, Michael, Pollnabrone, Mount Hazel

Kerry
Crowley, James, Listowel
Moriarty, Timothy, Carrig, Ballylongford
Norton, John, 12 Castle Street, Tralee
Stack, John, Ballyconroy, Listowel

Kildare
Armstrong, Henry, Bodenstown
Baxter, Joseph, Harbour View, Kilcock
Behan, Thomas, Bridge Street, Rathangan
Boland, Michael James, Kildare town
Bradley, James, Barrack Street, Athy
Brady, Patrick, Kill, Naas
Breslin, Michael, Abbey View, Kildare
Brophy, John, Athy
Buckley, Cornelius, Main Street, Kilcock
Buggle, John, Blackhill, Kill, Naas
Burke, Frank, Coonaugh, Carbury
Butler, Patrick, Cappagh, Cloncurry
Byrne, Andrew, Two-Mile-House, Naas
Byrne, Andrew, Moortown Castle, Kilcullen
Byrne, Michael, Kilcullen Road, Naas
Byrne, Patrick, Kilcock
Clarke, Thomas, Newrow, Oughterard
Cleary, Denis, James's Street, Newbridge
Cleary, Henry, Courtown Road, Kilcock

INTERNED

Cleary, Joseph, Kishavanna, Carbury
Cleary, Peter, Kishavanna, Carbury
Conway, Alexander C., Maynooth
Cooney, John, Naas
Coughlan, Anthony, Sallins
Cranny, Edward, Ballyshannon, Kilrush
Crinnigan, Peter, Freagh, Carbury
Delahunt, Patrick, Tuckmilltown, Naas
Delahunt, Sylvester, 40 South Main Street, Naas
Dolan, David, Edward Street, Newbridge
Domican, Thomas, Hartwell, Kill
Dooley, Jeremiah, Rathangan
Doran, Christopher, Carbury
Dowling, John, Ballysax
Doyle, Joseph, Sillagh, Naas
Doyle, Michael, Blackchurch, Kill
Duff, John, Laragh, Kilcock
Dunne, Patrick J., Ballyshannon, Athy
Farrell, Andrew, Beggars End, Naas
Fitzgerald, Michael, Allen Cross, Kilmeague
Fitzgerald, Richard, Fontsown, Athy
Fitzharris, Michael, Mullacash, Naas
Fitzharris, Thomas, Mullacash, Naas
Fitzpatrick, Augustine, Naas
Fitzsimons, Thomas, Kilbrook, Cloncurry
Flaherty, Luke, Main Street, Rathangan
Flanagan, John, Fonstown, Athy
Flynn, Peter, Newtown, Kilcock
Foran, Thomas, Rathangan
Furlong, Richard, Bluebell Cottage, Naas
Geraghty, Patrick, Eyre Street, Newbridge
Graham, Seán, Kildare town
Grehan, John, 7 South Main Street, Naas
Harris, Richard, Prosperous

APPENDIX II

Haughey, Henry, Blackhalls, Kill
Hayden, John, Athy
Herbert, Frank, Kilmeague
Howe, William, Ballysax
Hubbard, John, Longhouse, Tipperkevin
Hughes, James, Francis Street, Newbridge
Johnston, Patrick, Kilcock
Kelly, James, Killeen, Narraghmore
Kelly, Jeremiah, Hartwell, Kill
Kelly, Peter, Kilbrook, Cloncurry
Kenny, Christopher, New Street, Rathangan
Kenny, Joseph, New Street, Rathangan
Ledwith, Joseph, Kilcock
Lee, Joseph, Broadleas, Ballymore Eustace
Liston, Thomas, Brownstown
Logan, James, Hill of Allen, Kilmeague
Magee, Patrick, Ballymore Eustace
Maguire, James, Kilcock
Maher, Patrick, Old Connell, Newbridge
Merlin, Michael, Patrick Street, Newbridge
Merlin, William, Patrick Street, Newbridge
Murphy, Michael, Nicholastown
Nolan, John, Hermitage, Monasterevin
O'Hara, Thomas, Harristown
O'Kelly, Michael, Gleann na Greine, Naas
O'Neill, Denis, Kildare town
O'Neill, Patrick, Broadleas, Ballymore Eustace
O'Neill, William, Suncroft
O'Neill, William, The Knocks, Naas
O'Reilly, Daniel, The Square, Kilcock
O'Rourke, Thomas, Grand Canal Harbour, Athy
Purcell, Francis, Cappagh, Kilcock
Quinn, Patrick, Moortown, Ballysax
Rafferty, John, Basin Street, Naas

INTERNED

Reardon, —, Rathangan
Redmond, Thomas, Cappagh
Rourke, Edward, Betagh, Clane
Smyth, Joseph, Monasterevin
Smyth, Thomas, Grangebeg, Ballymore Eustace
Swan, Edward, Bodenstown, Sallins
Timmons, John, Mullacash, Naas
Toomey, Michael, Ballymore Eustace
Toomey, Nicholas, Ballymore Eustace
Traynor, John, Haynestown, Kill
Traynor, Peter, Haynestown, Kill
Williams, Thomas J., Main Street, Naas
Wilmot, Thomas, Linden House, Athgarvan

Kilkenny
Lennon, Patrick, 32 High Street, Kilkenny

Laois (Queen's Co.)
Barrett, John, Conoboro, Rathdowney
Begadon, Martin, Aghmacart, Rathdowney
Bergin, James, Borris-in-Ossory
Bergin, Matthew, Kilbreedy, Rathdowney
Brophy, James, Mountmellick
Burke, Patrick, Fallowbeg, Upper Luggacurran
Byrne, Henry, Manor Cottage, Mountmellick
Byrne, James, Knocklaide, Timahoe
Byrne, John, Knocklaide, Timahoe
Campion, John, Cullahill, Durrow
Carroll, John, Killinure, Mountrath
Carroll, Stephen, Errill
Carthy, William, Church Street, Rathdowney
Casey, Patrick, Beladd, Portlaoise
Connolly, —, Shannon Street, Mountrath
Connolly, James, Courtwood, Ballybrittas
Conroy, Daniel, Clarehill, Mountmellick

APPENDIX II

Cullen, James, Mountmellick
Cullen, Matthew, Ballymorris, Portarlington
Culleton, James, Clonygowan, Ballyfin
Cummins, Joseph, Springhill, Killeshan
Deegan, Joseph, Mountrath
Delaney, Timothy, Clonard, Mountrath
Dorrie, Edward, Portlaoise
Dowling, Michael, O'Moore Street, Mountmellick
Dunne, John, Kilmalogue, Portarlington
Dunne, Peter, Market Street, Mountmellick
Dunne, Patrick, Roe, Ballyhupawn, Mountrath
Dunne, Timothy, Mountmellick
Egan, John, Kilcronan, Ballinakill
Fennelly, William, Mountmellick
Finlay, Patrick, Portarlington
Finlay, Peter, Portarlington
Fitzpatrick, Francis, Springhill, Borris-in-Ossory
Flanagan, Edward, Stradbally
Fox, Edward, Camlough, Mountmellick
Gorman, Robert, Kildangan, Durrow
Gorman, William, Kildangan, Durrow
Gray, James, The Heath, Portlaoise
Gray, Michael, Main Street, Portlaoise
Gray, Thomas, The Heath, Portlaoise
Hibbitts, Martin, Longbarn, Mountmellick
Hibbitts, William, St Joseph's Terrace, Mountmellick
Higgins, Brian, Timogue Cross, Stradbally
Hurley, Gerald, Mullaghmore, Wolfhill
Hyland, Joseph, Coolglass, Wolfhill
Hyland, Thomas, Portarlington
Keegan, Thomas, Ballyfin, Mountrath
Kelly, John, The Square, Abbeyleix
Keogh, John J., Kilbride, Portarlington
Keogh, Patrick, Rathleigh, Portarlington

INTERNED

Keys, Patrick, Lalors Mills, Portlaoise
Lawler, Patrick, The Mall, Portlaoise
Lawler, Michael, Ballickmoyler
Lynch, Edmond, Ballinree, Barrowhouse
Lynch, John T., Ballykineen, Clonaslee
Lynch, Martin, Portlaoise
Maher, James, Stanhope Street, Ballinakill
Maher, Peter, Borris-in-Ossory
Mahon, Peter, Maclone, Rosenallis
Malone, Francis, Market Street, Mountmellick
Malone, Thomas, Clonaghadoo, Mountmellick
Marnell, Michael, Springhill, Borris-in-Ossory
McCormack, Joseph, Portarlington
McDonald, Patrick, Ballycowan
McDonnell, Patrick, Barrowhouse, Ballylinan
McEvoy, Edward, Sunberry, Abbeyleix
McEvoy, John, Kilbride, Portarlington
McEvoy, John, Aughmacart, Rathdowney
McEvoy, Patrick, Kilbride, Portarlington
McEvoy, William, Aughmacart, Rathdowney
McGowan, Charles, Rathleash, Portarlington
McGrath, Martin, Durrow
McGrath, Michael, Glasna, Wolfhill
Miller, James, Mountrath
Muldowney, Myles, Church Street, Ballinakill
Mullally, Joseph, Stradbally
Murphy, Garrett, Luggacurran
Nolan, —, Portarlington
O'Connor, Michael, The Courthouse, Stradbally
O'Connor, Richard, Portarlington
O'Higgins, Brian, Stradbally
O'Higgins, Thomas F., Stradbally
O'Dea, William, Borris-in-Ossory
O'Riordan, Denis, Mountrath

O'Rourke, Timothy, Dublin Road, Portlaoise
O'Toole, John, Stradbally
Pender, Daniel, Killeshin
Pender, Patrick, Oldleigh, Ballickmoyler
Phelan, Thomas, Whitefields, Killinure, Mountrath
Quigley, Laurence, Killeshin, Ballickmoyler
Ramsbottom, P. J., Maryborough
Rigney, Thomas, Cremorgan, Timahoe
Reid, Hubert, Cappabeg
Revan, Denis, Borris-in-Ossory
Rock, Edward, Forge Street, Mountmellick
Scully, Henry, Mountmellick
Scully, James, Mountmellick
Scully, Patrick, Portarlington
Scully, Richard, Portarlington
Spooner, William, Bordwell, Clough
Sullivan, John, Sweetview, Abbeyleix
Tarrant, Edward, Castletown
Treacy, P. J., Mountrath
Troy, Daniel, Clonaslee
Tuttle, Seán, Stradbally
Tynan, Thomas, Ballybrittas
Tynan, William, Ballybrittas
Walsh, Seamus, Portlaoise
Whelan, Jeremiah, Sentry Hill, Borris-in-Ossory

Leitrim
Armstrong, Peter, Anaghboy, Carrick
Brady, Owen, Drumhallow, Clune
Byrne, Patrick, Manorhamilton
Conifry, Matthew, Drumshanbo
Conifry, Thomas, Doonera, Mohill
Cooper, Thomas, Manorhamilton
Costello, Patrick, Drumshanbo

INTERNED

Donohue, John, Carrigallen
Duffy, James, Cornguagh, Mohill, Drumshanbo
Duignan, Peter, Probagh, Ballinamore
Farrell, James, Meehagh, Drumod
Foley, Andrew, Beagh, Garvagh
Fox, James, Manorhamilton
Gaffney, Hugh, Glencar
Gaffney, John, Ballinamore
Gallagher, James, Carrownoona, Largydonnell
Gibblin, Anthony, Clogher
Gilroy, Thomas, Lismannagh, Drumsna
Gordon, Frank, Gurteen, Glencar
Greenan, James, Corlough, Foxfield
Guiheen, Frank, Stabraggan, Drumshanbo
Heary, Patrick, Fenagh
Hunt, Jack, Rinnacurran, Carrick-on-Shannon
Keaveny, Patrick, Corratymore, Dromahair
Keiran, John, Aughavas
Kerrigan, John, Glencar
Kiernan, Patrick, Carrigallen
Leyland, Joseph, Leitrim town
Maguire, Bernard, Glenfarne
Maguire, Hugh, Tullaghan
Maguire, John, Tullaghan
Maguire, Malachy, Tullaghan
Mahon, John Joe, Diffier, Drumshanbo
McBrien, James, Aughavas, Carrigallen
McCabe, Mathew, Aughavas
McCann, James, Gurteen, Glencar
McDonagh, James, Cashel, Cloonlough
McDonagh, John, Cloonlough
McGirl, William, Drumshanbo
McGiveny, Thomas, Mullagh, Dromahair
McGlynn, Joseph, Tullaghan

McGovern, Hugh, Garadice, Ballinamore
McGovern, Thomas, Garadice, Ballinamore
McGowan, John, Tullaghan
McGowan, Laurence, Tullaghan, Manorhamilton
McIntyre, Peter, Gradoge
McKenna, Thomas, Arigna, Carrick-on-Shannon
McKeon, Francis, Roscunnish, Moher
Mitchell, Joseph, Mohill
Mulvey, James, Drumshanbo
Murphy, Frank, Mohill
Murphy, William, Selton, Mohill
O'Brien, Frank
O'Brien, Henry
O'Brien, Thomas, Largan, Drumshanbo
O'Loughlin, Thomas, Main Street, Manorhamilton
Oats, John, Leitra, Drumshanbo
Quinn, John, Ballinamore
Reynolds, Michael, Corgor
Rooney, Hugh, Glencar
Rooney, Thomas, Glencar
Ryan, Bernard, Cloone
Sexton, Daniel, Gurteen
Shanley, Thomas, Clooneagh, Drumod
Sweeney, Frank, Killaneen, Ballinamore
Sweeney, Frank, Tullyoscar, Ballinamore
Sweeney, Michael, Tullyoscar, Ballinamore
Vaughan, Patrick

Limerick
Ryan, Thomas, Hospital, Knocklong

Longford
Ballesty, Michael, Lisdreenagh, Ardagh
Ballesty, Charles, Lisdreenagh, Ardagh
Baxter, James, Clonbroney, Ballinalee

INTERNED

Brady, James, The Workhouse, Granard
Casserley, James, Ards, Kinagh
Connolly, Joseph, Lismeen, Ballinalee
Croghan, Thomas, Glebe, Cloondara
Cusack, Paul, Granard
Deignan, Peter, Ballinamore
Doherty, John, Rhine, Killeagh
Donohue, Hugh, Ballinalee
Donohue, Michael, Drumeel, Ballinalee
Duffy, Owen, Moygara
Dyre, Hugh, Woodgurteen
Early, James, Ballinalee
Egan, Peter, Ballinahone
Fanning, Peter, Earl Street, Longford
Garrahan, Patrick, Clonbroney
Garrahan, Thomas, Clonbroney
Gavan, James, Ballinahassey, Ballinahone
Harron, Eddie, Gorteen
Haughney, Martin, Craigue
Hogan, Patrick, Rhine, Killeagh
Hopkins, Patrick, Keenagh, Ballymahon
Keenan, Michael, Lamagh, Newtownforbes
Kelleher, Michael, Gortnasillagh, Drumkeeran
Kelly, John, Longford town
Kelly, John, Lisbally
Kelly, William, Killeen, Legan
Kenny, John, Kilmore
Kenny, Patrick, Greevaghmore, Ballymahon
Kenny, William, Greevaghmore, Ballymahon
Kilbride, Bernard, Springtown, Granard
Killian, James J., Currygrane, Edgeworthstown
Leavy, James, Kilnasavogue
Leavy, Michael, Kilnasavogue
Lee, James, Soran, Killoe

APPENDIX II

Lynam, Joseph, Barne, Edgeworthstown
Malervy, James, Castlebrook, Edgeworthstown
McCabe, Felix, Lisnageeragh, Edgeworthstown
McCabe, Michael, Lisbellaw
McGoldrick, Francis, Ballinamore
McGoven, Hugh, Corramahon, Garadice
McGoven, Thomas, Corramahon, Garadice
McGrath, Peter, Drumeel
McManus, Thomas, Drumgort, Ballinamuck
Meehan, William, Mulloghroe
Molloy, Joseph, Edgeworthstown
Mulervy, Patrick, Castlebrook, Moat Farm, Ballinamore
Nedley, Patrick, Dublin Street, Granard
O'Donohue, Laurence, Ballymahon
O'Reilly, Leo, c/o Mrs Quinn, Ardragh, Edgeworthstown
O'Reilly, Michael, Granard
Ryan, Patrick, Listreena, Ardagh
Skelly, Michael, Clonmore, Killashee
Teacy, Charles, Aughacreagh
Turley, Edward, Brack, Ballinahone
Victory, James, Bracklon, Edgeworthstown

Louth
Brennan, James, Chapel Street, Dundalk
Burke, Thomas, 94 Dunlock Street, Drogheda
Carbery, Bernard, Collon
Cassidy, John J., Cloyne, Drumiskin
Conlan, Matthew, Artony
Cummins, Joseph, 3 Railway Terrace, Drogheda
Cunningham, William, Mullatee, Carlingford
Daly, Bernard, Old Hill, Drogheda
Gray, William, Collen
Halpin, John, 2 Stockwell Lane, Drogheda
Hughes, John, As Little, Knockbridge, Dundalk

INTERNED

Keenan, Thomas, 3 Shop Street, Drogheda
Larkin, Patrick, Grange, Carlingford
Martin, Thomas, Bellewstown, Drogheda
McCann, Timothy, Greenore
Minihan, S., Dundalk
Murphy, James, Drogheda
Rogan, James Joseph, Monksland, Mountpleasant, Dundalk

Mayo
Berrane, Michael, Knocknananny, Kilfian
Brennan, Thomas, Charlestown
Burke, Henry, Claremorris
Burke, Thomas, Carragh Castle, Ballyglass
Burke, Thomas, Westport
Burke, William, Drumlong, Newport
Byrne, John J., Kilkelly
Callaghan, Anthony, Bracklagh, Newport
Campbell, Thomas, Swinford
Casey, Martin, Gowlaun, Kilkelly
Caulfield, Daniel, Charlestown
Cleary, Lewis, Ballycroy
Cleary, Peter, Ballycroy
Clinton, James, Shanballyhoe
Cloonan, Patrick, Ballyhaunis
Collins, Thomas, Blakehill, Cong
Comber, William, Ballyhaunis
Connor, Peter, Westport
Conroy, John, The Neale, Ballinrobe
Conroy, Michael, Creevagh, Cong
Cosgrove, P., Foxford
Cosgrove, Patrick, Swinford
Crowley, John, Ballycastle
Cuddy, J., Ballinrobe
Daly, John, Ballycroy

APPENDIX II

Daly, William, Moynalty
Derrig, Thomas, Westport
Donnellan, Patrick, Ballyhaunis
Doran, Edward, Carralabinn, Ballina
Dunleavy, Patrick, Foxford
Dunleavy, Patrick, Sonvelaun, Kilkelly
Egan, James, Leccarow, Charlestown
Faragher, P., Ballinrobe
Feerick, Michael, Creevagh, Cong
Fergus, Joseph, Cahir, Louisburgh
Fergus, William, Cullin
Ferran, Francis P., Foxford
Finn, J., Ballyhaunis
Fitzgerald, Michael, Charlestown
Fitzgerald, Thomas P., Swinford
Flynn, Thomas, Ballinrobe
Foley, William, Carragh Castle
Fox, Mark, Cong
Foy, Peter, Cong
Gallagher, Michael, Currane, Achill
Gaughan, Martin, Foxford
Gavan, Charles, Mill Street, Westport
Gavan, John, Kilmeena, Westport
Gogan, Martin, Foxford
Griffin, John, Ballyhaunis
Griffin, John, Mayfield, Claremorris
Hanley, John, Ballygar
Harney, Thomas, Toureen, Louisburg
Heavy, Thomas, Kiltimagh
Hennelly, John, Cloongowla, Ballinrobe
Heraty, Richard, Brownstown, Ballinrobe
Higgins, John, Cong
Higgins, Patrick, Cloonygowan, Foxford
Huddy, John, Creevagh, Cong

INTERNED

Hynes, Joseph, Ballyglass, Claremorris
Hynes, Michael Joe, Coolcon, Ballyglass
Jordan, John, Cross Strand
Jordan, Michael, Main Street, Ballinrobe
Jordan, Seán P., Ballyhaunis
Joyce, Martin, Coonard, Hollymount
Joyce, William, Clogher, Westport
Keady, Patrick, The Neal, Ballinrobe
Keady, Thomas, Carrowmore, Ballinrobe
Kelly, Patrick, Ballyhaunis
Kelly, Peter, Ardkeel, Hollymount
Kelly, Peter, Ballinrobe
Kelly, Peter, Peter Street, Westport
Kettrick, Patrick, Lucan Street, Castlebar
Kilroy, John, Kilmenagh, Newport
Kissane, Thomas, Charlestown
Lamb, Martin, Rinbrack, Swinford
Langan, Richard, Ballyglass, Claremorris
Leydon, John, Spiddal
Loftus, Patrick, Bonniconlon, Ballina
Lynagh, Anthony, The Neale, Ballinrobe
Lynch, William, Abbey, Loughrea
Lyons, Hubert, Ballyhaunis
Mackin, James, Brownstown
Maguire, John, Barrackhill, Newport
Malone, Patrick, Leccarrow, Hollymount
Mannion, Edward, Brownstown, Ballinrobe
Maughan, John, Hollymount
May, James, Ballinamona, The Neale
McBride, Joe, Westport
McDermott, William, Ballinrobe
McHugh, Michael, New Antrim Street, Castlebar
McLoughlin, J., Doon
McLoughlin, Peter, Drummin, Westport

APPENDIX II

McLoughlin, Thomas, Westport
McMahon, James, Westport
McMahon, —, Spencer Street, Castlebar
McNamara, Anthony, Doagh, Achill
McNulty, Michael, Cloondaff, Glenhest, Newport
McNulty, Patrick, Pleasanthill, Castlebar
Monaghan, John, Aughness, Ballycroy
Moran, Laurence, Loughloon, Westport
Moran, Patrick, Ballinrobe
Moran, William, Main Street, Foxford
Muldowney, Andrew, Tullinacurra, Swinford
Mullee, Thomas, Ballyhaunis
Mullen, Thomas, Roemore, Breaffy
Mullens, Maurice, Aughamore
Mullins, Michael, Ballyhaunis
Murphy, Martin, Ballinrobe
Murphy, Michael, Ballinrobe
Murphy, Michael, Billypark, Cross
Murphy, Thomas, Belmullet
Needham, James, Cross, Killeen, Louisburgh
Needham, Patrick, Cuilleen, Kilsallagh
Newcombe, Thomas, Cashel, Carramore, Ballina
O'Boyle, Francis, Islandeady
O'Brien, Patrick, Knock
O'Connor, P., Loughloon, Westport
O'Doherty, Frederick, Charlestown
Prendergast, P. J., Louisburgh
Prendergast, Richard, Drummin, Claremorris
Prendergast, Thomas, Louisburgh
Rattigan, Michael, Ballindine
Reid, Hubert, Aughagower
Reidy, Thomas
Rodgers, J., Ballyhaunis
Ronan, Francis, Allen Street, Ballina

INTERNED

Ruttledge, P. J., Ballina
Sammon, James, Louisburgh
Sammon, John, Carrowmore, Louisburgh
Sammon, Thomas, Carrowmore, Louisburgh
Sheridan, Edward, Ballinrobe
Sheridan, H. W., Castlebar
Sheridan, Martin, Ballinrobe
Shouldice, John F., Ballaghaderreen
Skelly, Michael, Swinford
Stanton, Edward, Cloonoona, Claremorris
Tunney, Michael, Cushlough, Westport
Tunney, Patrick, Cushlough, Westport
Turney, Michael, Ballinrobe
Tuohy, Peter, Islandeady
Waldron, Patrick, Abbey Street, Ballyhaunis
Waldron, Peadar, Cong

Meath

Blake, Patrick, Dunshaughlin
Byrne, Charles, Sylvan Park, Kells
Carey, Patrick, Knockshangan, Athboy
Connell, John, Lowstown
Crotty, Michael, Old Cornmarket, Navan
Curran, James, Avondale, Moynalty
Dardis, John, Kells
Durr, Hugh, Trimgate, Navan
Farrelly, Michael, Cloongowna, Kells
Govern, Thomas, Moynalty
Grehan, Robert, Castlejordan
Hart, John Joseph, 38 St Finian Terrace, Navan
Hayes, John, Drumbaragh, Kells
Kelly, Hugh, Flaxtown, Athboy
Kelly, James, Tankardstown, Clonalvy
Keogh, John, Smithstown, Oldcastle

Ledwidge, Patrick, Ballinderrin, Enfield
Lynch, Patrick, Newcastle, Moynalty, Kells
Lynch, Peter, Newcastle, Moynalty, Kells
Mallin, Thomas, Ferganstown, Navan
Masterson, John, Robinstown, Navan
McCormack, John, Pelletstown, Drumree
McDonald, Thomas, Stonefield House, Ballinlough
O'Connor, George, Kells
O'Connor, Peter, Petersville, Moynalty
Patterson, Patrick, Moyrath, Kildalkey
Plunkett, George, Picklestone, Kildalkey
Quinn, Daniel, Flourhill, Navan
Reilly, John, Feagh, Moynalty
Russell, Thomas, Moynalty
Sheridan, Harry, Oldcastle
Tevlin, Philip, Dulane, Kells
Tormey, David
Waters, Patrick, Ballygrey, Ballinlough

Monaghan
Connor, Peter, Carrickmacross
Hand, Michael, Clones
Hart, John, Newbliss
Little, John, Clare, Clones
Macklin, James, Braddocks, Tullycorbet
Martin, Francis, Carrickmacross
McCabe, Edward, Carrickmacross
McDonnell, Thomas, Clones
McGoldrick, Patrick, Clones
McKenna, Frank, Gloghfin, Emyvale
McKenna, John, Newbliss
McMahon, Peter, Castleblaney
McPhilips, James, Smithboro, Clones
Mulligan, Thomas, Drumsheeny, Stranooden

INTERNED

Murphy, James, Annaghlough, Castleshane
O'Connor, Thomas, Clontibret
O'Neill, Charles, Scotstown
Rafferty, Hugh, Corbally
Smyth, Joseph, Moys, Clontibret

Offaly (King's Co.)
Barry, John (Seán), Earl Street, Tullamore
Bergin, Michael, Derrykeel, Birr
Bergin, Patrick, Derrykeel, Birr
Berry, Thomas, Tullamore
Bracken, Michael, Sragh, Tullamore
Bracken, Peter, Sragh, Tullamore
Bracken, Peter, 8 High Street, Tullamore
Brien, Matthew, Ballinvally, Killeigh
Byrne, Barty, Croghan, Phillipstown
Carroll, Bernard, Boherbree, Edenderry
Carroll, John, Cadamstown
Carroll, Joseph, Cadamstown
Claffey, John, Tully
Claffey, Frank, Baddenmore, Belmont
Claffey, Patrick, Baddenmore, Belmont
Clavin, Nicholas, Derries, Raheen
Colgan, Michael, Cloghan
Conroy, James, Ross, Screggan
Conroy, Patrick, Ferbane
Conway, Richard, Killinure, Kinnitty
Cooke, Michael, Ballinvalley, Killeigh
Cooke, Patrick, Ballingar, Tullamore
Corcoran, Michael, Aghadonagh, Rahan
Cordial, William, Kinnity
Corrigan, Hugh, Clareen, Birr
Corrigan, Patrick, Killinure, Birr
Coughlan, James, Balliline, Belmont

APPENDIX II

Coughlan, John, Belmont, Banna
Coughlan, Martin, Balliline, Belmont
Cummins, Denis, Rathlyon, Mount Bolus
Cummins, Joseph, Ballycowan, Tullamore
Cummins, Michael, Bannagher
Daly, John, Newtown, Killeigh, Tullamore
Daly, Patrick, Charleville Parade, Tullamore
Deegan, John, Kilcappagh
Delahunt, John, Crinkill
Delahunty, James, Cadamstown, Birr
Delahunty, John, Birr
Diagan, Patrick, Ballycumber
Dillon, John, Birr
Dolan, Patrick, Noggusboy, Gallen
Donegan, James, Philipstown
Donegan, John, Walsh Island
Donegan, Michael, Walsh Island
Donnelly, Thomas, Cadamstown
Doody, John (Seán), Earl Street, Tullamore
Dooley, John, Killeenmore, Killeigh
Doyle, Denis, Philipstown
Dunne, William, Bridge House, Tullamore
Egan, James, Bridge House, Henry Street, Tullamore
Egan, Michael, Spring Park, Ballycumber
Egan, Patrick, Ferbane
Ennis, Michael, Rhode
Ennis, Patrick, Rhode Bridge, Edenderry
Feehan, Henry 'Harry', Tullamore
Feehan, William, Tullamore
Feeny, Maurice, Ferbane
Finlay, Patrick, Tullamore
Finlay, Thomas, Bracklin, Philipstown
Finley, Patrick, Killeenmore, Killeigh
Fitzpatrick, William, Earl Street, Tullamore

INTERNED

Foley, Michael P., Edenderry & Talbot Street, Dublin
Fox, Michael, Five Alley, Eglish
Fox, Patrick, Five Alley, Eglish
Fox, Thady, Laught, Clonaghadoo
Fox, William, Five Alley, Eglish
Gallagher, Michael, Tullamore
Galvin, John, Ardan, Tullamore
Garrahan, James, Cloghan
Garrahy, James, Birr
Graham, Robert, Edenderry
Grogan, John, Killourney, Cloghan
Grogan, Joseph, Killourney, Cloghan
Grogan, Kieran, Killinure, Killyon
Grogan, Patrick, Killinure, Birr
Guinan, Timothy, Clareen, Birr
Hernon, Joseph, Elye House, Clareen, Birr
Hernon, Joseph W., Coyle, Kinnitty
Hogan, James, O'Molloy Street (Pensioners Row), Tullamore
Horan, Cornelius, Derryclose
Horan, John, Coolnacreese, Cadamstown, Birr
Horan, Thomas, Cadamstown
Hyland, Denis, Cloneygowan
Hynes, John, Banagher
Jennings, Kieran, Killinure, Birr
Jones, Christopher, Tubberdaly, Rhode
Kane, James, Philipstown
Kelly, Denis, Killellery, Geashill
Kelly, James, 2 High Street, Tullamore
Kelly, William, Puttaghan, Tullamore
Kennedy, Thomas, Oratory Lane, Clara
Keys, Christy, Gageborough
Keys, Daniel, Ross, Screggan, Tullamore
Killeavy, John, William Street, Tullamore
Larkin, Michael, Edenderry

APPENDIX II

Lee, Joseph, Barrack Street, Tullamore
Lennon, John, Killeenmore, Killeagh
Longworth, James, O'Connell Street, Tullamore
Longworth, John, O'Connell Street, Tullamore
Lynam, Daniel, Tullamore
Lyons, James, Brackagh
Lyons, Michael, Brackagh
Mahon, Patrick, Mountbolus, Cooldarragh
McEvoy, John, Kilcooney
McGoven, Patrick, Cappincur, Tullamore
McIntyre, Martin, Galross, Cloghan
McRedmond, John, Cadamstown
Mitchell, John, Raddocks Lane, Tullamore
Molloy, Michael, Ballinree, Killyon, Birr
Mooney, Patrick, Killeigh
Mooney, William, Crow Street, Tullamore
Mulleen, Thomas, Charleville Square, Tullamore
Murray, Michael, Bannagher
Neville, Jeremiah, Lynally, Tullamore
Neville, Joseph, Lynally, Tullamore
Neville, Vincent, Lynally, Tullamore
Nolan, Patrick, Gurteen, Killeigh
O'Brien, Daniel, Ballinamore, Tullamore
O'Brien, Patrick, Tullamore
O'Connor, Richard, Tubberdaly, Rhode
O'Dea, William, Birr
Pender, Denis, Chapel Street, Tullamore
Pidgeon, Charles, Bracklin, Ballycommon
Pidgeon, Thomas, Bracklin, Ballycommon
Pidgeon, William, Bracklin, Ballycommon
Quinn, Patrick, Walsh Island
Ravenhill, Daniel, Ballycallaghan, Durrow
Ravenhill, John, Ballycallaghan, Durrow
Ravenhill, Patrick, Ballycallaghan, Durrow

INTERNED

Scully, James, Killeigh
Scully, John, Kilmore, Bluebell, Tullamore
Scully, William, Kilmore, Bluebell, Tullamore
Smyth, Michael, Cloghanhill
Spain, John, Clontarf Road, Tullamore
Sutton, John, Grattan House, Edenderry
Talbot, John, Barrack Street, Tullamore
Temple, Kieran, Shannon Harbour
Tobin, William, Gurteen, Killeigh
Walker, Stephen, Bannagher
Walsh, Denis, Barrack Street, Tullamore
Whelan, Michael, O'Connell Street, Tullamore
Whelan, Patrick, Cappincur, Tullamore

Roscommon
Appleby, Patrick, Donaldhill
Barry, Paddy, Knockvicar, Boyle
Beirne, James, Ballyroddy, Elphin
Beirne, Joseph, Shankill, Elphin
Beirne, Patrick, Clooncunny, Elphin
Brahenry, Michael, Portun
Brennan, James, Clooncraff, Ballymurray
Brennan, Michael, Clooncraff, Ballymurray
Burke, James, Kilgrave, Rooskey
Burke, Patrick, Kilgrave, Rooskey
Butler, Laurence, Curry, Curraghboy
Butler, Luke, Killunod
Campion, James, Brackloon, Castlerea
Caulfield, Timothy, Cemetery Lodge, Arm Castle, Castlerea
Compton, Henry, Kilgefin
Corr, Edmund A., Durham House, Derrane
Corr, Richard, Corrodine, Ballinmacurley
Cosgrove, George, 23 St Columbus, Athlone
Coyne, Bernard, Lisabrack, Curraghboy

APPENDIX II

Cullen, John, Tullynaha, Arigna
Dillon, John, Cloonfree, Strokestown
Dockery, William, Drumlish, Drummullan, Elphin
Doorley, James J., Castle Street, Roscommon
Doorley, Patrick, Castle Street, Roscommon
Doyle, John, Knockvicar, Boyle
Dyre, Patrick, Main Street, Castlerea
Egan, Edward, Curraghboy, Brideswell
Egan, John, Tunnymuck
Fallon, Patrick, Lurgan, Elphin
Farrell, James, Corramagrine, Whitehall, Tarmonbarry
Farrell, Patrick, Ballyleague, Lanesboro
Farrell, Peter, Gardenstown, Lanesboro
Feely, Henry, Greatmeadow, Boyle
Feely, James, Elphin Street, Boyle
Feeny, Patrick, Strokestown
Ford, Patrick, Moore, Castlerea
Forsythe, John, Ballaghaderreen
Galvin, Joe, Cloonlaughnan, Mount Talbot
Hannon, William, Bealnamulla
Hayden, Laurence, Kilteevan
Keaveny, Andrew, Aghadrestan, Loughglynn
Keigher, John, Arigna
Kelly, John, Cloonelt, Ballinalough
Kelly, Michael, Castlerea
Kelly, Patrick, Culleen, Lecarrow
Killalea, Martin, Doon, Boyle
King, James, Shankill, Elphin
King, Robert, Figh, Lisacul
Larkin, Joseph, Ardmore, Donamore
Larkin, Patrick, Grange
Lenehan, George, Carrownagullagh, Strokestown
Lenehan, John, Carrowreagh, Elphin
Lynch, Patrick, Church Street, Boyle

INTERNED

Mahon, Patrick, Cloonan, Castlerea
Mannion, Denis, Barry Beg, The Hill of Berries
Mannion, Thomas, Barry Beg, The Hill of Berries
Martin, Charles, Ballyfarnham
McDermott, Peter, Killygarry
McDonnell, James, Curraghboy, Lurgan
McGovern, Joseph, Emlagh, Ballintubber
McGrath, John, Lurgan, Elphin
McKenna, Thomas, Giddaun, Arigna
McNamara, Patrick, Culliagh, Strokestown
Mee, Richard, Curry, Curraghboy
Moran, Thomas, Crossna, Boyle
Mullaney, William, Culleenaghamore, Kilglass
Mullooly, Patrick, Luggs, Kiltrustan
Mulrenin, James, Creevy Bridge, Lisacul
Murphy, Hubert, St John's, Knockcroghery
Murray, Patrick, Manor, Tulsk
Murray, Philip, Elphin Street, Boyle
Nangle, Brian, Mongagh, Curraghroe
Neary, Michael, Cloonacool
Noone, Michael, Croghan, Boyle
O'Callaghan, Michael, Cloonboniffe, Castlerea
O'Connell, Patrick, Elphin
O'Connor, Martin, Strokestown
Pryall, John, Springfield, Elphin
Regan, Patrick, Leiterra House, Keadue
Roddy, Tom, Creevy, Lisacul, Ballaghaderreen
Rogers, James, Loughlin, Castlerea
Rogers, Joseph, Loughlin, Castlerea
Rogers, Patrick, Rathcrogan, Mantua
Tennant, Patrick, Lisnahoon, Knockcroghery
Tracey, Patrick, Ballinturly
Treacy, Francis, Ratenagh, Strokestown

APPENDIX II

Turnan, Patrick, Kilrooskey
Waldron, Thomas, Moor, Castlerea

Sligo
Alcock, Bert, Cloonamona, Ballymoate
Barrett, Thomas, Skreen, Toberpatrick
Bradley, Patrick, Glencar
Brennan, Luke, Rathscanlon, Tuppercurry
Carroll, Michael, Seaview, Gregg
Conlan, Patrick, Flagfield, Gerva
Conlan, Thomas, Flagfield, Gerva
Connolly, Roger, Kiltykere, Grange
Costello, John, Carrowdurney, Geevagh
Costello, John, St James's Well, Sligo
Costello, Joseph, Carrowdurney, Geevagh
Crean, Andrew, Ballyogan, Culleens
Danagher, Michael, Ballindoon, Riverstown
Devine, Thomas, Castlegall
Doocy, Andrew, Adelaide Street, Sligo town
Dowd, Martin, Drumacool, Riverstown
Dyer, Patrick
Feeny, Dominic, Castlegarran
Flynn, Augustus, Masreagh, Skreen
Gibson, James, Grangebeg
Gibson, John, Annaglass, Grange
Gibson, Thomas, Grangebeg
Gillen, James, Ballinfull
Gillen, Thomas, Grangebeg, Skreen
Gillen, Thomas, Skreen
Gilmartin, Peter, Gortnaleck
Gingan, Thomas, Masreagh
Gorevan, Thomas, Castlegarran
Jordan, Michael, Easkey
Kearns, Michael, Dunflin

INTERNED

Kelly, John, Lisbaleely, Gurteen
Kelly, Thomas, Lisbaleely, Gurteen
Kilcullen, Anthony, Cloonkeelaun
Kilcullen, Edward, Inniscrone
Kilgannon, Thaddeus, Tawnatruffaun, Drumore West
Kivlehan, Francis, Creggyconnell, Rosses Point
Lavin, John, Culfadda
Leonard, Michael, Owenbeg, Ballina
Marren, John, Carroweaden, Coolaney
McCabe, Alex, Keash, Ballymote
McCann, Martin, Carrowhubbock
McCarrick, Thomas, Tubbercurry
McGettrick, Bertie, Cluid, Ballymote
McManus, Bernard, Geeva
McManus, Michael, Coolmeen, Geeva
Moffitt, Edward, Gortnaleck
Mulcahy, Denis, Oakfield Road, Sligo town
Mullaney, James, Cloonticarn, Gurteen
Murren, Charles, Annaghcor, Castlebaldwin
Neary, Michael, Cloonacool, Tubbercurry
O'Donnell, Michael, Cloonacool, Tubbercurry
Oats, Michael, Castlegarran
Queenan, James, Moygara
Rogan, Martin, Ballymoneen, Castle Connor
Taheny, Michael, Castlebaldwin
Tansey, Joseph, Gurteen Cross, Ballymote
Tuffy, Denis, Lackan, Kilglass
Tuffy, Thomas, Culleens
Tully, James, Owenbeg, Easkey
Wimsey, Thomas, Gurteen, Cuilmore
Young, Harry, Clooneen, Drumcliff

Tipperary
Hough, Michael James, Davis Street, Tipperary

Luddy, W., Tipperary
O'Keefe, Daniel, Glenough, Hollyford

Tyrone
Carney, Thomas, Fintona
Cassidy, John, Kilbrackey, Dungannon
Clark, Peter, Gorteen
Hernon, Francis, Garvagh, Donaghmore
Leonard, Thomas, Charlemont Street, Dungannon
McCann, Patrick, Donaghmore
McShane, Patrick, Newchurch Rock
Murphy, Arthur, Donaghmore
Rice, Edward, Inniskeen, Clogher

Westmeath
Berry, Thomas, Athlone
Boyne, John, Cortuloe, Rochfortbridge, Mullingar
Bracken, Patrick, Kinnegad
Burke, David, Mullingar
Byrne, E., Main Street, Delvin
Byrne, Hugh, Athlone
Coke, George, Lake View Terrace, Athlone
Colgan, Joseph, Comagh Road, Kilbeggan
Concannon, Michael, Coosan, Athlone
Conlon, John, Creeve, Mount Temple
Cosgrove, George, Columbus Terrace, Athlone
Cunningham, James, Castlepollard
Cunningham, Michael, Bealin, Moate
Daly, David, Faheran, Moate
Daly, James, Clonoecan, Mount Temple
Davitt, James, Castlepollard
Donohue, Andrew, Mount Temple, Moate
Doolan, James, Ballykeenan, Athlone
Dowling, Edward, Carricknaughton, Athlone
Duffy, Joseph, Milltownpass, Mullingar

INTERNED

Edwards, Thomas, Tinamuck, Moate
Egan, Thomas, Tullymoat
Eggenton, Patrick, Brownstown, Collinstown
Elliot, John, Killamore
Fagan, Joseph, Killshallow, Coole
Fagan, Patrick, Killshallow, Coole
Fleming, Peter, Tinamuck, Moate
Flynn, Christopher, Glenidan, Castlepollard
Flynn, Éamonn, Kinnegad
Flynn, James, Glenidan, Castlepollard
Flynn, Owen, Ankerland, Fore
Gaffey, Michael, Blyry, Athlone
Gavigan, John J., Streete, Coole
Geraghty, William, Ballymore
Ginnell, Michael, Corbally, Castlepollard
Grennan, Simon, Moynore
Guilfoyle, James, Kilbeggan
Heffernan, Edward, Blackhill, Dublin Road, Kilbeggan
Hogan, John, Moate
Horan, Michael, St Loman's Terrace, Mullingar
Hynes, James, 1 Military Road, Mullingar
Johnston, James, Rockfield, Moate
Johnston, William, Tinamuck, Moate
Judge, Francis, Tyrellspass
Kearney, Dan, Law Street, Ballymore
Kearney, Patrick, Law Street, Ballymore
Kearney, Thomas, Law Street, Ballymore
Langan, John, Ardnaglue, Kilbeggan
Lennon, Thomas, 58 Earl Street, Mullingar
Leonard, Thomas, Athlone
Mahon, Michael, Ballinakill, Moate
Malone, John Joe, Ballinlassy, Ballinahown
Manning, Denis, The Berries, Athlone
McAuley, Philip, Killomenaghan, Tubbrit

APPENDIX II

McCormack, James, Kilbeggan
McCormack, James, Tonlegee, Ballymahon
McCormack, Michael, Ardboro, Drumraney
McCormack, Patrick, Ardboro, Drumraney
McCoy, Michael, Glenmore, Mullingar
McEllin, William, Glasson
McGuinness, Frank, Kilbeggan
McKenna, James, Kilbeggan
McQuinn, John, Milltown, Castlepollard
Molloy, Martin, Rockfield, Moate
Moore, Patrick, Williamstown
Mulvehill, Thomas, Coosan, Athlone
Nester, Thomas, Athlone
O'Brien, Arthur, Baylin, Athlone
O'Brien, Cornelius, Keenans Hotel, Mardyke Street, Athlone
O'Byrne, Conor, Ballynacargy
O'Reilly, Patrick, Crookedwood, Mullingar
Quinn, Thomas, Shinglass, Ballymore
Ramsey, Frank, Ballybeg, Athlone
Ramsey, John, Ballybeg, Athlone
Rattigan, John, 6 Patrick Street, Athlone
Rooney, William, Main Street, Delvin
Salmon, John, Cummerstown
Savage, James, Bishopstown
Tormey, David, Moate
Tully, John, Athlone
White, James, Rashina, Ballinahown, Athlone

Wexford
Clince, John, Wexford Street, Gorey
McCann, Andrew, Ballinamona, Gorey
Vize, Joe, Wexford town

Wicklow
Brien, James, 4 Elmgrove Terrace, Bray

INTERNED

Brien, Patrick, 4 Elmgrove Terrace, Bray
Burke, William, Donard
Byrne, Garrett, Glenealy
Byrne, John, Tinahely
Cleary, William, Arklow
Condren, John, Kilquiggan
Cullen, Christopher, Donard
Deering, Joseph, Milltown, Dunlavin
Donnelly, Thomas, Clonmore
Doran, Patrick, Blessington
Doyle, Peter, Knockinderragh
English, Henry, Dunlavin
Frith, Paul, Arklow
Grennan, John, Dunlavin
Harte, J., Bray
Hoey, John, 33 Duncan Avenue, Bray
Kavanagh, John, 61 Main Street, Arklow
Kearns, Luke, Rathvilly
Kearns, Patrick, Rathvilly
Keogh, Thomas, Eadestown, Stratford-on-Slaney
Lawler, John P., Dunlavin
Lee, Hugh, Mill Lane, Bray
Leggett, Frank, 9 Ravenswell Road, Bray
Martin, John, 24 Dargan Street, Bray
Martin, Thomas, 34 Dargan Street, Bray
McCann, John, 3 Castle Terrace, Bray
Morrissey, Jeremiah, Main Street, Rathdrum
Mulvey, Stephen, 6 Bruces Yard, Bray
Murphy, William, Clonmore
O'Brien, John, 23 Old Chapel Ground, Arklow
O'Toole, James, 3 Brennan Parade, Bray
Porter, James J., Ballinacooley, Glenealy
Redmond, M., Killenure
Reilly, Patrick, 15 Upper Connell's Lane, Arklow

Stankard, Martin, 41 Ferrybank, Arklow
Sutton, Thomas, 2 Bruces Terrace, Bray
Whelan, Daniel, Brittas, Manor Kilbride

England
Bowden, John, 11 Menai Street, Liverpool
Clarke, Patrick, 22 Virgil Street, Bootle, Liverpool
Coghlan, Patrick, 42 Woodsworth Street, Bootle, Liverpool
Delaney, Patrick, Shaftesbury Road, Ravenscourt Park, London & 6 Ardbrugh Road, Dalkey, Co. Dublin
Faughan, Thomas, 44 Mayfield Road, Dechally Range, Manchester
Geraghty, William, 21 Wavertree Road, Liverpool
Hayes, James, 8 Loraine Road, Holloway, London
Kerr, Thomas, 6 Florida Street, Bootle, Liverpool
Lanagan, Stephen, 432 Stanley Road, Bootle, Liverpool
Murphy, Fintan, 16 Effra Road, Brixton, London
Murphy, William, Old Trafford, Manchester
O'Leary, Denis, 9 Townsend Street, Liverpool
O'Leary, Michael (Ó Laoghaire, Micheál), 9 Townsend Street, Liverpool

No address or further information given
Butler, John
Connolly, Columbkille
Crowley, D.
Dunne, Christopher (Kildare/Offaly)
Harrold, Andy
Hynes, B.
McCaul, S.
O'Dwyer
O'Grady
O'Kane, Hugh
Shaughnessy, Joe

APPENDIX III
ESCAPERS FROM THE RATH CAMP, 9 SEPTEMBER 1921

Details of the known escapers.

C. S. 'Todd' Andrews, Terenure, Dublin. In March 1917, when he was fifteen, he joined Rathfarnham Company, Irish Volunteers. Arrested in April 1920, he was released after ten days' hunger strike; arrested again in March 1921. He was held in Arbour Hill Prison before being transferred to the Rath Camp.

John Barry, Earl Street, Tullamore, Co. Offaly. As a youth he spent three months in custody for singing a seditious song and lost his job in the post office service. In Belfast Gaol, aged nineteen, he joined a hunger strike. He was OC Offaly Brigade flying column when arrested in Ballydaly, Tullamore.

Patrick 'Paddy' Barry, Knockvicar, Boyle, Co. Roscommon. [No further details available.]

Seán Beaumont, 1 Clare Street, Dublin. A native of Mayo and a lecturer/teacher in Irish and maths, he was a prominent member of the Gaelic League.

Patrick 'Pat' Beirne, Clooncunny, Strokestown, Co. Roscommon. Adjutant for the 2nd Battalion, North Roscommon. He was arrested in a military swoop on 27 January 1921 and held at Boyle and Athlone Military Barracks before being transferred to the Rath Camp.

Jim Brady, Bailieboro, Co. Cavan. A member of 4th Battalion, North Roscommon Brigade. A miner by trade, he began the digging of the 'Tullamore Tunnel'.

APPENDIX III

Henry 'Harry' Burke, Claremorris, Co. Mayo. Commandant, South Mayo Brigade. Arrested in 1921, he was taken first to Galway Gaol, where he was OC republican prisoners, and then to internment in the Rath Camp.

Bernard Byrne. He was a member of the North King Street, Church Street and Four Courts garrisons in Easter Week 1916. Captured by Auxiliaries at Blackhall, Dublin, in April 1921, when he was a member of the Active Service Unit, Dublin Brigade. He was a brother of Charles Byrne, who also escaped.

Charles Byrne, captain of D Company, 1st Battalion, Dublin Brigade. He was in the garrisons of North King Street, Church Street and the Four Courts during Easter Week 1916. Captured by Auxiliaries at Blackhall, Dublin, in April 1921.

Hugh Byrne, Athlone, Co. Westmeath and Dublin. Adjutant 3rd Battalion, Dublin Brigade.

Tom Byrne, Carrickmacross, Co. Monaghan and Dublin. A veteran of Easter Week, when he led fourteen Kildare Volunteers to Dublin. He was interned in Brixton Prison, London, for five months in 1919. Byrne was commandant of the 1st Battalion, Dublin Brigade when he was arrested.

Henry Compton, Kilgefin, Co. Roscommon. A member of the 3rd Battalion South Roscommon Brigade's flying column and served as OC Kilgefin Company.

Connolly, Columbkille. [No further details available.]

Isaiah Conroy, Dublin. He joined E Company, 2nd Battalion, Dublin Brigade in early 1917. Arrested in January 1921.

John 'Jack' Conroy, The Neale, Ballinrobe, Co. Mayo. A commandant in South Mayo.

David Daly, Faheran, Moate, Co. Westmeath. He joined the Irish Volunteers in 1914 and the IRB four years later, becoming chief organiser of the IRB and Volunteers in the Athlone area. He was

275

OC 1st Battalion, Athlone Brigade and was arrested in April 1921 in Moate, Co. Westmeath.

Patrick Leo 'Paddy' Darcy, 'Woodside', Dalkey, Co. Dublin. A Volunteer with the 3rd Battalion, Dublin Brigade, he was a member of the Jacob's Biscuit Factory garrison during Easter Week 1916, when he was seventeen. He was subsequently interned at Frongoch. Arrested in May 1921, he was held in Dublin Castle, Kilmainham Gaol and Arbour Hill before being transferred to the Rath Camp.

John Francis 'Seán' Doody, Earl Street, Tullamore. He was a member of Tullamore Company and subsequently served with No. 1 Offaly Brigade flying column. He was arrested on 6 March 1921.

James 'Jim' Farrell, Corramagrine, Whitehall, Tarmonbarry, Co. Roscommon. Captain of D Company, 3rd Battalion, North Roscommon Brigade. He was arrested in February 1921 and subsequently sent to the Curragh.

Peter C. Feeney, Kinvara, Co. Galway. A Volunteer with Kinvara Company whose family home was burned down by crown forces in September 1920.

Michael 'Miko' Fleming, Clarinbridge, Co. Galway. He was a Volunteer with Clarinbridge Company. Arrested after the 1916 Rising and sentenced to twelve months' imprisonment, he was released in 1917. He was subsequently rearrested and sentenced to two years' imprisonment. While in Mountjoy Gaol he took part in the hunger strike that resulted in the death of Thomas Ashe. He later served time in Dundalk Gaol, and after his release was arrested once again, in November 1920.

Patrick 'Paddy' Fleming, Clarinbridge, Co. Galway. A Volunteer with Clarinbridge Company, he mobilised with the Galway Volunteers at Easter 1916. He was interned in Richmond Barracks, Dublin

APPENDIX III

and subsequently in Wakefield Prison in England and Frongoch. He was arrested in November 1920.

Éamonn Flynn, Kinnegad, Co. Westmeath. [No further details available.]

Myles Ford, Rathgar Road, Rathmines, Dublin. He was wounded in an attack on a military lorry at Rathmines church. A British officer was wounded in the attack, and Ford and another Volunteer, Joseph Devoy, were also injured. They were transferred to King George V Hospital. On his recovery, Ford was transferred to the Rath Camp.

Joseph 'Joe' Galvin, Cloonlaughnan, Mount Talbot, Co. Roscommon. An IRB member and OC Four Roads Company, Roscommon Brigade. Arrested in March 1921, he was held at Roscommon Jail and Athlone Barracks before being transferred to the Curragh.

Charles 'Charlie' Gavan, Mill Street, Westport, Co. Mayo. A member of Westport Na Fianna Éireann, he was jailed in 1918 for riotous behaviour, serving six months in Belfast Gaol. As adjutant of Westport Battalion he was arrested early in 1921 at Loughloon, Owenwee, and interned at the Rath Camp.

Hugh Green, Donegal. [No further details available.]

Robert P. Grehan, Castlejordan, Co. Meath. He was one of the planners of the escape.

Patrick Hopkins, Keenagh, Ballymahon, Co. Longford. [No further details available.]

Joseph Kelly, The Green, Lusk, Co. Dublin. A member of Fingal Company, he took part in the Battle of Ashbourne during the Easter Rising.

John 'Jack' Killeavy, William Street, Tullamore, Co. Offaly. He was from a prominent Tullamore nationalist family.

John Mannion (Manning), Abbey, Ballinasloe, Co. Galway. [No further details available.]

Patrick 'Pat' McNamara, Culliagh, Scramogue, Strokestown, Co. Roscommon. A member of 3rd Battalion, North Roscommon Brigade.

Richard 'Dick' Mee, Curry, Curraghboy, Co. Roscommon. Joined the Irish Volunteers in 1917 and was OC Curraghboy Company. He was arrested in March 1921.

Thomas 'Tom' Moran, Crossna, Boyle, Co. Roscommon. OC Crossna Company and subsequently OC 4th Battalion North Roscommon. He was arrested on 1 February 1921 and held at Boyle and Athlone Military Barracks before being transferred to the Curragh.

Thomas Mullen (Tomás Ó Maoláin), Roemore, Breaffy, Co. Mayo. A national schoolteacher, he served in the Irish Volunteers in Galway (1917–19) and Tullamore, Co. Offaly (1920–21).

Hubert Murphy, St John's, Knockcroghery. He was OC of St John's Company and was also involved with the republican courts. He was arrested after the Truce and interned in the Curragh.

Michael 'Mick' Murphy, Billypark, Cross, Co. Mayo. Adjutant Cross Company, 1st Battalion.

William P. 'Liam' Murphy, Aberdeen Street, Dublin. A member of the Boland's Mill garrison during Easter Week 1916; subsequently lieutenant in the 3rd Battalion, Dublin Brigade. He was arrested in February 1921.

Michael Neary, Cloonacool, Co. Sligo. He was a member of the Dublin Brigade.

John 'Jack' Noud, Kimmage Road, Dublin. Arrested in January 1921 and held at Dublin Castle before being transferred to the Rath Camp.

Walter J. O'Brien, Dublin. He was a lieutenant with the Dublin Brigade.

Anthony 'Tony' O'Connor, Westport, Co. Mayo. He was a native of Kingscourt, Co. Cavan.

O'Dwyer. [No further details available.]

Patrick 'Scottie' Regan, Leitarra House, Keadue, Co. Roscommon. A member of 4th Battalion, North Roscommon Brigade.

Robinson, Joseph, Dartry Road, Rathfarnham [No further details available.]

Michael Roseingrave, Tubber, Tuam, Co. Galway. [No further details available.]

Michael Scanlon, Ringsend Park, Dublin. A member of 3rd Battalion, Dublin Brigade.

John Schley, Ardrahan, Clifden, Co. Galway. Arrested in March 1921 by the Auxiliaries.

John Short, Crossmaglen, Co. Armagh and 78 Lower Irish Street, Armagh city. He was an officer in the Irish Volunteers.

Michael Skelly, Longford. Served in the Royal Navy during the First World War. He was captured by crown forces in April 1921.

Kieran Temple, Shannon Harbour, Co. Offaly. He was an officer with the 2nd Battalion, No. 2 Offaly Brigade.

Patrick 'Pat' Tennant, Lisnahoon, Knockcroghery, Co. Roscommon. He was 2nd lieutenant, Knockcroghery Company and worked with the republican police. He was captured in January 1921 by the Black and Tans and whipped severely. He was held at Athlone Military Barracks before being transferred to the Curragh.

Joe Vize, Wexford town and Dublin. Served with D Company 2nd Battalion, Dublin Brigade, and was a member of the Jacob's Biscuit Factory garrison during Easter Week. Later that week he reinforced St Stephen's Green with troops under Countess Markievicz; subsequently interned in Stafford Prison in England and Frongoch. In 1920 he was appointed director of purchases and OC Scotland and Britain with the rank of commandant general, responsible for the acquisition and importation of arms. He was arrested on 2 May 1921.

APPENDIX IV

SONGS OF FREEDOM

The September 1921 escape led to an appropriately entitled ballad 'The Ferrets of Kildare', sung to the tune of 'The Boys of Wexford'.

THE FERRETS OF KILDARE

Now all you lads and lassies
Come listen to my song
'Tis about some Irish Prisoners
I won't detain you long
'Twas way down in the Curragh Camp
Most truly I declare,
Right underground, they freedom found
The Ferrets of Kildare.

CHORUS
'Twas way down in the Curragh Camp
Most truly I declare,
Right underground, they freedom found
The Ferrets of Kildare.

Sure many days an' nights they worked
The tunnel to cut through,
No one complained or ever shirked
For there was work to do
The secret it was guarded well
By each man working there

APPENDIX IV

An' victory crowned the labours
Of the Ferrets of Kildare.

The Curragh Camp is in a stew
No prisoners could they find
The Major swore at everyone
An' said 'now strike me blind
Go make a search all through the camp
The fields or anywhere
An' see if anyone can find
The Ferrets of Kildare.'

So high and low they searched around
But it was all in vain
The 'Ferrets' have got safely through
And won't return again
It's hard to keep the Irish down
As England's well aware
So here's a 'Slainte Agut'
To the Ferrets of Kildare.
Source: National Library EPH C423

A BALLAD OF 1920

'Come-all-of-Yes' and listen to the story I will tell
About two youthful lovyers and all that thim befell;
Of gallant Tommy Domican – a carpenter by trade,
Who was courtin' lovely Martha Magee, a captivating maid.
And sure, all the neighbours round about, did ivery wan declare,
That there wasn't 'a purtier couple' in the County of Kildare.

Now trouble, troubles 'Lovyers' of high and low degree,
And sore sorrow nearly bruk the heart of charming Miss Magee,
For the 'Polis' came for Tommy one could and wintry day,
To the shop where he was working and carried him away,

INTERNED

An' put him in a cruel cell in the place that they prepare
In the Military Ditintion Camp, on the Curragh of Kildare.

And there the gallant hayro on bread and water kape,
And faith there's little rayson to think he can escape
For the Camp is all surrounded by wicked 'barbarous wire'
An' 'sintries' wid loaded rifles, all ready for to fire.
There he lies in cruel sorrow and filled with dark despair
In the Military Ditintion Camp on the Curragh of Kildare.

Then up spoke 'Nobel Martha' whom danger never daunts
'I'll go an' see my Tommy, an' bring him all he wants,
Tobacco, cakes an' matches, wid chocolate galore,
For I won't forget my darling, though my heart is feeling sore.'
So now Tommy's aytin av the best, instead av prison fare,
An' is getting' quite continted on the Curragh of Kildare.

Here's a message that I'm sendin' to each 'Pat and Colleen Bawn'
There's brighter times that's comin', though it's dark before the dawn,
Whin the people's made continted, and the troubles all have ceased,
An' the prison doors are opened, an' the prisoners all released
Then the bands will all be playin' an' the streets be like a Fair,
And they'll close the cruel Ditintion Camps on the Curragh of Kildare.

Whin the good old times have come agin, and I hope it won't be long,
I'll sing yez some more verses av a different sort av song,
To show how both were married to the darling av their heart,
And have reared a tidy family, an' niver more will part,
Thin we'll wish long life an' happiness to both the loving pair.
And trust they'll soon forgit about 'The Curragh of Kildare!'

Source: Copy given to the author by Brian McCabe, Kill Local History Group. Tommy Domican was from Hartwell, Kill, Co. Kildare and married Martha Magee, from Rathmore, Naas, in 1926.

To Maura from Wicklow

My dearest Maura, I'm sadly pining,
Where summer's beauty is ever drear,
But the star of love is still brightly shining
Although I'm parted from you, my dear.
Oh, I miss the charms and fond embrace
Of the only colleen that's dear to me,
But none on earth can take the place
My darling Maura, *asthore machree.*

Your love so tender, oh fairest maiden,
I often miss on the Curragh plains –
To your traits so gentle, with meekness laden –
I will be true whilst life remains,
Your true affection I often cherish,
Though now, my love, I am miles from thee,
Soon, soon, I'll see you or sadly perish,
My darling Maura, *asthore machree.*

No time or distance will ever change me,
No matter where I may chance to go,
No other fair one will e'er derange me –
My pride you'll be in lone West Wicklow.
Though vile oppressors may thus divide us
My undying love they can't take from me
But for a time they can sadly chide us,
My darling Maura, *asthore machree.*

Oh, the dawn of freedom will soon be beaming,
And I'll return to you, *asthore*!
In the Curragh dungeons I'll cease my dreaming,
And from my Maura I'll part no more,
'Mid Wicklow's mountains I'll live contented,
My native Erin, I'll be true to thee,

My hand and love I have now presented
To my darling Maura, *asthore machree*.

Source: True sentimental lines written in the Rath Camp, 1921, to an old Irish air by Patrick Tunney, Cushlough, Co. Mayo. *Wicklow News-Letter*, 4 October 1924.

ENDNOTES

INTRODUCTION
1 Female political prisoners were not interned, but usually charged and convicted of an offence.

1 INTERNMENT
1 John Maguire, *IRA Internments and the Irish Government: Subversives and the State 1939–62* (Irish Academic Press, Dublin, 2008), pp. 7–8.
2 *Ibid.*, p. 8.
3 Durney, James, *Foremost and Ready: Kildare and the 1916 Rising* (Gaul House, Naas, 2015), p. 131.
4 *Ibid.*, pp. 131–3, 146.
5 *Ibid.*, p. 149.
6 *Leinster Leader*, 25 August 1917.
7 Townshend, Charles, *The Republic: The Fight for Irish Independence* (Penguin, London, 2014), pp. 61, 64.
8 Coogan, Tim Pat, *The Twelve Apostles: Michael Collins, the Squad and Ireland's Fight for Freedom* (Head of Zeus, London, 2016), p. 61.
9 McGuffin, John, *Internment* (Anvil Books, Tralee, 1973), p. 33.
10 Flynn, Barry, *Pawns in the Game: Irish Hunger Strikes 1912–1981* (The Collins Press, Cork, 2011), pp. 45–8; Townshend, *The Republic*, pp. 142–3.
11 Townshend, *The Republic*, pp. 151–2.
12 Campbell, Colm, *Emergency Law in Ireland 1918–1925* (Clarendon Press, Oxford, 1994), p. 27.
13 Townshend, *The Republic*, p. 151.
14 Townshend, Charles, *The British Campaign in Ireland 1919–1921: The Development of Political and Military Policies* (Oxford Historical Monographs) (Oxford University Press, Oxford, 1975), p. 106; *Irish Independent*, 21 August 1920.

15 Sheehan, William, *Hearts & Mines: The British 5th Division, Ireland, 1919–1922* (The Collins Press, Cork, 2009), pp. 52, 54.
16 *Irish Independent*, 25 November 1920.
17 *The Freeman's Journal*, 27 November 1920; *Irish Independent*, 9 December 1920.
18 *The Freeman's Journal*, 4 December 1920; *Donegal News*, 4 December 1920.
19 Ó Duibhir, Liam, *Prisoners of War: Ballykinlar Internment Camp 1920–1921* (Mercier Press, Cork, 2013), pp. 58, 63.
20 Francis O'Duffy, Bureau of Military History (henceforth BMH) Witness Statement (henceforth WS) 665, pp. 2–3.
21 *Belfast Telegraph*, 29 November 1920.
22 Campbell, *Emergency Law in Ireland*, p. 106.
23 *Ibid.*, pp. 106–8.
24 *Irish Independent*, 24 December 1920.
25 Townshend, *The British Campaign in Ireland*, p. 223.
26 *The Kerryman*, 5 February 1921.
27 *The Freeman's Journal*, 17 February 1921; *Belfast Newsletter*, 21 February 1921.
28 Townshend, *The British Campaign in Ireland*, p. 223.
29 Durney, James, 'The Curragh internees, 1921–24: From defiance to defeat', *Journal of the County Kildare Archaeological Society* 2010–2011, Vol. XX (Part II), p. 8.
30 *Leinster Leader*, 12 March 1921.

2 THE RATH CAMP

1 Townshend, *The British Campaign in Ireland*, p. 223.
2 Sheehan, *Hearts & Mines*, p. 78.
3 Evans, Inez G., 'Life on the Curragh Camp 1919', *The Irish Times*, 17 May 1919.
4 Corrigan, Mario, *All the Delirium of the Brave: Kildare in 1798* (Kildare County Council, Naas, 1998), pp. 60–1.
5 Durney, 'The Curragh internees', p. 8.
6 Micheál Ó Laoghaire, BMH WS 797, p. 58. On 7 June 1914 Gibbet Rath was selected for a show of strength when 1,000 Irish

Volunteers from twelve locally formed companies paraded within yards of quartered British troops to listen to loud patriotic speeches delivered by Thomas MacDonagh and Michael J. O'Rahilly.

7 Harvey, Dan, *Soldiers of the Short Grass: A History of the Curragh Camp* (Merrion Press, Sallins, 2016), p. 3.
8 Durney, *Foremost and Ready*, p. 93.
9 *Ibid.*, pp. 123–4, 149–50.
10 *Irish Independent*, 24 April 1920.
11 *The Freeman's Journal*, 19 February 1921.
12 *Ibid.*; *Leinster Leader*, 19 February, 6 August and 17 September 1921; *Donegal News*, 19 March 1921.
13 *Leinster Leader*, 20 September 1924.
14 Sheehan, *Hearts & Mines*, pp. 4, 9.
15 The description of the Rath Camp comes from accounts in the BMH witness statements of Joseph Lawless (1043) and Mícheál Ó Laoghaire (797), and from C. S. Andrews' *Dublin Made Me* (The Lilliput Press, Dublin, 2001), pp. 173–86. The individual experiences of many of the internees are available through the BMH witness statements.
16 Sheehan, *Hearts & Mines*, p. 131; Mícheál Ó Laoghaire, BMH WS 797.
17 *Leinster Leader*, 12 March 1921.
18 *The Freeman's Journal*, 26 March 1921; *Leinster Leader*, 8 October 1921.
19 Joseph Lawless, BMH WS 1043, pp. 373–6.
20 Sheehan, *Hearts & Mines*, p. 78.
21 Joseph Lawless, BMH WS 1043, pp. 377–8.
22 Sheehan, *Hearts & Mines*, p. 299.
23 Sheehan, William, *British Voices from the Irish War of Independence: The Words of British Servicemen Who Were There* (The Collins Press, Cork, 2007), pp. 46–8.
24 Mícheál Ó Laoghaire, BMH WS 797, pp. 59–62.
25 Brian A. Cusack, BMH WS 736, pp. 12–13.
26 Byrne, Thomas, 'A tunnel to freedom: Escape from Kildare Camp', undated newspaper article. Copy in author's possession.

27 Micheál Ó Laoghaire, BMH WS 797, pp. 65–6. Captain F. H. Vinden, in his memoir *By Chance, a Soldier* (IWM manuscript 96/36/1), denied that the military authorities planted spies in the Rath Camp.
28 Sheehan, *British Voices*, p. 50.
29 Swan, Lt-Col Desmond, 'The Curragh', in *Handbook of the Curragh Camp* (Defence Forces Press, The Curragh, 1984), p. 21.
30 Swan, 'The Curragh', p. 21.
31 *The Freeman's Journal*, 23 April 1921.
32 Sheehan, *British Voices*, p. 49.
33 Hart, Peter (ed.), *British Intelligence in Ireland 1920–21: The Final Reports* (Cork University Press, Cork, 2002), p. 69.
34 *Ibid.*, p. 57.
35 *Ibid.*, pp. 56–7.
36 Campbell, *Emergency Law in Ireland*, p. 109.
37 Joseph Lawless, BMH WS 1043, p. 378A.
38 Peadar McMahon, BMH WS 1730, p. 5. Peadar McMahon became chief of staff of the National Army in 1924.
39 Campbell, *Emergency Law in Ireland*, p. 108.
40 Ó Súilleabháin, Adhamhnán, *Domhnall Ua Buachalla. Rebellious Nationalist, Reluctant Governor* (Merrion Press, Sallins, 2015), pp. 142–3.
41 Sheehan, *Hearts & Mines*, p. 141.

3 THE MEN BEHIND THE WIRE

1 Micheál Ó Laoghaire, BMH WS 797, p. 62.
2 Townshend, *The Republic*, pp. 136–7.
3 Campbell, *Emergency Law in Ireland*, p. 111.
4 Yeates, Pádraig, *A City in Turmoil: Dublin 1919–21* (Gill & Macmillan, Dublin, 2012), pp. 163, 257.
5 These numbers are drawn from the list of internees given in Appendix II.
6 Micheál Ó Laoghaire, BMH WS 797.
7 Foster, R. F., *Vivid Faces: The Revolutionary Generation in Ireland 1890–1923* (W. W. Norton, London, 2014), p. 190.

ENDNOTES

8 Micheál Ó Laoghaire, BMH WS 797, p. 62.
9 Peadar McMahon, BMH WS 1730; Maguire, James and Quinn, James (eds), *Dictionary of Irish Biography: From the Earliest Times to the Year 2000* (Cambridge University Press, Cambridge, 2010) Vol. 6, p. 90.
10 Joseph Lawless, BMH WS 1043, pp. 358, 361.
11 Collier, Tola, 'Joseph Lawless. Fingal's Finest', https://fingalsfinest1916.com.
12 Joseph Lawless, BMH WS 1043, pp. 373–4.
13 The Lawless Collection, Collections and Research, National Museum of Ireland. Cameras were prohibited in internment camps and prisons, but some prisoners did manage to smuggle them in; there were several camera smugglers in the Rath Camp.
14 Maguire and Quinn (eds), *Dictionary of Irish Biography*, Vol. 7, pp. 271–2.
15 Townshend, *The Republic*, p. 95.
16 FitzGerald, Garret, *All in a Life: An Autobiography* (Gill & Macmillan, Dublin, 1991), pp. 4–9; Maguire and Quinn (eds), *Dictionary of Irish Biography*, Vol. 3, pp. 820–2.
17 Sheehan, *British Voices*, p. 49.
18 Andrews, *Dublin Made Me*, pp. 13, 44–9, 63, 95, 122, 135, 143, 165–9.
19 Murphy, William, *Political Imprisonment and the Irish, 1912–1921* (Oxford University Press, Oxford, 2014), p. 207.
20 'Obituary, Thomas Derrig', *The Connaught Telegraph*, 24 November 1956. Tom Derrig was released in December 1921. He was subsequently against the Treaty, and a member of the IRA Executive while active in Dublin and the east. Captured in April 1923, he was shot in the eye while trying to escape and was subsequently jailed in Mountjoy and the Curragh.
21 Michael McHugh, BMH WS 1632.
22 Wren, Jimmy, *The Four Courts Garrison, Easter Week 1916: A Biographical Dictionary* (Geography Publications, Dublin, 2016), p. 154.
23 Michael Noyk, BMH WS 707; Dwyer, T. Ryle, *The Squad and the Intelligence Operations of Michael Collins* (Mercier Press, Cork, 2005), pp. 210–12.

INTERNED

24 Michael Byrne, Offaly Historical Studies, Tullamore, correspondence to the author, 25 January 2018.
25 'Obituary, Fr. P. Smith', *The Anglo-Celt*, 26 October 1940.
26 Liam Ó Briain, BMH WS 7, p. 15.
27 Alice Ginnell, BMH WS 982, pp. 12–13; *Meath Chronicle*, 6 October 1917. On Fr Smith's 1917 appeal against his imprisonment, Mr T. Healy being the counsel, his fine was reduced to £50 and the term of imprisonment reduced to three weeks.
28 Andrews, *Dublin Made Me*, p. 180.
29 Micheál Ó Laoghaire, BMH WS 797, p. 61.
30 Durney, James, 'Frank Burke: Teacher, Sportsman and Patriot', *Kildare Nationalist*, 17 April 2016.
31 Cummins, Gerry and De Búrca, Éanna, *The Frank Burke Story: Patriot, Scholar, GAA Dual-star. Guardian of Pearse's Vision and Legacy* (published privately, Naas, 2016), pp. 116–17.

4 'NO PLACE LIKE HOME'

1 Brigid Ryan (née Brophy), BMH WS 1573, p. 4.
2 *The Freeman's Journal*, 9 August 1921. Because of its support for the prisoners, *The Freeman's Journal* was occasionally 'banned'.
3 Costello, Con, *A Most Delightful Station: The British Army on the Curragh of Kildare 1855–1922* (The Collins Press, Cork, 1999), p. 219.
4 Micheál Ó Laoghaire, BMH WS 797, pp. 62–3. About 600 parcels per day arrived at the Curragh. Many families could not afford to send parcels, though this was alleviated by the tendency of most prisoners to share their parcels' contents.
5 *Nationalist and Leinster Times*, 4 June 1921. Derry-born Dr Francis P. Ferran was interned again in the Curragh during the Civil War and died of pneumonia on 10 June 1923 in the Curragh Military Hospital.
6 Andrews, *Dublin Made Me*, pp. 173–6.
7 *Meath Chronicle*, 28 May 1921.
8 Andrews, *Dublin Made Me*, p. 176.
9 Joseph Lawless, BMH WS 1043, pp. 380–1.

ENDNOTES

10 *The Freeman's Journal*, 17 October 1921.
11 According to research by the *Irish Red Cross Journal*, 12,000 young Irish adults died of TB in 1904. Mortality remained high in the 1920s; 'The silent terror that consumed so many', Dan Buckley, *Irish Examiner*, 24 August 2010; figures taken from a search of 425 deaths recorded in the Naas Registration District from 1 January to 31 December 1921, which covers the Curragh Camp and the Kildare Infirmary. Source: www.irishgenealogy.ie.
12 Joseph Tonge, Military Service Pensions Collection (henceforth MSPC) 24SP147. According to his death certificate he was twenty-two, but he was in fact born in 1898.
13 Michael Horan, MSPC DP23836.
14 *The Freeman's Journal*, 9 August 1921; *Irish Independent*, 10 August 1921.
15 Tunney, Patrick, 'Told at the fireside', *Western People*, 1 October 1949.
16 House of Commons Debate, 9 June 1921, sourced online from https://api.parliament.uk/historic-hansard/commons/1921/jun/09/internment-camp-rath#S5CV0142P0_19210609_HOC_94.
17 'Sir Hamar and Cork Burnings', *Irish Independent*, 14 December 1920.
18 Tunney, 'Told at the fireside'.
19 *Kildare Observer*, 27 August 1921.
20 *Irish Independent*, 10 August 1921; *The Freeman's Journal*, 9 November 1921.
21 Dooley, Frank, 'Humour in War', *Connacht Tribune*, 6 August 1976. Another interned doctor in the Rath Camp was Limerick-born Dr Edward Dundon of Borris, Co. Carlow, who was interned from March to December 1921.
22 John J. Martin, MSPC 1P134. John Martin was awarded a 40 per cent disability pension in 1922; he died in 1942.
23 Daniel Murray 'Bushwhacked: The loss of the Carlow Flying Column, April 1921', *The Irish Story*, Irish history online; Michael Ryan, MSPC MSP34REF17277.

24 Ó Súilleabháin, Cormac, *Leitrim's Republican Story 1900–2000* (Cumann Cabhrach Liatroma, USA, 2014), p. 90.
25 Correspondence from Philip McConway, 7 September 2018.
26 Thomas Berry, MSPC MSP34REF2550.
27 O'Callaghan, Micheál, *For Ireland and Freedom: Roscommon's Contribution to the Fight for Independence* (Mercier Press, Cork, 2012), p. 145.
28 Micheál Ó Laoghaire, BMH WS 797, p. 66.
29 *The Freeman's Journal*, 21 July 1921.
30 Ó Maoláin, Tomás, 'The inside story of famous I.R.A. escape from the Curragh Camp', *The Mayo News*, 17 January 1959.
31 Daniel E. Ryan, BMH WS 1673, pp. 4–5.
32 *Ibid.*, p. 5.
33 'Obituary, Mr C. Kenny', *The Irish Press*, 30 January 1949; Joseph Lawless, BMH WS 1043, p. 379. In his witness statement Lawless claimed that he asked Ryan to delay the escape and that two wounded Volunteers, Mick Ryan and Larry O'Neill, be given the first chance of escape when they recovered. However, as Ryan and O'Connor escaped on 12 March 1921, and Mick Ryan and Larry O'Neill were not captured until 18 April 1921, Lawless's account must be taken as a lapse of memory or an attempt to discredit Rory O'Connor.
34 Daniel E. Ryan, BMH WS 1673, pp. 7–8.
35 *Ibid.*, p. 9.
36 Joseph Lawless, BMH WS 1043, p. 380.
37 *Fermanagh Herald*, 19 March 1921.
38 O'Callaghan, *For Ireland and Freedom*, pp. 128–30.
39 Conroy, John F., 'Escape from the Rath Internment Camp, Curragh, 1921', *Western People*, 6 June 1964.
40 O'Callaghan, *For Ireland and Freedom*, p. 130. In his pension application (MSPC 24SP8027), Isaiah Conroy of Dublin also claimed to have worked on this first tunnel and the second Brady tunnel.
41 Conroy, 'Escape from the Rath Internment Camp'.
42 O'Callaghan, *For Ireland and Freedom*, p. 131.
43 Moran, May, *Executed for Ireland: The Patrick Moran Story* (Mercier Press, Cork, 2010), pp. 179–80.

44 Swan, 'The Curragh', p. 22.
45 Moran, *Executed for Ireland*, p. 180; O'Callaghan, *For Ireland and Freedom*, p. 131.

5 SPORT AND PASTIMES

1 Coogan, Tim Pat, *Ireland in the Twentieth Century* (Hutchinson, London, 2003), p. 16.
2 McElligott, Richard, 'Football finds its feet amid 1916 rebellion against Empire', *The Irish Times*, 16 April 2016.
3 Ó Tuathaigh, Gearóid (ed.), *The GAA and Revolution in Ireland 1913–1923* (The Collins Press, Cork, 2015), pp. 174, 178.
4 Andrews, *Dublin Made Me*, p. 178.
5 Ó Tuathaigh, *The GAA*, p. 171; *Leinster Leader*, 19 March 1921.
6 'Cavan man's part in escape of republican prisoners', *The Anglo-Celt*, 4 January 1936; Crowley, J., Ó Drisceoil, D. and Murphy, M. (eds), *Atlas of the Irish Revolution* (Cork University Press, Cork, 2017), p. 897. On the page there is a photograph of the Offaly hurling team in the Rath Camp, but there is a lack of detail on hurling matches in the camp. The Offaly county hurling team for the 1921 Championship was made up of former inmates from the Rath Camp who had formed a team there during their incarceration. The successful completion of GAA competitions, at both local and national levels, became very difficult, and the GAA championships were greatly disrupted during 1920 and 1921. Because of the number of players imprisoned, many counties could not field full teams and the 1920 All-Ireland hurling final was not played until May 1922, and the football final in June 1922. The 1921 All-Ireland hurling final was played in March 1923 and the football final in June 1923.
7 *Leinster Leader*, 28 May 1921.
8 *Nationalist and Leinster Times*, 26 February 1966; Durney, James, 'Brothers in arms' – article, Co. Kildare online electronic history journal, 12 November 2010.
9 *The Irish Press*, 4 June 1947. Tom Behan was killed 'trying to escape' on 12 December 1922. The circumstances of his death are still disputed.

10 *Leinster Leader*, 18 June 1921.
11 *The Anglo-Celt*, 4 January 1936.
12 Micheál Ó Laoghaire, BMH WS 797, p. 59.
13 *Leinster Leader*, 16 July 1921.
14 *Ireland's Own*, 18 January 1922; 'Historic athletic meeting in strange setting', *Irish Independent*, 7 June 1963.
15 Shouldice, Frank, *Grandpa the Sniper: The Remarkable Story of a 1916 Volunteer* (The Liffey Press, Dublin, 2015), p. 306; John F. Shouldice, MSPC MSP34REF21842; Wren, *The Four Courts Garrison*, p. 245.
16 *Ireland's Own*, 18 January 1922.
17 *Leinster Leader*, 6 August 1921.
18 *Nationalist and Leinster Times*, 13 August 1921.
19 *Leinster Leader*, 13 August 1921.
20 *Nationalist and Leinster Times*, 13 August 1921.
21 *Meath Chronicle*, 3 December 1921; *Nationalist and Leinster Times*, 18 March 1950.
22 'Liam Ó Briain' by Paul Rouse – UCD Decade of Centenaries. Available at: http://centenaries.ucd.ie/wp-content/uploads/2015/04/%C3%93_Briain-Liam.pdf.
23 'Poems', Tom Behan, copy in author's possession.
24 *Nationalist and Leinster Times*, 4 June 1921. The three brothers Behan from Graiguecullen, Carlow, were Michael, Thomas and Seamus.
25 'Obituary, John Murray', *Donegal Democrat*, 16 November 1935.
26 Andrews, *Dublin Made Me*, p. 173.
27 O'Donovan, Donal, *Kevin Barry and His Time* (Glendale Publishing, Dublin, 1989), pp. 183–5.
28 *Irish Independent*, 10 June 1921.
29 *The Freeman's Journal*, 23 September 1921.
30 *Leinster Leader*, 2 July 1921.

6 TRUCE OUTSIDE, DISSENT INSIDE

1 Joseph Lawless, BMH WS 1043, p. 380; *The Freeman's Journal*, 9 August 1921; *Leinster Leader*, 12 November 1921.

ENDNOTES

2 Campbell, *Emergency Law in Ireland*, p. 108.
3 Ó Ruairc, Pádraig Óg, *Truce: Murder, Myth and the Last Days of the Irish War of Independence* (Mercier Press, Cork, 2016), p. 51.
4 Andrews, *Dublin Made Me*, p. 178. The Dublin Brigade IRA burned the Custom House on 25 May 1921. It was the headquarters of the Local Government Board and the finest classical building in the city.
5 Kautt, William H., *The Anglo-Irish War, 1916–1921: A People's War* (Praeger, Westport, CT, USA, 1999), pp. 80–1; Hopkinson, Michael, *Green Against Green: The Irish Civil War* (Gill & Macmillan, Dublin, 1988), p. 13; O'Malley, Cormac K. H. and Ó Comhraí, Cormac (eds), *The Men Will Talk to Me: Galway Interviews by Ernie O'Malley* (Mercier Press, Cork, 2013), p. 85.
6 Ó Ruairc, *Truce*, p. 51.
7 Abbott, Richard, *Police Casualties in Ireland 1919–1922* (Mercier Press, Cork, 2019); www.cairogang.com/soldiers-killed/list-1921.html (accessed 7 February 2018.)
8 Ó Ruairc, *Truce*, p. 57.
9 Jackson, Alvin, *Ireland 1798–1998. War, Peace and Beyond* (2nd edn, Wiley-Blackwell, Chichester, 2010), pp. 253–4.
10 Copy of original document, donated by Karen Woodstock (uncategorised), in the Local Studies Department, Newbridge Library, Newbridge, Co. Kildare.
11 Durney, James, *On the One Road: Political Unrest in Kildare 1913–1994* (Gaul House, Naas, 2001), p. 84.
12 Hopkinson, *The War of Independence*, p. 196.
13 First Eastern Division general order, copy in author's possession.
14 Ó Ruairc, *Truce*, p. 61.
15 Smyth, Michael, 'Kildare Battalion, 1920' (copy in Local Studies, Archives and Genealogy Department, Newbridge Library, Newbridge, Co. Kildare).
16 Durney, *The War of Independence in Kildare*, p . 206.
17 *Ibid.*, p. 207; *Leinster Leader*, 9 July 1921.
18 *The Irish Exile*, December 1921, p. 13.
19 Andrews, *Dublin Made Me*, p. 188.

INTERNED

20 Joseph Lawless, BMH WS 1043, pp. 384–5.
21 *Evening Telegraph*, 20 July 1921.
22 *The Freeman's Journal*, 23 July 1921.
23 *Ibid.*, 28 July 1921.
24 Younger, Calton, *Ireland's Civil War* (Frederick Muller, London, 1968), pp. 148–9; Hopkinson, *Green Against Green*, p. 24.
25 *Leinster Leader*, 5 August 1921.
26 Sheehan, *British Voices*, p. 51.
27 Younger, *Ireland's Civil War*, p. 149; Hopkinson, *Green Against Green*, p. 24; Mitchell, Arthur, *Revolutionary Government in Ireland: Dáil Éireann 1919–22* (Gill & Macmillan, Dublin, 1995), pp. 302–3.
28 Tunney, 'Told at the fireside'.
29 Durney, 'The Curragh internees', p. 14.
30 *Kildare Observer*, 27 August 1921; *Nationalist and Leinster Times*, 27 August 1921; *Irish Independent*, 7 October 1921.
31 *Irish Bulletin*, 24 August 1921.
32 *Nationalist and Leinster Times*, 3 September 1921.
33 Murphy, *Political Imprisonment and the Irish*, p. 222.
34 *Irish Independent*, 10 August 1921.
35 *Ibid.*, 24 August 1921.
36 Murphy, *Political Imprisonment and the Irish*, p. 220.
37 Micheál Ó Laoghaire, BMH WS 797, pp. 69–70. The officer in question was Colonel J. C. Hanna.
38 *The Freeman's Journal*, 31 August 1921.
39 *Irish Independent*, 3 September 1921.
40 *The Freeman's Journal*, 20 September 1921.
41 Tobin, Fergal, *The Irish Revolution: An Illustrated History 1912–25* (Gill & Macmillan, Dublin, 2013), p. 184.

7 A TUNNEL TO FREEDOM

1 Michael McCoy, BMH WS 1610, p. 33; *Donegal Democrat*, 16 September 1921.
2 Joseph Lawless, BMH WS 1043, pp. 380–1.
3 O'Callaghan, *For Ireland and Freedom*, pp. 131–2.

4. Ó Maoláin, 'The inside story of famous I.R.A. escape from the Curragh Camp'. Ó Maoláin's phrase 'we simply removed the kid gloves' implies that camp spies were dealt with in the same way as spies on the outside, meaning with violence, but there are no records of beatings or killings within the camp.
5. *The Anglo-Celt*, 4 January 1936.
6. 'Rath Camp Escape', *Evening Herald*, 6 January 1936.
7. Liam P. Murphy, MSPC 24SP7310.
8. Conroy, 'Escapes from the Rath Internment Camp, Curragh, 1921'; Ó Maoláin, 'The inside story of famous I.R.A. escape from the Curragh Camp'.
9. Byrne, 'A tunnel to freedom: Escape from Kildare Camp'.
10. 'Rath Camp Escape', *Evening Herald*, 6 January 1936; Ó Maoláin, 'The inside story of famous I.R.A. escape from the Curragh Camp'; Joseph Lawless, BMH WS 1043, p. 383.
11. *Connacht Tribune*, 7 January 1922.
12. Ó Maoláin, 'The inside story of famous I.R.A. escape from the Curragh Camp'.
13. 'Old I.R.A. man's death recalls daring prison escape', *The Anglo-Celt*, 10 March 1978.
14. Kelly, Bill, 'Mass escape of internees from the Curragh Camp', in *IRA Jailbreaks 1918–1924* (Mercier Press, Cork, 2010), p. 243.
15. Conroy, 'Escapes from the Rath Internment Camp, Curragh, 1921'; Ó Maoláin, 'The inside story of famous I.R.A. escape from the Curragh Camp'.
16. Kelly, 'Mass escape of internees from the Curragh Camp', p. 243; Ó Maoláin, 'The inside story of famous I.R.A. escape from the Curragh Camp'.
17. *The Tuam Herald*, 8 January 1966. Ó Maoláin also escaped by tunnel from Tintown No. 1 Camp in 1923. He subsequently became a Fianna Fáil TD for Dublin county, 1938–43. In a two-part article in *The Mayo News* (1959), Ó Maoláin said, 'I should know the facts, especially as I took the precaution of jotting them down many years ago, because even then I knew that of all liars the smoothest and most convincing may be memory.'

18 Ó Maoláin, Tomás, 'Mayo men feature in famous I.R.A. escapes from the Curragh Camp', *The Mayo News*, 24 January 1959; Ó Maoláin, 'The inside story of famous I.R.A. escape from the Curragh Camp'. 'Heery' is possibly Patrick Heary, of Fenagh, Co. Leitrim.
19 Kelly, 'Mass escape of internees from the Curragh Camp', p. 244.
20 Byrne, 'A tunnel to freedom: Escape from Kildare Camp'.
21 Andrews, *Dublin Made Me*, p. 187.
22 Conroy, 'Escapes from the Rath Internment Camp'.
23 Byrne, 'A tunnel to freedom'.
24 Ó Maoláin, 'Mayo men feature in famous I.R.A. escapes from the Curragh Camp'.
25 *Ibid*.
26 Byrne, 'A tunnel to freedom: Escape from Kildare Camp'.
27 Kelly, 'Mass escape of internees from the Curragh Camp', p. 244.
28 *Ibid*.
29 *The Anglo-Celt*, 4 January 1936.
30 'Rath Camp Escape', *Evening Herald*, 6 January 1936.
31 Gillis, Liz, *Women of the Irish Revolution* (Mercier Press, Cork, 2016), p. 132. Lucy Agnes Smyth joined Cumann na mBan on its inception and was a first lieutenant in Central (Árd Craobh) Branch. She helped Tom Byrne evade capture after the Easter Week surrender. They married on 28 April 1919 and Lucy became pregnant with her first child in December of that year.
32 Byrne, 'A tunnel to freedom'; *The Nenagh Guardian*, 17 September 1921.
33 Kelly, 'Mass escape of internees from the Curragh Camp', p. 245; Conroy, 'Escapes from the Rath Internment Camp'.
34 'Rath Camp Escape', *Evening Herald*, 6 January 1936.
35 Kelly, 'Mass escape of internees from the Curragh Camp', p. 245.
36 O'Callaghan, *For Ireland and Freedom*, p. 132.
37 Kelly, 'Mass escape of internees from the Curragh Camp', p. 246. In her pension application, Ellen Kearns, an officer in Cumann na mBan, claimed to have smuggled wire cutters into the Rath Camp in a box containing food on top and wire cutters underneath in a false bottom. She also claimed to have helped some of the escaped

prisoners get away to their home areas. (Handwritten letter to the Military Pensions Board, Dublin, from Ellen 'Nellie' Kearns Kilbride, dated 1 May 1936. Copy given to the author by John Stack, Newbridge, 10 January 2019.)
38 Kelly, 'Mass escape of internees from the Curragh Camp', p. 246.
39 O'Callaghan, *For Ireland and Freedom*, p. 133. Kennedy's of Main Street, Naas was the home of Philip Kennedy, an IRA intelligence officer based in Kingstown (Dún Laoghaire).

8 THE FOGGY DEW

1 'Rath Camp Escape', *Evening Herald*; Conroy, 'Escapes from the Rath Internment Camp'; Michael McCoy, BMH WS 1610, p. 35.
2 Conroy, 'Escapes from the Rath Internment Camp'.
3 Byrne, 'A tunnel to freedom'; Wren, *The Four Courts Garrison*, pp. 20–1.
4 'How an Arigna miner dug for freedom', *Leitrim Observer*, 18 July 1942.
5 *The Anglo-Celt*, 4 January 1936.
6 Andrews, *Dublin Made Me*, pp. 187–8.
7 *Ibid.*, p. 188.
8 Ó Maoláin, 'Mayo men feature in famous I.R.A. escapes from the Curragh Camp'.
9 'Rath Camp Escape', *Evening Herald*, 6 January 1936.
10 Byrne, 'A tunnel to freedom'.
11 'Cavan man's part in escape of republican prisoners', *The Anglo-Celt*, 4 January 1936.
12 Andrews, *Dublin Made Me*, pp. 188–90.
13 *Roscommon Herald*, 17 December 1921.
14 Moran, *Executed for Ireland*, p. 124.
15 *Ibid.*, pp. 182–4; O'Callaghan, *For Ireland and Freedom*, pp. 126–7.
16 Moran, *Executed for Ireland*, p. 183.
17 *Ibid.*, p. 184.
18 *Irish Independent*, 13 September 1921.
19 'Obituary, Michael Cunningham', *The Irish Press*, 31 March 1955; Co. Kildare Local Studies Executive Librarian Mario Corrigan

in conversation with Michael McWey, 26 April 2018. Michael McWey confirmed that his grandfather, Michael Cunningham, was involved in the Rath Camp escape by supplying clothing to an escaper and transporting him to Dublin.
20 Kelly, 'Mass escape of internees from the Curragh Camp,' p. 247; 'Rath Camp Escape', *Evening Herald*, 6 January 1936.
21 David Daly, BMH WS 1337, p. 26.
22 Ó Maoláin, 'Mayo men feature in famous I.R.A. escapes from the Curragh Camp'.
23 Andrews, *Dublin Made Me*, p. 190.
24 'Curragh tunnel escape recalled', *Irish Independent*, 6 March 1955. Patrick Dunne was the man Éamonn Flynn met at Greenhills. In this interview on his retirement from CIÉ as a supervisor, Flynn said the first man he met when he took up office at Aston Quay as supervisor of the Irish Omnibus Company was Dunne's son, bus driver Jack Dunne.
25 *Leinster Leader*, 17 September 1921; *The Irish Times*, 10 September 1921.
26 *Leinster Leader*, 17 September 1921; *Belfast Newsletter*, 12 September 1921.
27 *Donegal Democrat*, 16 September 1921. There was a story often repeated that a sentry had seen men emerging from a hole in the ground, screamed with fright, dropped his rifle and then fainted. Three more prisoners were alleged to have escaped before the sentry recovered and shouted, 'There are Paddies leaving the camp like rabbits'. More fanciful reports record the sentry said 'Shinners' instead of 'Paddies'.
28 Flanagan, Edward, 'Curragh Internment Diary', copy donated to Kildare Library and Arts Service, Local Studies Department, by Karen Woodstock (June 2008).
29 Joseph Lawless, BMH WS 1043, pp. 387–8.
30 Michael McCoy, BMH WS 1610, p. 35.
31 *Roscommon Herald*, 17 December 1921.
32 *The Freeman's Journal*, 13 September 1921; 'Escape from the Curragh', *The Irish Press*, 8 September 1978.

33 *Leinster Leader*, 17 September 1921.
34 Kelly, 'Mass escape of internees from the Curragh Camp', pp. 247–8.
35 *Fermanagh Herald*, 17 September 1921.
36 Flanagan, 'Curragh Internment Diary'.
37 Micheál Ó Laoghaire, BMH WS 797, p. 68.
38 Flanagan, 'Curragh Internment Diary'.
39 Michael McCoy, BMH WS 1610, p. 37.

9 PRISON BREAKS

1 *The Freeman's Journal*, 6 October 1921.
2 *Ibid.*; *Donegal News*, 8 October 1921; *The Skibbereen Eagle*, 8 October 1921.
3 As told to the author *c.* June 2001 by Peadar Bracken's son, Enda, at his home in Naas, Co. Kildare.
4 *The Freeman's Journal*, 8 October 1921.
5 *The Irish Press*, 3 May 1937.
6 Wren, Jimmy, *The GPO Garrison, Easter Week 1916: A Biographical Dictionary* (Geography Publications, Dublin, 2015), p. 12.
7 Joseph Lawless, BMH WS 1043, pp. 388–9.
8 Aiken, S., Mac Bhloscaidh, F., Ó Duibhir, L. and Ó Tuama, D. (eds), *The Men Will Talk to Me: Ernie O'Malley's Interviews with the Northern Division* (Merrion Press, Newbridge, 2018), p. 81.
9 Joseph Lawless, BMH WS 1043, p. 389.
10 *Ibid.*, pp. 389–93.
11 *Evening Herald*, 4 October 1921.
12 Joseph Lawless BMH WS 1043, p. 395.
13 *Ibid.*; Tom Glennon, Pension Application MSPC 24SP10231.
14 Wren, *The Four Courts Garrison*, p. 249.
15 Dooley, 'Humour in war', *Connacht Tribune*, 6 August 1976.
16 Michael McCoy, BMH WS 1610, pp. 35–6.
17 O'Malley, Cormac and Keane, Vincent (eds), *The Men Will Talk to Me: Mayo Interviews by Ernie O'Malley* (Mercier Press, Cork, 2014), p. 193; Wren, *The GPO Garrison, Easter Week 1916*, p. 333.
18 Michael Staines, BMH WS 944, p. 33.
19 *Irish Independent*, 21 October 1921.

20 *Ibid.*
21 *The Freeman's Journal*, 22 October 1921.
22 *Nationalist and Leinster Times*, 2 October 1987.
23 *The Freeman's Journal*, 22 October 1921.
24 *Nationalist and Leinster Times*, 2 October 1987.
25 *The Freeman's Journal*, 22 October 1921.
26 *Irish Independent*, 21 October 1921.
27 *Roscommon Herald*, 17 December 1921.
28 Michael McCoy, BMH WS 1610, pp. 36–7.
29 Aiken, S. *et al.*, *The Men Will Talk to Me*, pp. 181–4.
30 *Connaught Tribune*, 24 January 1959.
31 For a full account of this jailbreak, see O'Donoghue, Florence (foreword), *I.R.A. Jailbreaks 1918–1924* (Mercier Press, Cork, 2010), pp. 285–95.
32 Sheehan, *British Voices*, p. 50.
33 *The Irish Times*, 20 October 1921; *Irish Independent*, 21 October and 16 November 1921. A three-day riot in late October wrecked the internment camp on Spike Island and left several internees in hospital.
34 Sheehan, *British Voices*, pp. 49–50.
35 *Leinster Leader*, 17 December 1921.
36 Information supplied by Karel Kiely, Genealogy Department, Newbridge Library, Newbridge, Co. Kildare.
37 *Leinster Leader*, 14 January 1922.
38 Death certificate of John J. Scuffil, information supplied by Karel Kiely, Genealogy Department, Newbridge Library, Newbridge, Co. Kildare.

18 *FÉ GHLAS AG GALLAIBH* – LOCKED UP BY FOREIGNERS

1 *Leinster Leader*, 22 October 1921.
2 John Timmons' Rath Camp Autograph Book, courtesy of Kevin Timmons, Newbridge, Co. Kildare.
3 *The Freeman's Journal*, 10 October 1921.
4 *Ibid.*, 17 October 1921. The Naas District Committee operated from 40 South Main Street and received money and gifts to make

up parcels collectively for local prisoners in the Rath Camp and Ballykinlar Camp; 40 South Main Street was also the address of Rath Camp internee Sylvester Delahunt, who had been arrested there in March 1921.
5 Cited in Campbell, *Emergency Law in Ireland*, p. 110.
6 *The Freeman's Journal*, 10 October 1921.
7 *Irish Independent*, 19 October 1921.
8 *Ibid.*, 21 October 1921.
9 *Leinster Leader*, 29 October 1921.
10 Murphy, *Political Imprisonment and the Irish*, pp. 220–1.
11 *Irish Weekly Independent*, 15 October 1921.
12 Murphy, *Political Imprisonment and the Irish*, p. 221.
13 *The Freeman's Journal*, 10 October 1921.
14 Murphy, *Political Imprisonment and the Irish*, p. 221. Frank Gallagher was deputy director of the first Dáil's Department of Publicity. Under the pseudonym David Hogan, Gallagher wrote *The Four Glorious Years* (Irish Press, Dublin, 1953).
15 Lyons, F. S. L., *Ireland Since the Famine* (Fontana, London, 1973), p. 429. The Irish delegation consisted of Arthur Griffith, Michael Collins and Robert Barton, and two lawyers, Gavan Duffy and Eamonn Duggan. Providing secretarial assistance were Erskine Childers, Fionán Lynch, Diarmuid O'Hegarty and John Smith Chartres. The formidable British team was led by the prime minister, David Lloyd George, and consisted of Winston Churchill, Austen Chamberlain, F. E. Smith (Lord Birkenhead), Sir Laming Worthington-Evans, Sir Hamar Greenwood and the attorney general, Sir Gordon Hewart, along with two civil servants, Tom Jones and Lionel Curtis.
16 Townshend, *The Republic*, p. 336.
17 Murphy, *Political Imprisonment and the Irish*, p. 221.
18 *Irish Weekly Independent*, 15 October 1921.
19 *Irish Independent*, 21 October 1921.
20 *Ibid.*, 24 October 1921. Fintan Murphy had joined the Irish Volunteers in London and was an Easter Week veteran. T. A. Andrus was the former CO of the 7th Battalion, North

Staffordshire Regiment and a First World War veteran. Horatio John Chippindall (reported as Chippendale in the Irish and British press at the time) was governor of Maryborough Gaol from 1916 to 1919; he was subsequently appointed inspector, General Prisons Board for Ireland, based at Armagh Gaol (reference: Ancestry.com; 1901/1911 Census of Ireland).

21 Michael Staines, BMH WS 944, p. 30.
22 Murphy, *Political Imprisonment and the Irish*, p. 229.
23 *Irish Independent*, 16 November 1921.
24 *The Freeman's Journal*, 9 November 1921.
25 *Ibid.*, 26 October 1921; Campbell, *Emergency Law in Ireland*, p. 110.
26 *Evening Herald*, 14 November 1921.
27 *The Freeman's Journal*, 16 November 1921.
28 *Leinster Leader*, 29 November 1921.
29 Murphy, *Political Imprisonment and the Irish*, p. 222; *The Freeman's Journal*, 12 November 1921.
30 *The Freeman's Journal*, 9 November and 30 November 1921.
31 Murphy, *Political Imprisonment and the Irish*, pp. 222–3; *Irish Independent*, 15 November 1921.
32 McNally, Frank, 'Locked out of history. An Irishman's Diary about a forgotten son of Cork', *The Irish Times*, 25 July 2013.
33 Murphy, *Political Imprisonment and the Irish*, pp. 223–4.
34 *The Freeman's Journal*, 24 October 1921; *Irish Independent*, 9 November and 16 November 1921. There are a surprising number of surviving photographs of life inside the Rath Camp and I have viewed four collections of prints.
35 *Irish Independent*, 3 December 1921.
36 *The Freeman's Journal*, 5 December 1921.
37 *Ibid.*, 28 November 1921.
38 *The Cork Examiner*, 23 November 1921.
39 *Irish Independent*, 25 November 1921.
40 *Ibid.*, 20 December 1921.

ENDNOTES

11 AND THE GATES FLEW OPEN

1. *Penrith Observer*, 13 December 1921.
2. Younger, *Ireland's Civil War*, p. 193.
3. *Penrith Observer*, 13 December 1921.
4. *Irish Independent*, 9 December 1921; *Leinster Leader*, 10 December 1921. William Murphy tried to escape by sitting on the axle of a lorry that was leaving the camp. He was captured when the vehicle was outside the main gate. Leo Close, Patrick Dyer and Martin Thompson attempted to escape when they were patients in the camp hospital.
5. *Irish Independent*, 9 December 1921.
6. *Kildare Observer*, 10 December 1921.
7. *Irish Independent*, 9 December 1921.
8. *Leinster Leader*, 10 December 1921; *Kildare Observer*, 10 December 1921.
9. Micheál Ó Laoghaire, BMH WS 797, pp. 63–4.
10. *The Freeman's Journal*, 12 December 1921.
11. *Leinster Leader*, 15 December 1921.
12. Micheál Ó Laoghaire, BMH WS 797, pp. 70–1.
13. *Irish Independent*, 9 December 1921.
14. Costello, *A Most Delightful Station*, p. 325.
15. *Ibid.*, pp. 328–9.
16. *The Freeman's Journal*, 4 February 1922.
17. Micheál Ó Laoghaire, BMH WS 797, p. 59.

BIBLIOGRAPHY

Newspapers

Anglo-Celt, The
Belfast Newsletter
Belfast Telegraph
Connacht Tribune
Connaught Telegraph, The
Donegal Democrat
Donegal News
Evening Herald
Evening Telegraph
Fermanagh Herald
Freeman's Journal, The
Meath Chronicle
Irish Bulletin
Irish Exile, The
Irish Press, The
Irish Times, The
Irish Independent
Irish Weekly Independent
Kerryman, The
Kildare Observer
Nationalist and Leinster Times
Leinster Express
Leinster Leader
Leitrim Observer
Mayo News, The
Meath Chronicle
Nenagh Guardian, The
Penrith Observer
Roscommon Herald
Skibbereen Eagle, The
Tuam Herald, The
Wicklow News-Letter

Witness Statements (WS), Bureau of Military Archives (BMH), Cathal Brugha Barracks, Dublin

Liam Ó Briain, WS 7
Francis O'Duffy, WS 665
Michael Noyk, WS 707
Brian A. Cusack, WS 736
Micheál Ó Laoghaire, WS 797
Alice Ginnell, WS 982
Michael Staines, WS 944
Joseph Lawless, WS 1043
David Daly, WS 1337
Brigid Ryan (née Brophy), WS 1573
Michael McCoy, WS 1610
Michael McHugh, WS 1632
Daniel E. Ryan, WS 1673
Peadar McMahon, WS 1730

BIBLIOGRAPHY

MILITARY SERVICE PENSION COLLECTION
Thomas Berry, MSP34REF2550
Isaiah Conroy, 24SP8027
Michael Fleming, W24SP7310
Thomas Henry Glennon, 24SP10231
Michael Horan, DP23836
John J. Martin, 1P134
Liam P. Murphy, 24SP7310
Michael Ryan, MSP34REF17277
John F. Shouldice, MSP34REF21842
Joseph Tonge, 24SP147

MISCELLANEOUS SOURCES
Delahunt, Sylvester, autograph book, courtesy of Áine Delahunt
Flanagan, Edward, 'Curragh Internment Diary', copy donated to Kildare Library and Arts Service, Local Studies Department by Karen Woodstock (June 2008)
Kearns Kilbride, Ellen 'Nellie', handwritten letter to the Military Pensions Board, Dublin, dated 1 May 1936. Copy given to the author by John Stack, Newbridge, 10 January 2019
Smyth, Michael, 'Kildare Battalion, 1920' (copy in Local Studies and Genealogy Department, Newbridge Library, Newbridge, Co. Kildare)

BOOKS
Abbott, Richard, *Police Casualties in Ireland 1919–1922* (Mercier Press, Cork, 2019)
Aiken, S., Mac Bhloscaidh, F., Ó Duibhir, L. and Ó Tuama, D. (eds), *The Men Will Talk to Me: Ernie O'Malley's Interviews with the Northern Division* (Merrion Press, Newbridge, 2018)
Andrews, C. S., *Dublin Made Me* (The Lilliput Press, Dublin, 2001)
Campbell, Colm, *Emergency Law in Ireland 1918–1925* (Clarendon Press, Oxford, 1994)
Collins, Lorcan, *1916: The Rising Handbook* (The O'Brien Press, Dublin, 2016)

Coogan, Tim Pat, *Ireland in the Twentieth Century* (Hutchinson, London, 2003)

— *The Twelve Apostles: Michael Collins, the Squad and Ireland's Fight for Freedom* (Head of Zeus, London, 2016)

Corrigan, Mario, *All the Delirium of the Brave: Kildare in 1798* (Kildare County Council, Naas, 1998)

Costello, Con, *A Most Delightful Station: The British Army on the Curragh of Kildare 1855–1922* (The Collins Press, Cork, 1999)

Cronin, Mike, Murphy, William and Rouse, Paul, *The Gaelic Athletic Association 1884–2009* (Irish Academic Press, Dublin, 2009)

Crowley, John, Ó Drisceoil, Donal and Murphy, Mike (eds), *Atlas of the Irish Revolution* (Cork University Press, Cork, 2017)

Cummins, Gerry and De Búrca, Éanna, *The Frank Burke Story: Patriot, Scholar, GAA Dual-star. Guardian of Pearse's Vision and Legacy* (published privately, Naas, 2016)

De Vere White, Terence, *Kevin O'Higgins* (Anvil Books, Dublin, 1987)

Durney, James, *On the One Road: Political Unrest in Kildare 1913–1994* (Gaul House, Naas, 2001)

— *The War of Independence in Kildare* (Mercier Press, Cork, 2013)

— *Foremost and Ready: Kildare and the 1916 Rising* (Gaul House, Naas, 2015)

Dwyer, T. Ryle, *The Squad and the Intelligence Operations of Michael Collins* (Mercier Press, Cork, 2005)

Feehan, John, *Cuírrech Life: The Curragh of Kildare, Ireland* (UCD, Dublin, 2007)

FitzGerald, Garret, *All in a Life. An Autobiography* (Gill & Macmillan, Dublin, 1991)

Flynn, Barry, *Pawns in the Game: Irish Hunger Strikes 1912–1981* (The Collins Press, Cork, 2011)

Foster, R. F., *Vivid Faces: The Revolutionary Generation in Ireland 1890–1923* (W. W. Norton, London, 2014)

Gillis, Liz, *Women of the Irish Revolution* (Mercier Press, Cork, 2016)

BIBLIOGRAPHY

Hart, Peter (ed.), *British Intelligence in Ireland 1920–21: The Final Reports* (Cork University Press, Cork, 2002)

— *The I.R.A. at War 1916–1923* (Oxford University Press, Oxford, 2003)

Harvey, Dan, *Soldiers of the Short Grass: A History of the Curragh Camp* (Merrion Press, Sallins, 2016)

Hogan, David (pseudonym of Frank Gallagher), *The Four Glorious Years* (Irish Press, Dublin, 1953)

Hopkinson, Michael, *Green Against Green: The Irish Civil War* (Gill & Macmillan, Dublin, 1988)

Jackson, Alvin, *Ireland 1798–1998: War, Peace and Beyond* (2nd edn, Wiley-Blackwell, Chichester, 2010)

Kautt, William H., *The Anglo-Irish War, 1916–1921: A People's War* (Praeger, Westport, CT, USA, 1999)

Kotsonouris, Mary *Retreat from Revolution: The Dáil Courts, 1920–24* (Irish Academic Press, Dublin, 1994)

Lyons, F. S. L., *Ireland Since the Famine* (Fontana, London, 2010)

Maguire, James and Quinn, James (eds), *Dictionary of Irish Biography: From the Earliest Times to the Year 2000*, Vols 1–9 (Cambridge University Press, Cambridge, 2010)

Maguire, John, *IRA Internments and the Irish Government: Subversives and the State 1939–1962* (Irish Academic Press, Dublin, 2008)

McGuffin, John, *Internment* (Anvil Books, Tralee, 1973)

Mitchell, Arthur, *Revolutionary Government in Ireland: Dáil Éireann 1919–22* (Gill & Macmillan, Dublin, 1995)

Moran, May, *Executed for Ireland: The Patrick Moran Story* (Mercier Press, Cork, 2010)

Murphy, William, *Political Imprisonment and the Irish, 1912–1921* (Oxford University Press, Oxford, 2014)

O'Callaghan, Micheál, *For Ireland and Freedom: Roscommon's Contribution to the Fight for Independence* (Mercier Press, Cork, 2012)

Ó Comhraí, Cormac, *Revolution in Connacht: A Photographic History 1913–23* (Mercier Press, Cork, 2013)

O'Donoghue, Florence (foreword), *I.R.A. Jailbreaks 1918–1924* (Mercier Press, Cork, 2010)

O'Donovan, Donal, *Kevin Barry and His Time* (Glendale Publishing, Dublin, 1989)

Ó Duibhir, Liam, *Prisoners of War: Ballykinlar Internment Camp 1920–1921* (Mercier Press, Cork, 2013)

O'Malley, Cormac K. H. and Ó Comhraí, Cormac (eds), *The Men Will Talk to Me: Galway Interviews by Ernie O'Malley* (Mercier Press, Cork, 2013)

O'Malley, Cormac K. H. and Keane, Vincent (eds), *The Men Will Talk to Me: Mayo Interviews by Ernie O'Malley* (Mercier Press, Cork, 2014)

Ó Ruairc, Pádraig Óg, *Truce: Murder, Myth and the Last Days of the Irish War of Independence* (Mercier Press, Cork, 2016)

Ó Súilleabháin, Adhamhnán, *Domhnall Ua Buachalla. Rebellious Nationalist, Reluctant Governor* (Merrion Press, Sallins, 2015)

Ó Súilleabháin, Cormac, *Leitrim's Republican Story 1900–2000* (Cumann Cabhrach Liatroma, USA, 2014)

Ó Tuathaigh, Gearóid (ed.), *The GAA and Revolution in Ireland 1913–1923* (The Collins Press, Cork, 2015)

Rafter, Michael, *The Quiet County. Towards a History of the Laois Brigade, I.R.A. and Revolutionary Activity in the County 1913–23* (published privately, Castletown, 2016)

Sheehan, William, *British Voices from the Irish War of Independence: The Words of British Servicemen Who Were There* (The Collins Press, Cork, 2007)

— *Hearts & Mines: The British 5th Division, Ireland, 1920–1922* (The Collins Press, Cork, 2009)

Shouldice, Frank, *Grandpa the Sniper: The Remarkable Story of a 1916 Volunteer* (The Liffey Press, Dublin, 2015)

Tobin, Fergal, *The Irish Revolution: An Illustrated History 1912–25* (Gill & Macmillan, Dublin, 2013)

Toomey, Thomas, *The War of Independence in Limerick 1912–1921*, also

Covering Actions in the Border Areas of Tipperary, Cork, Kerry and Clare (self-published, Limerick, 2010)

Townshend, Charles, *The British Campaign in Ireland 1919–1921: The Development of Political and Military Policies* (Oxford Historical Monographs) (Oxford University Press, London, 1975)

— *The Republic: The Fight for Irish Independence* (Penguin, London, 2014)

Wren, Jimmy, *The GPO Garrison, Easter Week 1916: A Biographical Dictionary* (Geography Publications, Dublin, 2015)

— *The Four Courts Garrison, Easter Week 1916: A Biographical Dictionary* (Geography Publications, Dublin, 2016)

Yeates, Pádraig, *A City in Turmoil: Dublin 1919–21* (Gill & Macmillan, Dublin, 2012)

Younger, Calton, *Ireland's Civil War* (Frederick Muller, London, 1968)

Articles

Byrne, Thomas, 'A tunnel to freedom: Escape from Kildare Camp', undated newspaper article. Copy in author's possession

'Cavan man's part in escape of republican prisoners', *The Anglo-Celt*, 4 January 1936

Collier, Tola, 'Joseph Lawless: Fingal's Finest', https://fingalsfinest1916.com

Conroy, John F., 'Escapes from the Rath Internment Camp, Curragh, 1921', *Western People*, 6 June 1964

'Curragh tunnel escape recalled', *Irish Independent*, 6 March 1955

Dooley, Frank, 'Humour in war', *Connacht Tribune*, 6 August 1976

Durney, James, 'Brothers in arms', Co. Kildare online electronic history journal, 12 November 2010

— 'The Curragh internees, 1921–24: From defiance to defeat', *Journal of the County Kildare Archaeological Society* 2010–2011, Vol. XX (Part II)

— 'Frank Burke: Teacher, Sportsman and Patriot', *Kildare Nationalist*, 17 April 2016

'Escape from the Curragh', *The Irish Press*, 8 September 1978

Evans, Inez G., 'Life on the Curragh Camp 1919', *The Irish Times*, 17 May 1919

'Historic athletic meeting in strange setting', *Irish Independent*, 7 June 1963

'How an Arigna miner dug for freedom', *Leitrim Observer*, 18 July 1942

McElligott, Richard, 'Football finds its feet amid 1916 rebellion against Empire', *The Irish Times*, 16 April 2016

McNally, Frank, 'Locked out of history. An Irishman's Diary about a forgotten son of Cork', *The Irish Times*, 25 July 2013

Ó Maoláin, Tomás, 'The inside story of famous I.R.A. escape from the Curragh Camp', *The Mayo News*, 17 January 1959

— 'Mayo men feature in famous I.R.A. escapes from the Curragh Camp', *The Mayo News*, 24 January 1959

'Obituary, Michael Cunningham', *The Irish Press*, 31 March 1955

'Obituary, Thomas Derrig', *The Connaught Telegraph*, 24 November 1956

'Obituary, Mr C. Kenny', *The Irish Press*, 30 January 1949

'Obituary, John Murray', *Donegal Democrat*, 16 November 1935

'Obituary, Fr P. Smith', *The Anglo-Celt*, 26 October 1940

'Old I.R.A. man's death recalls daring prison escape', *The Anglo-Celt*, 10 March 1978

'Rath Camp Escape', *Evening Herald*, 6 January 1936

'Sir Hamar and Cork Burnings', *Irish Independent*, 14 December 1920

Swan, Lt.-Col. Desmond, 'The Curragh', in *Handbook of the Curragh Camp* (Defence Forces Press, The Curragh, 1984)

Tunney, Patrick, 'Told at the fireside', *Western People*, 1 and 8 October 1949

INDEX

A

'A Ballad of 1920' 281
Abbey, Thomas 97, 223
Aldington, Richard 51
Andrews, C. S. Todd 53, 54, 58, 64–68, 88, 91, 92, 103, 107, 114, 136, 145–148, 150–154, 159, 232, 274
Andrus, T. A. 202–204
Anglo-Irish Treaty 100, 200, 207, 211, 212, 219, 222
Arbour Hill Prison 15, 26, 32, 43, 45, 47, 48, 52, 53, 61, 81, 129, 274, 276
Archer-Shee, Lieutenant Colonel Martin 74
Armstrong, Henry 98, 224
Ashe, Thomas 11, 102, 276
Athgarvan 93, 111, 225, 246
Athlone 25, 79, 155, 156, 186, 196, 264, 269–271, 274–279
Athy 191, 243–245
Auxiliaries 27, 45, 75, 86, 108, 110, 275, 279

B

Baggallay, Captain G. T. 56
Bailieboro 87, 230, 274
Ballinalee 11, 180, 181, 251, 252
Ballinrobe 87, 95, 240, 241, 254–258, 275
Ballybay 44
Ballykinlar Camp 15–19, 25, 32, 47, 68, 206, 216, 221, 223
Ballymany, Newbridge 27, 112, 113, 176
Ballymore Eustace 102, 105, 215, 225, 245, 246
Ballymurphy 77
Ballyshannon 102, 231, 244
Barry, John 274

Barry, Kevin 103
Barry, Paddy 157, 264, 274
Barry, Seán 148, 149, 159, 260
Barry, Tadhg 206
Barton, Robert 110
Baxter, James 181, 251
Béaslaí, Piaras 50
Beaumont, Seán 232, 274
Beggars Bush Barracks 22
Behan, James (Seamus) 77, 223
Behan, Michael 77, 102, 223
Behan, Thomas 77, 223
Behan, Tom 93, 95, 96, 100, 119, 243
Beirne, Pat 157, 264, 274
Belfast 21, 55, 72, 99, 169, 171, 172, 181, 184, 213, 228, 274, 277
Belfast Boycott 72
Bere Island 17, 122
Berry, Thomas 78, 260
Birrell, Augustine 21
Black and Tans 22, 75, 78, 99, 108, 112, 142, 279
Bloody Sunday, 1920 7, 14, 56
Bodenstown 151, 243, 246
Bog of Allen 149, 159
Boyce, James 56, 232
Boyd, Donald 196, 200
Boyle 28, 29, 76, 77, 155, 264–266, 274, 278
Boyle, Andrew 93, 232
Brabazon, Tommy 136–138, 164, 232
Bracken, Peadar 169–171, 260
Brady, Jim 87, 88, 127–132, 134, 136–144, 147, 230, 274
Brock, Anthony 97, 98, 224
Broderick, Myles 122, 232
Broderick, Richard 122, 232
Broderick, Richard J. 122, 232
Brugha, Cathal 56, 117

INTERNED

Brunswick Street, Dublin 45, 234, 236, 237
Buckley, Cornelius 39, 243
Bulfin, Francis 117, 226
Burgoyne, John F. 21
Burke, Frank 43, 59–61, 92, 93, 243
Burke, Henry 'Harry' 254, 275
Burke, Tom 92, 95, 253
Byrne, Bernard 233, 275
Byrne, Charles 144, 233, 275
Byrne, Hugh 87, 88, 128, 139, 143, 149, 158, 269, 275
Byrne, John J. 209–211, 254
Byrne, Lucy 138
Byrne, Tom 'The Boer' 33, 44, 94, 129, 135–138, 143, 144, 149, 150, 233, 275

C

Carbury 59, 93, 156, 171, 243, 244
Cardiff, Matt 105
Carlow 35, 36, 62, 77, 97, 102, 103, 106, 124, 181, 182, 185, 186, 223, 224, 228, 229
Carney, T. J. 102, 224
Carolan, Michael 169–171, 228
Carrick-on-Shannon 77, 216, 250, 251
Casement Brigade 34
Castlebar 95, 217, 256–258
Castlepollard 57, 184, 269–271
Cavan 45, 52, 87, 101, 229, 230, 274, 278
Chippindall, Horatio John 202, 204
Churchill, Winston 109
Clongowes Wood College 50
Close, Leo 213, 228
Coan, Henry John 181–183, 228
College of Science, Dublin 50
Collins, Michael 11, 86, 99, 117, 118, 164, 165, 201, 206
Collinstown Camp 15, 32, 46
Compton, Henry 157, 264, 275
Connolly, Joseph 181, 252
Connolly, Seán 101

Connor, Elizabeth 29
Conroy, Isaiah 233, 275
Conroy, John F. 'Jack' 87, 254, 275
Coole District Council 154
Cootehill 52
Cope, Alfred 121
Cork 17, 50, 75, 122, 187, 206, 230
Cork Corporation 195
Cork Harbour 18
Cosgrave, Philip 117, 233
Cotter, John P. 68, 233
Cotter, Tom 205, 233
Crimean War 21
Crooksling Sanatorium 71
Crossna 155, 157, 266, 278
Crowley, James 117, 243
Crowley, John 118, 254
Crumlin Road Gaol 184
Culleenaghamore 78, 266
Cullen, James 136, 247
Cumann na mBan 22, 62, 64, 133, 214, 216, 218
Cunningham, Elizabeth 158
Cunningham, Michael 158
Curragh Military Hospital 76–78, 180
Curragh Racecourse 19, 23, 103, 138, 143, 145, 148–151, 156, 176, 221
Cusack, Dr Brian A. 31, 32, 72, 75, 96, 117, 241
Custom House, Dublin 107

D

Dáil Éireann 11, 52, 54, 58, 110, 114, 116–119, 195, 197, 207, 212, 218, 219
Dalton, Emmet 45
Daly, David 158, 269, 275
Daly, Ned 45
Darcy, Paddy 158, 159, 234, 276
Dardis, John 98, 258
De Valera, Éamon 58, 110, 116, 118, 119, 195, 202
Defence of the Realm Act (DORA) 9, 10, 12, 13, 51

INDEX

Delahunt, Sylvester 62, 244
Derrig, Tom 30, 54, 55, 95, 118, 255
Derry Gaol 55, 102
Devoy, John 160
Devoy, Joseph 277
Dollymount 15
Donegal 102, 117, 231, 277
Donohue, Hugh 181, 252
Donohue, Michael 181, 252
Donohue, William 'Bill' 185, 229
Doody, Seán 148, 149, 159, 261, 276
Dooley, Frank 178, 234
Doolittle, Hilda 51
Doran, Art 102, 225
Doran, Bridget 113
Doran, William 112
Down 15, 184, 221, 232
Doyle, Judge 42
Drogheda 92, 253, 254
Drumcondra 178, 205, 233, 238
Dublin 9–12, 14, 15, 21, 22, 30, 32–34, 39, 42, 44–46, 50, 52, 53, 55, 57, 59–61, 67, 71, 77, 81, 85, 86, 89, 93, 95–97, 108, 110, 115, 117, 118, 122, 124, 136, 142–145, 150, 152, 153, 158–160, 163, 169, 171, 177, 178, 181, 182, 184, 185, 189, 190, 196, 202, 208–210, 213–216, 219, 220, 224, 227, 228, 232–240, 262, 273–279
Dublin Bay 15
Dublin Brigade 39, 44, 46, 47, 55, 70, 76, 81, 82, 96, 126, 129, 135, 136, 138, 163, 164, 275, 276, 278, 279
Dublin Castle 11, 12, 17, 45, 47, 52, 54, 81, 109, 276, 278
Dublin District Division 19, 23
Duff, Major General Sir James 20
Duffy, Joseph 183, 184, 269
Duffy, Paddy 157
Duggan, Eamonn 110
Dundas, Ralph 19
Dundrum Bay 15
Dungannon 103, 269

Dunne, Christopher 184, 273
Dunne, Patrick 160
Dunne, Timothy 95, 247
Dyer, Patrick 213, 267

E

Early, James 181, 252
East Sussex Regiment 134
Easter Rising 10, 21, 44, 46, 50, 51, 55–57, 68, 91, 96, 99, 129, 133, 171, 276, 277

F

Fallon, Thomas 102, 223, 229
Farrell, Jim 157, 265, 276
Farrell, Peter 95, 265
Farrelly, Michael 104, 122, 258
Feehan, Harry 169, 170, 226, 261
Feeney, Peter 192, 241, 276
Fehilly, Dr Eugene 31, 179, 187, 230
Fermanagh 43
Ferran, Francis P. 64, 75, 118, 255
Fingal 46, 236, 277
FitzGerald, Desmond 43, 50–52, 68, 80, 118, 196, 200, 234
Fitzpatrick, Bernard 156
Fitzpatrick, Patrick 77, 223
Flanagan, Edward 161, 165, 166, 247
Flanagan, John 191, 244
Flavin, Father 153
Fleming, Michael 'Miko' 241, 276
Fleming, Patrick 'Paddy' 241, 276
Flint, F. S. 51
Flynn, Éamonn 149, 160, 270, 277
Fontstown 191
Ford, Myles 145–147, 150–154, 159, 234, 277
Fort Westmoreland 18
Foxford 64, 254, 255, 257
France 21, 99, 186, 190
Frongoch Internment Camp 45, 46, 55, 56, 60, 68, 99, 171, 276, 277, 279
Furlong, Dick 102, 225

315

G

Gaelic Athletic Association (GAA) 46, 60, 91–93, 95, 96
Gaelic League 43, 44, 46, 50, 98, 274
Gaffney, Jerry 82–84
Gaffney, Patrick 77, 224
Gallagher, Frank 200
Galvin, Joe 87, 88, 127, 129, 131, 137, 139–142, 265, 277
Galvin, Michael 97, 226
Galway 30, 32, 42–44, 55, 63, 99, 117, 136, 171, 195, 213, 217, 224, 240–243, 275–279
Garland, Edith 22
Garristown Barracks 46
Gavan, Charles 'Charlie' 255, 277
Gavigan, John J. 154, 155, 161, 183, 270
Germany 9, 29, 34
Gibbet Rath 18–20, 27, 69
Gibbons, Daniel 185, 186, 228
Glenageary 122, 232
Glennon, Thomas 228
Glennon, Tom 171–173, 176, 178
Glynn, Tom 95, 241
Goff, Robert J. 219, 220
Gormanstown 45
Graham, Seán 'Jack' 185, 186, 244
Graiguecullen 102, 223, 224
Green, Hugh 231, 277
Greenwood, Hamar 15, 73, 74, 75, 201
Grehan, James 11
Grehan, Robert P. 258, 277
Griffith, Arthur 52, 110, 117

H

Hacketstown 102, 185, 223, 224, 228, 229
Hanna, Francis B. 29
Hanna, John Connor 29, 73, 123, 187, 214
Hardy, Captain Jocelyn 'Hoppy' 47
Harold's Cross Hospice 71
Harrold, Andy 130, 273

Hill of Allen 156, 245
Hogan, Mick 60
Hopkins, Patrick 154, 252, 277
Horan, Michael 71, 72, 205, 270
Hulme, T. E. 51
Hunt, Jack 77, 78, 250
Hunt, Jim 205
Hyland, Joseph 166, 247
Hyland, Tom 186, 247

I

Igoe Gang 54, 81
Internees' Amusements Committee 101, 209
Internment Camps Inquiry Commission 180, 202, 204
Irish Citizen Army 9, 44, 99
Irish Parliamentary Party (IPP) 11, 55
Irish Republican Brotherhood (IRB) 9, 32, 46, 50, 51, 96, 99, 129, 172, 180, 275, 277
Irish Transport and General Workers' Union (ITGWU) 105
Irish Volunteer Dependents' Fund 193

J

Jacob's Biscuit Factory 45, 276, 279
Jeudwine, Major General Sir Hugh Sandham 23, 219
Jones, Bill 111, 112
Joyce, Martin 95, 256

K

Keadue 131, 266, 279
Kealey, Martin 186
Keane Barracks 11, 77, 185
Keane, Joe 105
Kearney, Peadar 45
Keegan, Willie 120, 226
Kells 57, 98, 104, 122, 258, 259
Kelly, Joseph 235, 277
Kenny, Christopher 83, 245
Kenny, Joe 95, 235
Kenworthy, J. M. 201

INDEX

Keogh, J. 105
Kerr, Tom 218, 273
Kerry 50, 51, 101, 117, 225, 243
Kilcoole 29
Kildare town 62, 158, 186, 214, 243–245
Kilgefin 264, 275
Kilglass 78, 266, 268
Kilkelly 209, 211, 254, 255
Kilkenny 45, 154, 186, 206, 246
Kill 160, 215, 243–246, 282
Killeavy, John 'Jack' 158, 159, 262, 277
Killowen 184, 232
Kilmainham Gaol 124, 276
Kilskyre 57
King, Captain William 'Tiny' 47
King's Own Scottish Borderers 67, 89
Kinvara 192, 241, 276
Knock 207, 257
Knockcroghery 156, 266, 278, 279
Knutsford Prison 45, 46, 56

L

Labour Party 105
Lake, Lieutenant General 20
Laois 11, 43, 98, 136, 161, 166, 185, 186, 226, 246–249
Lavin, Andrew 216
Lawless, Colm 45
Lawless, Frank 45, 68
Lawless, Jim 45
Lawless, Joseph 26, 28, 30, 38, 39, 45–49, 68, 83, 84, 114, 126, 161, 171–178, 236
Lawless, Ned 45
Lee, Joseph 105, 245
Leitrim 30, 45, 77, 205, 216, 249, 250
Lennon, Thomas 71, 270
Leonard, Tom 186, 270
Lillis, James 181, 182, 229
Limerick 45, 55, 251
Lintott, Alfred 189
Liverpool 30, 43, 77, 94, 190, 217, 273

Lloyd George, David 110, 116, 118, 119, 195, 201
Logue, Cardinal J. M. 200
London 43, 50–52, 56, 69, 74, 96, 99, 110, 116, 119, 125, 190, 196, 200, 201, 206, 212, 218, 273, 275
Longford 11, 79, 101, 117, 154, 184, 251–253, 277, 279
Longworth, James 217, 263
Louth 92, 117, 253, 254
Lurgan Battalion 184
Lynch, Patrick J. 96, 236

M

MacBride, Joseph 118
MacDonagh, Thomas 45
MacEoin, Seán 117, 158
Macready, General Nevil 109, 110, 120, 122, 123, 202, 212
Madden, Pat 157
Mallett, Lieutenant 31, 63, 123
Mallin, Michael 44, 99
Manchester 43, 50, 273
Manfredi, John 189
Mannion (Manning), John 242, 277
Mansion House, Dublin 110, 118
Markievicz, Constance 44, 279
Martin, John J. 76, 88, 128, 236
Martin, Thomas 35, 36
Maryborough Gaol 25
Maynooth 98, 200, 224, 225, 244
Mayo 30, 39, 43, 45, 54, 55, 64, 80, 87, 96, 101, 118, 128, 133, 195, 207, 209, 211, 217, 254–258, 274, 275, 277, 278, 284
McAleer, Gerry 103
McBride, Joe 44, 256
McCabe, Alexander 98, 118, 268
McCarrick, Tommy 95, 186, 268
McConnell, Mabel 51, 52
McCoy, Michael 162, 166, 180, 184, 216, 271
McDermott, Richard J. 63, 209, 242
McDonald, John 106, 229

McEllin, William 95, 271
McEvoy, Ed 49, 248
McGoldrick, Patrick J. 117, 231
McHugh, Michael 30, 218, 256
McKenna, Justin 117, 230
McKenna, William 77, 224
McMahon, Peadar 28, 30, 39, 44, 45, 48, 49, 73, 76, 84, 115, 187, 196, 214, 218, 259
McManus, Thomas 106, 229
McNamara, James J. 55, 56, 95, 237
McNamara, Patrick 157, 278
McSherry, Thomas 208, 237
Meath 30, 57, 98, 133, 171, 226, 258, 259, 277
Mee, Richard 'Dick' 156, 266, 278
Milltownpass 183, 269
Moate 158, 269–271, 275, 276
Molloy, Michael 78, 263
Molloy, Richard 'Dick' 136, 138, 237
Mooney, William 217, 263
Moore Street 60, 237
Moran, Cissie 157
Moran, Joe 157
Moran, Paddy 155, 157
Moran, Thomas 'Tom' 155, 157, 266, 278
Mount Talbot 87, 265, 277
Mountjoy Gaol 12, 13, 43, 54, 77, 103, 112, 117, 120, 180, 202, 276
Mullaney, William 78, 266
Mullee, Tom 95, 257
Mullen, Edward 133
Mullen, Mary 133
Mullen, Michael 133
Mullen, Thomas. *See* Ó Maoláin, Tomás
Mullingar 71, 183, 184, 205, 216, 269–271
Mullins, Tom 95
Murney, Michael 184–186, 232
Murphy, Fintan 69, 202, 205, 273
Murphy, Frank 205, 251
Murphy, Hubert 266, 278

Murphy, Jack 129
Murphy, James 117, 254
Murphy, Michael 'Mick' 156, 257, 278
Murphy, Richard 129
Murphy, William 213, 228
Murphy, William P. 'Liam' 88, 129, 134, 139, 143, 146, 149, 237, 278
Murray, John 102, 231

N

Naas 25, 75, 102, 105, 142, 151, 152, 160, 191, 205, 215, 218, 225, 243–246, 282
Na Fianna Éireann 46, 53, 120, 178, 277
Neary, Michael 266, 268, 278
Newbridge 19, 22, 64, 86, 102, 105, 112, 113, 142, 150–152, 163, 176, 177, 215, 216, 218–220, 224, 243–245
Newcastle Sanatorium 71
Nohilly, James 95, 242
Noud, John 'Jack' 146, 147, 150–154, 237, 278

O

O'Boyle, Manús 166, 228
Ó Briain, Liam 44, 57, 98, 99, 242
O'Brien, Daniel 98, 224
O'Brien, Patrick 207, 208, 257
O'Brien, Walter J. 143, 238, 278
O'Callaghan, Donal 206
O'Callaghan, Laurence 75, 205, 225
O'Carroll, Kevin 95, 238
O'Connor, Anthony 230, 278
O'Connor, Dick 93
O'Connor, George 104, 259
O'Connor, Joe 185, 186, 238
O'Connor, Rory 43, 47, 48, 50, 82–87, 238
O'Dairdis, Seán 98, 258
O'Doherty, Joseph 117, 231
O'Donovan, Con 47
O'Donovan Rossa, Jeremiah 46

INDEX

O'Farrell, Michael 179, 238
O'Higgins, Brian 102
O'Higgins, Kevin 31
O'Higgins, Thomas 31, 248
O'Kelly, Michael 25, 96, 225, 245
O'Kelly, Patrick 20
O'Kelly, Seámus (Kelly, James) 185, 262
O'Kelly, Seán T. 99
Ó Laoghaire, Micheál 20, 21, 30, 31, 33–35, 41, 43, 44, 58, 63, 79, 94, 122, 166, 215–218, 221, 273
Ó Maoláin, Tomás 80, 128, 132, 133, 135, 136, 148, 149, 158, 159, 257, 278
O'Neill, Charlie 103, 104
O'Neill, Laurence 'Larry' 77, 124, 224
O'Neill, T. J. 220
O'Sullivan, Gearóid 86
O'Toole, Seán 102, 225
Offaly 22, 43, 57, 58, 78, 93, 115, 117, 156, 171, 184, 185, 217, 226, 260–263, 274, 276–279

P

Parnell Street 46, 47, 56, 60, 235
Pearse, P. H. 53, 59
Prisoners Dependents' Fund 96

R

Rahan 22, 57, 58, 260
Ranelagh 59, 233, 238, 239
Rathangan 83, 95, 156, 157, 184, 243–246
Rathfarnham 53, 54, 59–61, 70, 164, 234, 236, 238, 239, 274
Rathvilly 97, 106, 223, 224, 228, 229, 272
Regan, Patrick 'Scottie' 131, 266, 279
Restoration of Order in Ireland Act (ROIA) 13, 14
Richmond Military Barracks 10, 276
Rinnacurran 77, 250
Robinson, Joe 159, 239, 279

Rochford, Joe 131, 132, 239
Rooney, John 'Jack' 181–183, 239
Roper, Sergeant 49
Roscommon 28, 30, 43, 50, 76, 87, 131, 155–157, 216, 264–266, 274 279
Roseingrave, Michael 242, 279
Ross, Sir John 42
Rotunda 44, 59
Round Tower House 158
Royal Engineers 24, 134, 188, 189, 191
Royal Irish Constabulary (RIC) 11, 22, 36, 41, 46, 51, 54, 60, 110, 117
Ruttledge, P. J. 118, 258
Ryan, Daniel 81–87, 239
Ryan, Mick 77, 124, 224

S

Sallins 150, 151, 153, 154, 244, 246
Scanlon, James 105
Scanlon, Michael 239, 279
Schley, John 242, 279
Scuffil, Albert J. 189, 190
Scuffil, Sapper John J. 189, 190
Scully, James 98
Shaughnessy, Joe 131, 132, 273
Short, John 228, 279
Shouldice, John F. 'Jack' 96, 258
Simons, Frank 157
Sinn Féin 10, 11, 14, 15, 39, 41, 43, 50, 52, 55, 60, 74, 99, 102, 109, 112, 118, 121, 171
Skelly, Michael 253, 279
Skinner, Brigadier General Percy Cyriac Burrell 23, 100
Sligo 30, 95, 98, 118, 185, 186, 213, 267, 268, 278
Smith, Fr Patrick 22, 57, 58, 96, 104, 172, 187, 226
Smith, Thomas P. 209, 239
Smyth, Michael 111, 112, 225
Soloheadbeg 11
Spike Island 18, 187

St Enda's College 53, 54, 59–61, 164
St Mary's College 50
Stack, Austin 50, 117
Stafford Detention Barracks 60
Staines, Henry Vincent 120, 178–180, 239
Staines, James 'Jim' 119–121, 178, 224
Staines, Michael 120, 178, 180, 202–204
Storer, Edward 51
Stradbally 31, 98, 161, 226, 247–249
Straffan 62
Strangeways Prison 50
Strokestown 78, 157, 265, 266, 274, 278
Suffolk Regiment 28, 29
Sullivan, W. 42
Synge Street Christian Brothers School (CBS) 53, 54

T

Temple, Kieran 158, 159, 264, 279
Tennant, Patrick 'Pat' 156, 266, 279
Terenure 53, 67, 232, 238, 274
'The Ferrets of Kildare' 280
Thompson, Martin 213, 242
Tipperary 11, 60, 81, 96, 171, 268, 269
'To Maura from Wicklow' 283
Tobin, Michael 56
Tomeagh 103
Tonge, Joseph Leo 70, 71, 239
Traynor, Patrick 169, 170, 240
Truce 32, 39, 42, 52, 77, 92, 111, 113–116, 119, 121, 137, 158, 165, 178, 180, 200, 202, 207, 222, 278
Tuberculosis (TB) 70–72
Tullamore 30, 57, 78, 97, 116, 120, 129, 148, 169, 185, 196, 217, 226, 260–264, 274–278
Tullow 181, 228, 229
Tuttle, Seán 98, 249
Tyrellspass 57, 270
Tyrone 103, 195, 269

U

Ua Buachalla, Domhnall 40
Ulster Volunteer Force (UVF) 9
University College Dublin (UCD) 50, 54, 55
University College Galway (UCG) 44, 55, 99, 242
Usk Prison 96

V

Victory, James 31, 253
Vinden, Lieutenant Hubert Frederick 29, 35, 37, 52, 53, 109, 113–115, 118, 168, 185, 186, 188
Vize, Joe 31, 44, 138, 143, 144, 150, 271, 279

W

Walsh, John J. 96
Wandsworth Prison 99
Waterford 43
West Ham 50
Westmeath 43, 57, 117, 149, 158, 162, 171, 216, 269–271, 275–277
Westport 54, 55, 231, 254–258, 277, 278
Whelan, Thomas 56, 57
White Cross 64, 71, 216
Wicklow 29, 30, 51, 71, 123, 226, 271, 272, 283
Wilmot, Tom 93, 246
Wilson, Henry 109
Wood, Major Murdoch Mackenzie 73, 74